INSIDE IMMIGRATION

INSIDE
IMMIGRATION
DETENTION

MARY BOSWORTH

OXFORD
UNIVERSITY PRESS

OXFORD
UNIVERSITY PRESS

Great Clarendon Street, Oxford, OX2 6DP,
United Kingdom

Oxford University Press is a department of the University of Oxford.
It furthers the University's objective of excellence in research, scholarship,
and education by publishing worldwide. Oxford is a registered trade mark of
Oxford University Press in the UK and in certain other countries

Published in the United States of America by Oxford University Press
198 Madison Avenue, New York, NY 10016, United States of America

British Library Cataloguing in Publication Data
Data available

Library of Congress Control Number: 2014939072

ISBN 978-0-19-872257-1

For my parents, Richard and Michal Bosworth

Acknowledgements

This project has benefited from the assistance and support of a range of people. Above all, I owe a great debt to the women and men in the detention centres who participated in the project, filling out surveys, chatting, and generally engaging with me, even when they were enduring a period of great uncertainty and sorrow, or were busy at work.

I could not have completed the study without Blerina Kellezi and Gavin Slade who conducted significant parts of the fieldwork in Tinsley House, Yarl's Wood, and Morton Hall. Alison Liebling, Ben Crewe, and John Dring gave early advice that proved vital in gaining access, while Jim Gomersall, Walter McGowan, Jamie Bennett, Alex Sweeney, Paul Morrison, Michael Guy, Victoria Colloby, Dawn Elaine, James Wilkinson, Karen Head, and Marie Walker opened the doors of their establishments. At the Home Office, Alan Kittle and Karen Abdel-Hady offered key support from the outset, while Jonathan Nanceville-Smith, Duncan Partridge, Simon Edwards, and Helen Morgan each facilitated various parts of the research.

I am fortunate in those whom I work alongside at Oxford. Carolyn Hoyle, Lucia Zedner, Inês Hasselberg, and Sarah Turnbull have offered not just ideas but glasses of wine when needed, while a number of my students, some of whom have gone onto academic positions of their own, or are just about to, have provided intellectual inspiration and research assistance. Thank you Emma Kaufman, Ana Aliverti, Bonnie Ernst, Sophie Eser, Emily Ross, Lea Sitkin, and Michelle Miao.

I have benefited from discussions with colleagues some of whom read and commented on draft chapters and related articles including Katja Aas, Ana Aliverti, Vanessa Barker, Ben Bradford, Mina Fazel, Andriani Fili, Matthew Gibney, Alex Hall, Nick Gill, Ambrose Lee, Ian Loader, Dominique Moran, Coretta Philips, Sharon Pickering, Emma Plugge, Marie Segrave, Imogen Tyler, Thomas Ugelvik, Leanne Weber, and Lucia Zedner. Those who have read whole drafts of the manuscript deserve special thanks: Jamie Bennett, Hindpal Singh Bhui, Sophie Eser, Emma Kaufman, and Sarah Turnbull. I appreciate also the advice and assistance of Luigi Gariglio who selected the cover image from a number of photographs I had taken in IRC Colnbrook.

The book and the fieldwork on which it is based would not have been possible without generous financial support from a number of institutions. In 2009, the Nuffield Foundation, under their small grants scheme ('Understanding Immigration Detention: A qualitative analysis, SGS/37597'), covered the costs of the first months of fieldwork, while the national study was supported by a 2010–12 British Academy Research Development Award BR100060, and by a 2010–11 research award from the University of Oxford John Fell OUP Research Fund ('Understanding Immigration Detention, 092/233'), that paid for a two-year part time research officer (Dr Blerina Kellezi). The writing-up occurred during my 2012–17 European Research Council Starting Grant 313362, 'Subjectivity, Identity and Penal Power'. Throughout, I have benefited from teaching relief, administrative, and technical support from the Centre for Criminology and the Faculty of Law at the University of Oxford. For all of this assistance, I am very grateful.

Finally, my family has borne the brunt of my labour on this project since 2009 and helped me through the hard parts. Anthony, Ella, and Sophia have provided respite, love, and welcome distraction. My parents, Richard and Michal Bosworth, not only did many 'after school pick ups', but also subedited the final draft of the manuscript despite being busy on writing projects of their own, catching and castigating me for my unclear jargon, unintended Americanisms, and 'floating phrases'. In so doing they have greatly improved the text. I thank them and dedicate this book to them.

Mary Bosworth

Contents

List of illustrations

Cover photo Women's Short Stay Unit, IRC Colnbrook
(Photo credit: MF Bosworth)

List of abbreviations

ACDT	Assessment Care in Detention and Teamwork
AVID	Association of Visitors to Immigration Detainees
AVR	Assisted Voluntary Return
BH	IRC Brook House
BID	Bail for Immigration Detainees
BOC	British Overseas Citizen
C&R	Control and Restraint
CB	IRC Colnbrook
CH	IRC Campsfield House
CPS	Crown Prosecution Service
DCM	Detention Custody Manager
DCO	Detention Custody Officer
DEPMU	Detainee Escorting and Population Management Unit
DRC	Democratic Republic of Congo
ECHR	European Convention on Human Rights
EEA	European Economic Area
ESOL	English as a Second Language
EU	European Union
FNP	Foreign National Prisoner
HMIP	Her Majesty's Inspectorate of Prisons
ICIBI	Independent Chief Inspector of Borders and Immigration
IEP	Incentives and Earned Privileges
IMB	Independent Monitoring Board
IOM	International Organization for Migration
IRC	Immigration Removal Centre
JCWI	Joint Council for the Welfare of Immigrants
MH	IRC Morton Hall
MQLD	Measure of the Quality of Life in Detention
MQPL	Measure of the Quality of Prison Life

NOMS	National Offender Management Service
NGO	Non-Governmental Organization
NHS	National Health Service
PCT	Primary Care Trust
PFI	Private Finance Initiative
PPO	Prison and Probation Ombudsman
SIR	Security Incident Report
SMT	Senior Management Team
SSU	Short Stay Unit
STHF	Short-Term Holding Facility
TH	IRC Tinsley House
UKBA	United Kingdom Border Agency
UKIP	United Kingdom Independence Party
YOI	Young Offenders Institution
YW	IRC Yarl's Wood

Introduction

Inside immigration detention

Today is the Chinese women's welfare focus meeting in Yarl's Wood. Nobody comes. Staff members sit around waiting. Eventually Tina[1] appears. A long-term British resident originally from Taiwan, she has been personally invited since she is the informal interpreter for the Chinese women in Yarl's Wood. As it turns out, she has come to complain. 'Every day they ask me for things', she moans. 'I'm an old lady. I'm 56. And I have to run everywhere'. She also wants the staff to stop asking her to interpret. Amir, the Welfare Officer, suggests that the women could ask the weekly Buddhist preacher for help and reminds Tina that the centre has employed a Chinese woman to come in weekly to interpret. All detainees need to do, he says, is post a note in a special black box in the library asking to see her. Tina rebuffs both suggestions, reporting that the preacher 'tells us he can't help us with anything', and that the official interpreter has not been in for a fortnight. The issues are urgent Tina points out: 'There are lots of them who need help with forms. A lot of these Chinese people get a solicitor. He says £500 I help you. Then he says £4000 and then £8000. Yesterday there was a girl whose solicitor had taken £1500 and wanted more money but she has no more. So I had to fill it out for her. It was very stressful.' Amir is sympathetic but has no other solution. He then turns to the agenda:

AMIR: 'The next issue is activities. Are there any problems?'

TINA: 'We have spoken to the Pastor and IMB[2] about this. There is a cleaner who comes to the vacuuming during our Chinese prayer meeting and makes a lot of noise.'

AMIR: 'They are dealing with this but if the problem persists, please speak to us.'

TINA: 'When we have a service in the evening the black persons come in and are very rude. They interrupt our meeting. The other women are very angry

---

1. Not her real name. All participants have been allocated pseudonyms.
2. Independent Monitoring Board; a group of volunteers screened and appointed by the Ministry of Justice in the UK with a permanent presence in prisons and immigration removal centres (IRCs). Along with HM Inspectorate of Prisons (HMIP) and the Prison and Probation Ombudsman (PPO) they provide official mechanisms of accountability. The IMB produce annual reports about each IRC. More information about them can be found on the Ministry of Justice website <http://www.justice.gov.uk/about/imb>.

because they can't speak English. I can, but I do it gently. They think I'm too weak. The Chinese think the Pastor is on their side because he is black.'

AMIR: 'No, no! Healthcare?'

TINA: 'I run here and there. Every time I go to healthcare there are Chinese talking, talking. They ask me to interpret. Some nurses are very appreciative, but one was very rude saying this is confidential.'

AMIR: 'Tell them there is Language Line.'

TINA: 'Oh Language Line! They don't use it. They think they know what is wrong . . . When patients are waiting and angry you need to calm them down. She is so frustrated. She don't know how to speak English. She doesn't want to talk on the phone. They are anxious that the service makes mistakes.'

After more complaints about other matters, Tina raises a final set of issues:

TINA: 'One thing my Chinese say whenever they asked for anything they have to wait for months and they see black people are released quickly because they speak English.'

AMIR: 'I will say this: Black people aren't released because they speak English. Each case is different. The main delay is the embassy. Another delay might be if they have a solicitor who is putting up barriers.'

TINA: 'I think my Chinese are angry. I wrote to the Embassy five times about Hui-Ying [a young woman who had been in Yarl's Wood for over a year despite agreeing to return to China]. I write and say she has tried to kill herself two times. But I got no answer.'

AMIR: 'We can't get involved' (Fieldnotes, July 2010).

Nearly 3,000 foreign national citizens are detained under Immigration Act powers in the UK on any given day in one of 10 Immigration Removal Centres (IRCs) scattered throughout the country (see Figure 1).[3] The government spends £100 per person per night to house them in this way (AVID, 2014).[4] An additional, undisclosed number of men, women, and children are held in police cells, immigration reporting centres, or in

3. An 11th establishment, IRC The Verne, was due to open in March 2014. That month, due to fears about prison overcrowding elsewhere, its official reclassification from HMP The Verne was put on hold until September 2014, even though its cells had been emptied of prisoners and were being filled with immigration detainees (HC Deb 3 April 2014, col 757).

4. See also HC Deb 17 January 2014, cols 720–1, House of Commons Written Answers for 17 January 2014. Available at <http://www.publications.parliament.uk/pa/cm201314/cmhansrd/cm140117/text/140117w0002.htm>.

hospital. Since May 2013, the government has made available an additional 1,000 bed spaces in prison, most of which are set aside for ex-prisoners who have finished their sentence and are awaiting deportation.[5] Around 100 others are held for up to five days in short-term holding facilities at ports and airports.[6] Finally, the Home Office operates a so-called 'Pre-departure accommodation' facility for up to nine families near Gatwick airport (HMIP, 2013). Families may be held at Cedars, or in Tinsley House down the road, for 72 hours at a time.[7]

These are not enormous numbers being confined, particularly in comparison to the far greater population living in the community without legal documentation,[8] or to the sum of foreigners in prison.[9] Yet, their small size belies the considerable moral, ethical, and legal dilemmas they raise, issues that demand careful academic scrutiny. These institutions are volatile and contested sites. They are also places about which we know very little. What is their goal? How are they justified?

As this book will demonstrate, these two fundamental questions are surprisingly hard to answer. There is no clearly defined objective of detention. Instead, the aim, the 2001 Detention Centre Rules state, is to detain:

> 3. (1) The purpose of detention centres shall be to provide for the secure but humane accommodation of detained persons in a relaxed regime with as much freedom of movement and association as possible, consistent with maintaining a safe and secure environment, and to encourage and assist detained persons to make the most productive use of their time, whilst respecting in particular their dignity and the right to individual expression.

5. The sum of available beds in prison for this purpose changes frequently. According to the most recently available figures made in response to a Parliamentary question from Philip Davies, the Conservative Member for Shipley, on 31 December 2013 there were 1,214 men and women being held in prison under Immigration Act powers (HC Deb 9 April 2014, col 248).
6. The numbers of which are unclear. In a 2013 report, for instance, the government body with responsibility for monitoring such places, the HMIP, discovered several new ones previously undeclared to it operating on French territory (HMIP and CGPL, 2013).
7. In exceptional circumstances, and only with ministerial authority, the period of confinement may be extended to one week.
8. A population that was estimated at between 417,000–863,000 in 2007 (Gordon et al, 2009).
9. Who, as of June 2013, accounted for 13% of the total prison population of England and Wales in March 2013, at 10,786 women and men (Prison Reform Trust, 2013).

Immigration Removal Centres
April 2014*

Edinburgh

IRC Dungavel

IRC Morton Hall

IRC Yarl's Wood

IRC Campsfield House

IRC Colnbrook

IRC Harmondsworth

London

Cedars

IRC Dover

IRC Tinsley House & IRC Brook House

IRC Haslar

*The underlined establishments were included in this study.

Figure 1. Map of UK Immigration Removal Centres, April 2014.

Signs recently erected in the gatehouses of IRCs entitled 'Detention Operations Mission' offer a little more explanation, yet do not stray far from this text:[10]

> Detention operations, part of immigration enforcement, serves the public by escorting and holding people detained under immigration law and by assisting in the removal of those not entitled to stay in the United Kingdom.

10. These signs are usually placed next to another outlining the 'Immigration Enforcement Customer Charter for Immigration Removal Centres' which 'sets out how you [the detainee] will be treated whilst in our care, and how we expect you [the detainee] to behave in return'.

Our purpose is to ensure that they are held securely and cared for with humanity.

Unlike other parts of the government, it is hard to find an official statement of purpose, 'vision', or a set of 'values' of immigration detention or those in charge of these facilities. While opting briefly for a slogan: 'detain, protect, remove', the Home Office soon abandoned even that descriptive ambition. It is likewise difficult to identify the name, scope, and nature of the government department responsible for these institutions. During the research project and since it finished, the immigration service within the Home Office has been relabelled several times, and seen its internal organization and leadership change as well.[11] The private contractors also alter frequently, while centres are closed and new ones opened with some regularity.

Such institutional uncertainty has been no barrier to debate or to expansion. For its proponents, immigration detention is a necessary part of border control, both a right and an obligation of the British sovereign state. Those without visas and immigration status are not entitled to stay and, if they will not go voluntarily, they must be detained to prompt their deportation. For critics, however, immigration removal centres should be abolished. They cause long-term psychological distress, are used in an arbitrary fashion, and are expensive and inefficient. Notwithstanding official claims that people are detained only briefly prior to their departure, such opponents point out a growing number languish in detention for months and even years (Phelps, 2009; HMIP and ICIBI, 2012).

In either set of arguments about immigration detention, little detail is given about the experience of confinement or the lives and identities of those detained. For the most part, due to the difficulties in gaining research access, critical scholarship has relied either on purely theoretical arguments about state power and sovereignty or on secondary material produced by NGOs, the media or the government. If commentators gather original empirical material about such places, and most do not, they typically do so through interviews with detainees in visits halls arranged by local NGOs, or speak to individuals who have been released.[12] As a result, and notwithstanding

---

11. At the time of writing, IRCs are now part of a section of the Home Office referred to as 'Immigration Enforcement'.

12. There are important exceptions to this claim, most obviously in the work of HMIP, as well as BID and other voluntary sector organizations who try to give voice to detainees and illuminate their experiences of incarceration.

a growing, interdisciplinary set of publications on border control practices around the world, we simply have very little sense of the social and cultural world of immigration detention centres. What do detainees do all day? How do they get along with the staff? How does detention make them feel? Where are they from? How do they cope? What are they like?

This book presents material from the first national study of life in British IRCs. Based on 20 months of fieldwork in six institutions, it draws on a large amount of empirical data, including 250 detainee surveys, over 500 unstructured detainee interviews (including life histories), 130 structured and unstructured staff interviews, over 2,400 hours of observation (the equivalent of three days per week over 20 months), and detailed field notes. This account presents more than just a description of life behind bars. Instead, it uses staff and detainee testimonies to revisit key assumptions about state power and the legacies of colonialism under conditions of globalization, exploring how IRCs designate certain people as strangers no matter how familiar. By focusing on the tensions between identification and identity, this study exposes the shifting and uneasy relational nature of power in the face of mass mobility. In so doing, it draws on and develops literature on the criminalization of migration and border criminologies, also known as the criminology of mobility (Stumpf, 2006; Aas, 2011; Aas and Bosworth, 2013), as well as utilizing longstanding ideas and approaches from the field of punishment and society (Simon and Sparks, 2012; Bosworth, 2012; Bosworth and Kaufman, 2013).

In a short period of time, immigration detention has attracted considerable academic attention. Some seek to delineate its parameters (Flynn, 2012; Guild, 2005), others to define its goals (Broeders, 2010; Hailbronner, 2007; Leerkes and Broeders, 2010; 2013; Mainwearing, 2012), and map its legal framework (Wilsher, 2012; Stevens, 2011; Cornelisse, 2010; Thwaites, 2014). In addition to a small (but growing) body of criminological research (see, for example, Miller, 2002; Pratt, 2005; Malloch and Stanley, 2005; Grewcock, 2010; Bosworth, 2012; 2013; Larsen and Piché, 2009; Leerkes and Brodeurs, 2010; Welch, 2002; Ugelvik and Ugelvik, 2013), there is a considerable quantity of reports produced each year by NGOs and government agencies around the world (see, inter alia, HMIP, 2013; IMB, 2013; Phelps, 2009; BID, 2013; Amnesty International, 2013; PICUM, 2013).[13]

---

13. See also the work of the Global Detention Project <http://www.globaldetentionproject.org>.

Scholars in refugee and migration studies (Silverman and Massa, 2012), political science (Gibney, 2004; 2008; Squire, 2010; Walters, 2002; 2006; Ceccorulli and Lebanca, 2014), human rights (Dembour, 2006; Dembour and Kelly, 2011), anthropology (Hall, 2010; 2012; Makaremi, 2009a; 2009b; Fassin, 2011; Fischer, 2013a; 2013b; De Genova, 2002; 2010; Griffiths, 2012; 2013), geography (Gill, 2009; Coleman and Kocher, 2011; Mountz, 2010; 2011a; 2011b), law (Wilsher, 2012; Cornelisse, 2010; Stumpf, 2006), and sociology (Bigo, 2008; Barker, 2012; 2013a; Schuster, 2005; Sanchez and Romero, 2010; Schuster and Bloch, 2005; Schuster and Majidi, 2013) locate immigration detention in larger debates about border control. Authors in political theory (Fraser, 2008; Benhabib, 2004; 2006; Walters, 2006), feminist (Butler, 2009; Butler and Spivak, 2009; Brown, 2010), and critical race theory (Ahmed, 2000; Sanchez and Romero, 2010; Hernandez, 2008) do the same. Primarily theoretical, much of this literature draws on Michel Foucault's (1991; 2004) writings on governmentality and biopower, and Giorgio Agamben's (1998; 2005) ideas of the state of exception and the Camp.

Whereas Foucault's notions of governmentality and biopower focus on the productive and controlling nature of power, the strategies and technologies by which the state manages populations and sets minimum thresholds of care, Agamben's work deliberately, and provocatively, invokes the horrors of the Nazi Concentration Camp to examine how the state annihilates and sacrifices the unwanted. An actual as well as metaphorical space, 'the camp' is directly connected to the 'state of exception', the power inherent in the liberal rule of law to suspend the usual rights in moments of emergencies. For Agamben, 'The camp is the space that is opened when the state of exception begins to become the rule' (Agamben, 1998: 63). It is 'the fundamental biopolitical paradigm of the West' (Agamben, 1998: 181). A system of governance outside the law.

All this work provides clues for a consideration of the nature and effect of this form of custody. Yet, in its predominantly theoretical bent, academic scholarship is sometimes difficult to square with life in detention. We receive little information about the texture of the institutions, how they differ from one another, their ambiguities, points of tension, or commonalities. In the priority given to Foucault and Agamben, other factors, most predicatably, race, gender (Bosworth and Kellezi, 2014), class (De Giorgi, 2010), and the role of the private sector (Bacon, 2005) tend to be overlooked. Foucault and Agamben also propose notoriously bleak world-views, offering little cause for hope or strategies for change.

[handwritten marginal note: was authordity – looking at a macro level]

Consequently, notwithstanding a handful of important exceptions (Hall, 2010; 2012; Fischer, 2013a; 2013b) and in marked contrast to the rich ethnographic studies of refugee camps elsewhere (and, we might add, of prisons), 'knowledge of these new detention sites, at the doors of Europe, remains limited' (Fassin, 2011: 219). It is that gap that this book starts to fill.

Who is detained and why?

Unlike other immigration systems in Australia, Italy, and Greece, where people are predominantly detained on arrival, removal centres in the UK are meant to be the final point in someone's migration. Non-British citizens may be detained following a criminal conviction, for over-staying a visa, for failing to possess a visa of any sort, or for working while on a holiday or student visa.[14] Foreigners may be held 'whilst identity and basis of claim are established, where there is a risk of absconding, as part of fast-track asylum procedures (in the case of straightforward asylum claims that can be decided quickly)' (Home Office, 2013a: 71). Former asylum seekers, whose claims have been rejected, may also be detained prior to their removal.

As with other countries, the UK is a signatory to various UN protocols, most importantly the 1951 UN Convention on Refugees and its 1967 Protocol, that are meant to restrict the kinds of people who can be detained, as well as the conditions under which they can be held.[15] In addition to observing the strictures on the *non-refoulement* of refugees set out in the 1951 Convention, unaccompanied minors, those who have been trafficked, and victims of torture should not be confined. Neither should anyone with serious mental or physical health problems 'if the condition cannot be satisfactorily managed' in detention.[16] Britain ought also be guided by

---

14. Most students are entitled to work a limited number of hours per week while studying although, like much of British immigration law, this arrangement is currently under review.

15. Other relevant human rights agreements which Britain has ratified include the 1966 International Convention on Civil and Political Rights, the 1966 International Covenant on Economic, Social and Cultural Rights, the 2000 Convention against Transnational Organized Crime, and its protocols on Human Trafficking (2003) and Smuggling of Migrants (2004), and the 2005 Council of Europe's Convention on Action Against Trafficking in Human Beings.

16. Although bureaucratic systems exist to weed out all these populations, they are not always successful. All the centres I visited included 'age-disputed' minors, ie individuals who were claiming to be younger than 18, as well as some who said they had been trafficked and/or tortured. Many appeared to be suffering from quite severe mental health problems, and

Article 5 of the European Convention on Human Rights (ECHR), which stipulates that:

1. Everyone has the right to liberty and security of person. No one shall be deprived of his liberty save in [particular] cases and in accordance with a procedure prescribed by law....

(f) the lawful arrest or detention of a person is only allowed to prevent his effecting an unauthorized entry into the country or of a person against whom action is being taken with a view to deportation or extradition....

2. Everyone who is arrested shall be informed promptly, in a language which he understands, of the reasons for his arrest and of any charge against him....

4. Everyone who is deprived of his liberty by arrest or detention shall be entitled to take proceedings by which the lawfulness of his detention shall be decided speedily by a court and his release ordered if the detention is not lawful.

5. Everyone who has been the victim of arrest or detention in contravention of the provisions of this article shall have an enforceable right to compensation.

Such international instruments are implemented at the national level, in the UK via the Human Rights Act 1998, in an ever-expanding body of criminal justice, immigration, and asylum legislation, and in various pieces of case law. More locally, Article 5 has been written into Chapter 55 of the UKBA *Operation Enforcement Manual* (OEM)[17] and is part of the 2001 Detention Centre Rules.[18]

---

some were clearly physically unwell. While we were conducting research in IRC Yarl's Wood, for example, one of the detainees had a (non-fatal) heart attack. In the period since my research ended, a 40-year-old woman, Christine Case, died of a heart attack at the same institution, while a number of men have expired in Colnbrook, and one man just hours after he was released. In February 2014, Alois Dvorzac, an elderly Canadian man, who had been detained in Harmondsworth upon arrival at Heathrow, died while handcuffed in hospital as centre staff belatedly sought assistance for his dementia (Allison, 2013; D. Taylor, 2014; Rawlinson, 2014).

17. Revised most recently in 2011 (UKBA, 2011).
18. On some matters, the guidelines surrounding detention seem unambiguous. Individuals should only be detained for a clear purpose, for a reasonable period of time, and under acceptable conditions. They must be informed of the reason for their detention and their

Most detention centres house relatively young men, the majority of whom are aged between 18 and 45 years. They are drawn from all over the world, but tend to originate from the global south. Most come from former colonies—India, Pakistan, Jamaica, Bangladesh—with a consistent minority haling from states in which the UK is, or was until recently, at war—eg Iraq and Afghanistan. There are exceptions to these generalizations: all detention centres hold a significant number of Chinese and a smaller sum of Vietnamese nationals, both from countries with which the UK has only had limited colonial involvement (outside Hong Kong). There are also, far more predictably, very few individuals from white former colonies. I met one white Australian citizen, one white Zimbabwean, and one white South African. I saw no New Zealanders or Canadians. One (black) man claimed to be from the US, although the authorities were disputing his nationality.

The women and men described in this study had entered Britain in a variety of ways: as members of a family group who sought asylum, often many years previously; as a spouse or fiancée; on a work permit; on a holiday visa; in the back of a lorry.[19] David, who was taken to the airport for deportation twice while I was in Colnbrook and returned each time when the paperwork for a judicial review of his immigration case was accepted for last minute consideration, arrived in the UK from Uganda when he was just three years old, part of a family fleeing persecution: 'that was the last time I was on a plane, man. Can you believe it?' he said, shaking his head (Uganda, CB). Now in his 20s, and despite having no remaining family members in Uganda, David was being forced out of the UK due to a string of criminal convictions for firearm offences that had nullified his indefinite leave to remain.

---

cases must be subject to regular (albeit administrative, internal, and undisclosed) review. On the other hand, however, such statements may come into conflict with contractual arrangements, particularly if the contract in question is rather old. Thus, while the operating standards require certain levels of medical care, the contract may not have budgeted for sufficient nursing staff. Similarly while the Detention Centre Rules advocates a 'productive use' of detainees' time, contracts stipulate only minimal training in ESOL classes and art and craft. In any case, they fail to articulate a clear goal, aim, or principle.

19. It is worth noting that most of those interviewed were far more comfortable listing their reasons for coming and desiring to stay than the practicalities of their arrival. Such reticence was, as expected, more marked among those who had either purchased false documents or arrived without any. IRCs are very low-trust environments and it was apparent that questions about the logistics of border crossing made many people uncomfortable, presumably due to their fear that I might report on them.

Another long-term Colnbrook detainee, Samien described his journey to the UK, during parts of which he hid under the axle of a lorry, as 'terrifying' (Palestine, CB). Deeply depressed,[20] alluding to experiences of torture and rape in Israel, Samien told me: 'When you are afraid, you can run, it doesn't matter. I just ran'. For Wali, a Turkish Kurd, forced to leave his home due to threats from the military, the journey was expensive. 'I paid 10,000 to come here', he disclosed. 'I travelled for 3–4 days in the lorry. There was a space in the middle, and we were covered by merchandise. There was no bed we just slept on the floor. The lorry driver gave us food and drinks because he knew about it. It was expensive but my brother paid for it as we have a farm' (Turkey, TH).

While Samien and Wali purchased false documents before leaving their country of origin, others, like Ena and Deb, paid for them through sex work during the voyage and after arrival in the UK. Chinese nationals, like Fen and Da-Xia were smuggled in on condition they would work in a restaurant, sell counterfeit DVDs, or cultivate marijuana. The more fortunate were sponsored by family members, assisted by acquaintances, or had simply qualified for a visa in their own right. Rana, from Bangladesh, for instance, whom I met in Brook House, had obtained a 'Tier two' visa to manage an Indian restaurant in London. He had lived in the UK for nine years, during which he had obtained an MBA from a British university. The physical border for this man had been legitimately traversed. It seemed as though he would succeed. Yet, he ended up in detention nonetheless, when he broke the terms of his visa, taking on a second job to earn more money.

Allocation to detention

Detainees like Samien, Rana, and Da-Xia are allocated to IRCs by Home Office staff working within the Detainee Escorting and Population Management Unit (DEPMU) upon receipt of a form known as an IS91 or 'warrant of detention', that must be completed by an immigration officer.[21] This warrant should only be issued if deportation is imminent,

---

20. Soon after our interview Samien was awarded temporary admission to the UK by the Home Office.
21. According to Chapter 31 of the June 2013 Immigration Directorates Instructions, 'in very few cases where neither the detention nor the movement of a detainee is being arranged

or if the individual is considered a flight risk. These conditions are not always observed. Not only are some people held for many months, suggesting their deportation was not imminent when they were first detained, but, staff made clear, detention could be used for other reasons altogether. 'The other day', one immigration officer at Colnbrook said angrily,

> we got sent a flea-infested vagrant. He was disgusting. They had to put him in segregation because he refused to wash . . . Lin Homer [the former head of what was then called UKBA[22]] had taken a personal interest in him; people had been complaining. So he was put on a bus from Leeds. Why did they pick him up in the first place? Does he have removal orders? I don't know. When he got here he smelled, but he is refusing to have a bath. We can't make him take a bath; he refused everything we offered him. He refused all blood tests. He scratched his head and you wouldn't want to know what came out (Elle, Home Office, CB).

There is no formal classification scheme for IRCs. Consequently, allocation decisions are, for the most part, made on the basis of bed space. Nevertheless, certain centres tend to attract particular kinds of cases. Home Office and custodial staff at Colnbrook, for instance, referred to it as a 'centre of last resort', claiming they often received men allocated whom other establishments would not accept due to their precarious mental health or serious criminal record.[23] 'A lot of problems here', Elle alleged, 'is that Colnbrook has a healthcare suite which has 6 beds, nurses, and an on-call doctor.[24] So we get sent difficult people. Other centres take less vulnerable persons. This is the last stop' (Home Office, CB). Alternatively, after enduring a number of disturbances and an escape in the first few years of the twenty-first century, Campsfield House capped the proportion of ex-prisoners whom they

---

via DEPMU. The form [IS91M] must be completed and used to notify both the detaining authority and the escorting agency of the proposed move' (Home Office, 2013b: para 8.3, p. 14).

22. The United Kingdom Border Agency (UKBA). The Agency's status was revoked in 2013 and its responsibilities returned to ministerial oversight within the Home Office. Despite this official shift in terminology and autonomy, at the time of writing in Spring 2014, UKBA continues to be used by many alongside immigration, 'immigration enforcement', and the Home Office. Throughout the book I use 'Immigration' and 'Home Office' interchangeably as well as UKBA when referring to the term used by the respondent.

23. On its website, the Home Office refers to Colnbrook as 'the most secure removal centre within the UK Border Agency estate' <http://www.ukba.homeoffice.gov.uk/aboutus/organisation/immigrationremovalcentres/colnbrook>.

24. 'The health care unit', Kevin, a member of the Senior Management Team (SMT) at Colnbrook noted, 'is filled with mental health cases waiting for beds at the PCT' (Primary Care Trust, ie local hospital) (SMT, CB).

would accept, leaving them with a higher proportion of visa over-stayers and those without documents.[25]

Staff in IRCs (via the centre manager) can ask DEPMU to transfer detainees to prison[26] or to another establishment, on the basis of good order and discipline or in response to a request from the detainee. Some women and men ask to be moved in order to be closer to their family and friends. Others are attracted by the reputation of certain establishments. Men in this project were particularly positive about Dungavel, also singling out Tinsley House and Campsfield House for praise. Most were critical of the high-security establishments, Colnbrook and Brook House, relieved to be away from them, or upset they were there. Long-term detainees sometimes request a move in order to alleviate their boredom. Everyone hopes that the immigration judge associated with a different establishment might take another view of their case (BID, 2010).[27] In all these respects women are far more limited in their options, able to circulate only between Yarl's Wood and prison, although they may be held for up to a week in the women's sections of Colnbrook (in a short-stay unit),[28] or Dungavel. If they are part of family groups, they may be held briefly in Tinsley House or at Cedars.

Transfer and release decisions can be made on other grounds as well. Once someone has removal directions he or she can be shifted to a short-term holding facility in or near a port. Such places hold women, men and families. The Home Office may temporarily admit detainees to the UK who are proving difficult to deport or remove, while individuals may also be granted bail by an immigration judge. Decisions about transfer and admission may also reflect factors unrelated to the person's case. On one occasion, for instance, during the research in Campsfield House, four men were temporarily admitted to the UK at the same time, an unusual occasion

---

25. As a strategy to avoid disruption, this was only mildly successful. In November 2013, one man who did not wish to be removed caused a conflagration which destroyed one of the two main housing blocks. He subsequently admitted to his crime in the Oxford Crown Court, and was sentenced to 32 months in prison.

26. In May 2013 the government announced a plan to ring-fence 1,000 beds in prison, in order to reduce the number of ex-prisoners in the detention estate, in order to reduce the average stay in an IRC and increase the 'throughput'. According to a senior civil servant, the Home Office wants to speed up the whole process yet again.

27. For more about decision-making in asylum tribunals, see Thomas, 2011; on the treatment of women in particular, see Baillot, Cowan, and Munro, 2013.

28. If the sum outnumbers the 27 available beds in Colnbrook, women may also find themselves held alongside men in the centre's far more austere Short-Term Holding Facility (STHF).

explained to me by reception staff as a result of a planned mass deportation. 'They must have chartered a flight', Keith deduced. 'When that happens, they gather together everyone who is going from all over and send them to Colnbrook and Brook House. That means we get people from those places so they have enough room' (DCO, CH). Similarly I was told by a number of people that around Christmas a higher proportion of detainees are temporarily admitted to Britain (ie released from detention), irrespective of the state of their immigration case.

What are detention centres like?

There is considerable variation among the centres in terms of their physical environment and how they are managed. Although the Home Office published a set of national operating standards in 2008 (UKBA, 2008), which all IRCs are required to follow, the institutions are each quite different from one another in terms of physical layout, population, and in the fine details of their contract. Such differences inevitably have an impact on the lived experience of detention.

Material conditions can be particularly significant. For instance, whereas Colnbrook (adjacent to Heathrow) and Brook House (next to the runway at Gatwick) were both built according to highly restricted Category B Prison security standards, Campsfield House, outside Oxford, is a much older institution that has served a number of purposes from military barracks to a Young Offenders Institution (YOI). Campsfield House operates a 'free flow' regime, where detainees can walk freely around the building and access a grassy outdoor area all day from early in the morning until late at night. At Colnbrook and Brook House, in contrast, movements are more circumscribed and there is far greater time spent locked on the units or in the rooms with no fresh air.

Within each centre there are multiple layers of governance. While the private contractors, or HM Prison Service, are responsible for the day-to-day running of the removal centres, they are accountable to an onsite 'immigration manager' whose job is to check that the contract is followed. Such people usually have limited prior experience of working in a custodial environment, and may hold different expectations about such places and their inhabitants than HM Prison Service or the private custody firms.

The immigration manager oversees a number of local immigration officers who mediate between the detainees and their immigration case-workers based elsewhere. Immigration officers meet with detainees in 'legal visits', passing documents and information between them and their case workers. They represent the face of the Home Office in detention, serving removal directions and communicating decisions about bail, temporary admission, and asylum. They do not, however, make those decisions.

All centres contract out their cleaning and healthcare services. The healthcare contract is usually awarded to a local GP practice, and a doctor will be available most days. In removal centres run by the prison service, healthcare is provided by the National Health Service (NHS).[29] Some centres employ counsellors and education staff, others do not, opting instead to use Detention Custody Officers to run art and craft courses. Some—like Colnbrook—train detainees to act as 'Buddies' offering advice to new arrivals and anyone feeling depressed. Others have no such organized arrangements relying instead on informal networks among the detainees and religious volunteers to offer additional support to those in need.

The daily regime in detention is limited. According to the operating standards (UKBA, 2008), the contractors must offer lessons in English as a second language (ESOL), art and craft and leisure activities, including gym. They must also make available internet access and offer some level of IT training. There is no requirement for any paid work, vocational training, or higher education.

All removal centres rely on voluntary organizations to supplement their daily regime. They are required to work with a local visitor group, that is part of the national body, the Association of Visitors to Immigration Detainees (AVID). Members of these organizations visit detainees socially, and, on occasion, provide them with small sums of money or phone cards. They also can direct them to other groups or immigration solicitors who may be able to offer advice and assistance. Bail for Immigration Detainees (BID) operate in most centres helping detainees fill out bail applications and lodge asylum claims, while other volunteer groups are also active. Music in Detention runs workshops in many detention centres, in Colnbrook

29. After the fieldwork ended, the government announced that it would be handing over the medical care in all centres to the NHS. However, the process of transferring from private healthcare contractors to the public sector has been slow and, at the time of writing, is still incomplete.

producing CDs with detainees in a purpose-built recording studio. Finally, until April 2014 representatives from the International Organisation of Migration (IOM) or Refugee Action, who sought to encourage individuals to return voluntarily to their country of origin by offering them financial assistance to set up businesses or to undergo training upon their return, held regular workshops for detainees.[30]

What are removal centres for?

In both their population and their institutional make-up, removal centres defy simple taxonomy. Ostensibly the destination for people en route to the airport, they also house women and men for upwards of six months and sometimes longer. Although deportation and the detention that precedes it is a matter of administrative law, foreign offenders are now routinely given deportation orders by judges and magistrates as part of their criminal sentence. Considerable ambivalence and confusion remain, however, about the precise or desired relationship between the immigration and criminal justice systems.

There is a national immigration detention system. Yet, there is no single national service provider. Rather, the institutions are divided between companies and HM Prison Service and are run by them according to terms set out in their private contracts. Ultimately, the Home Office is responsible for the centres, yet, on a day-to-day level, they have devolved this duty via the contract. Centre managers meet collectively throughout the year with the Home Office, while the head of detention services or his or her deputy chairs regular committee meetings with centre staff addressing particular issues like Safer Custody. During the research there was also a committee known as the 'Detention Users Group' that brought together representatives from the voluntary sector with the Home Office staff to discuss their concerns about immigration detention, although this has since been disbanded. In any case, among these various groups there is little shared corporate culture and no cohesive statement of values or approach. The contractors, after all, are competitors with one another, and often with the voluntary sector who are among their harshest critics.

---

30. For a critical account of the role of humanitarian agencies in border control, see Walters, 2011 and Lee, 2013.

The fragmented and complex system of governance and responsibility contributes to a lack of clarity over the aims of detention. Among those I met, the bases for the decisions to detain, admit, or remove as well as the duration of confinement were also poorly understood.[31] Would I 'be asking how UKBA made their decisions about who to release and who to keep?' Keith, and others, wanted to know (DCO, CH).[32] Such uncertainty over the duration and justification for detention at all levels of IRCs, from the detainees to the Home Office, are compounded by the variety of pathways to detention. Only by going inside can we try to make better sense of IRCs. Bearing witness to daily life, and observing how women and men interact, reveal the trials of living and working in such a liminal space. As subsequent chapters will show, whereas detention centres were initially founded to offer some due process protections, rather like the lower criminal courts observed by Malcolm Feeley (1979) in the 1970s, such aspirations had unintended consequences, that have lead to a system with few proponents.

The field of immigration detention is a fluid one. Not only does immigration law and policy frequently change, but removal centres have high staff turnover at all levels. Such developments pose considerable challenges to the researcher, both in obtaining access and in reporting findings. It is important, in other words, to recognize the shifting context, and to accept, that by the time this book is published some aspects of the system will have altered again. At the same time, it is equally necessary to accept that generalizations can be made and lessons learned. With this ambition, this book starts by tracing the longer history of detention.

In order to make sense of the current system, the book proceeds as follows. Chapter 1 establishes the historical development of the current system and refines the image of it that has been sketched in this introduction. Chapter 2 sets out the practicalities of the study, while Chapters 3–7 draw on staff and detainee testimonies to flesh out our understanding of

---

31. Recent work in geography (eg Gill, 2009; Michalon, 2013; Moran, Conlon, and Gill, 2013) has emphasized the need to concentrate on transfers and what they refer to as the 'forced mobility' within networks of detention and border control more generally. See also Herd, 2011.

32. While I interviewed some staff in DEPMU for this project, I did not speak with the 'case owners' or others with the power to detain. Subsequently, however, I have administered a survey and conducted focus group interviews with a series of such staff. The findings from that project can be found in Bosworth and Bradford, forthcoming.

immigration detention. In these chapters, I explore matters of identity and community, paying particular attention to matters of race and gender. Despite the undeniable vulnerabilities of detainees, I find considerable ambivalence and uncertainty about border control under conditions of mass mobility.

IRCs identify their inhabitants as strangers, constructing them as unfamiliar, ambiguous, and uncertain. In this endeavour, they are greatly assisted by their resemblance to prisons and by familiar racialized narratives about foreigners and nationality. However, as staff and detainee testimonies reveal, in their interactions and day-to-day life, women and men find many points of commonality. In their interactions and recognition of one another, the goal and effect of detention is shown to be incomplete. Denial requires effort. It can be challenged.

In order to minimize the effort it must expend, the state 'governs at distance', via the contract. It also splits itself in two, deploying some immigration staff onsite, while keeping the actual decision-makers (the caseworkers) elsewhere, sequestered from the potentially destabilizing effects of facing up to those they wish to remove. Such distancing, while bureaucratically effective, contributes to the uncertainty of daily life in detention, and is often the source of considerable criticism and unease. Denial and familiarity are embodied and localized activities, whose pains and contradictions inhere in concrete relationships. Such matters, which become visible through applied research, raise profound questions about the limits and pains of denial under conditions of mass mobility. These matters form the basis of the conclusion in which I argue for a more moderate approach to border control.

Conclusion

Despite the best efforts of those working in detention, detainees across the board—whether former prisoners or visa over-stayers—articulate a number of common concerns. Reflecting the enduring nature of Empire, as well as their period of residence in the UK, most of those confined speak some English. However, few are fully literate. Many have great difficulty reading the Home Office documentation relating to their immigration case or the signs around the removal centres advertising courses or events. They may also find it hard to communicate with custody officers and one another. Many are confused about why they are detained and nobody knows how long they will be there. They find it difficult, despite the availability of mobile phones, to maintain contact with their families and, even though centres arrange family-day visits to assist with contact with children, few take this option.

Detainees are often unable to obtain a trustworthy and effective immigration solicitor. Fewer and fewer of them are entitled to legal aid. Many are frustrated by the limited amount of paid work and education in detention, particularly if they have served a prison sentence during which they have taken advantage of a wide range of courses and programmes. Healthcare remains, across the board, a source of great anxiety.

Such complaints are likely to be disheartening for centre managers and staff, as well as for those working in immigration, some of whom are actively striving to improve conditions behind bars. The findings do not make for optimistic reading for detainees, their families, or their supporters. For all concerned, these problems are also likely to be familiar. The question remains, then, why are these failings so entrenched and why do they have such little impact on the legitimacy of the practice of immigration detention?

It seems plausible that there may be limitations inherent in the contracts—although, since these are protected, private documents, it is not possible to be sure about their content. Likewise, it is clear that most people in detention do not wish to be deported, so they are hardly likely to be satisfied with their treatment. Instead, they are anxious, depressed, and often angry.

Yet, there is also a more substantive point to be made about the utilitarian justification of detention as no more than a means to the end of enforcing deportation. Just as legal scholars (von Hirsch, 1976) argued in the 1970s that approaching punishment in a purely utilitarian fashion was unjust, so too it seems clear that considering detention in this way is a large part of the problem. What we need instead is greater attention to detention centres and a tougher examination of those they house in their own terms. To do so effectively, we must uncouple detention from a criminal justice imagination and generate new ideas and language to understand them.

In so doing, we may need to leave behind the traditional vocabulary that centres on legitimacy in our analysis of state power (Beetham, 1991). On what basis might we find a shared perspective and beliefs? In a global world, and in institutions situated at the limits of the nation state, how useful is this term anyway? Instead, we should concentrate on why we detain *foreign-ers* and treat them in the way we do. In terms of the IRCs, such questions become quite simple. What is detention like? What is it for? What is its effect?

Why do foreigners, particularly in a postcolonialist multicultural coun-try like the UK, generate such a response? What is it about those without citizenship that enables us (morally and ethically) to perceive them differ-ently from ourselves? What are the costs to us, to those who work with them and to detainees of this estrangement? Given the enormous financial and personal burdens, which will be elucidated in the coming pages, what might it take to think and act otherwise? Although detainees may not, by law, have the right to remain, they do have the right to call on us as fellow human beings. In their current form, detention centres make it hard to rec-ognize that right and this situation needs to change. This book will make that case.

I

The historical development of immigration detention in Britain

They seem to think that all foreigners are liars, and there is an underlying assumption that all the black people in the world want to come and live in Britain ('Asian detainee' in Harmondsworth, cited in Wilson, 1975: 12).

This country has a precious gift of geography which Continental nations envy . . . no internal control is as efficient as one at the entrance. If this country has not yet reached a state of civilisation whereby front doors can be abolished and the individual's home left open to all comers, how much less can it afford to fling wide the national front door! (Roche, 1969: 254).

The British government has long had the power to confine or expel foreign nationals simply because of their citizenship either as they arrived or once they were already resident (Wilsher, 2012; Weber and Bowling, 2008). The composition of the population over whom this power has been wielded has shifted over time from Irish immigrants looking for work, Central and Eastern European Jews escaping the pogroms of the late nineteenth and early twentieth centuries, Commonwealth citizens in the post-war era, to, more recently, those whose claims of persecution are not believed, terror suspects, economic migrants, ex-prisoners, and students (Cohen, 1994; Panayi, 1994; Holmes, 1988; 1991; Hansen, 2000; Bloch and Schuster, 2005). During the two world wars, Britain created internment camps for citizens of their enemies, fearful of their divided loyalties (Wilsher, 2012; Simpson, 1992; Panayi, 1994; Cohen, 1994; Cesarani and

Kushner, 1993).[1] In addition to these camps, between 1941 and 1945, Britain screened arrivals from occupied Europe for possible adversaries, housing them in two reception centres in Wandsworth, London.[2] More recently, they have held failed and current asylum seekers, undocumented migrants, visa overstayers, and former foreign offenders in prisons and in detention centres.

In this chapter I expose the longer roots of current practice. Although I examine legislation from earlier periods, I locate the origins of the contemporary British immigration detention system in the opening of the Harmondsworth Detention Unit in 1970. Designed to house Commonwealth citizens denied entry at the border who had been given in-country right of appeal under the Immigration Appeals Act 1969, Harmondsworth and its sister institution in Dover Castle linked custody and border control in new ways. Although tiny in comparison with the number of beds used in prison to hold foreigners at the time, they unlocked the potential for administrative confinement of foreign nationals, thereby expanding state power. In their population, they also revealed an early racialization that has yet to abate (see Figure 2).

In giving an historical overview, I do not seek to draw a straight line from the past to the present, but rather to argue for the importance of context and nuance. As this chapter will demonstrate, migration control has always been contested. While there are particular debates surrounding contemporary practice, putting immigration detention in an historical setting will not only help us understand Immigration Removal Centres today but also reveals enduring ambiguities and disjunctures. Voices from the past are sometimes difficult to understand. At other points they sound remarkably familiar. Issues that appear throughout this book can be found in the historical record, where concerns about crime and community cohesion jostle with calls for compassion and sanctuary. Starting with the law, before turning to the detention centres themselves, I trace the key debates over border control and confinement in order to illuminate these enduring debates. Taking a longer view unearths varied and intersecting motivations for border control as well an enduring ambivalence about it.

---

1. On the Second World War, records held in the National Archives, London, in series HO 396 (1939–47) give some details of individual cases.
2. Information about this scheme can be found in the National Archives in a number of files including: KV2, KV4, KV 4/339, and KV 4/342.

Figure 2. Harmondsworth detainees, 1980 (Photo credit: *Hillingdon Mirror,* Trinity Group).

The promise of the past

In any era, voices of critique can be found wondering whether the state should regulate mobility at all and bemoaning the methods of doing so. Specific populations, particularly individuals seeking protection, children, and those with lengthy residency and family ties to Britain, have always been troubling. While voices of moderation are usually drowned out by the more strident, their concerns remain remarkably consistent. As such they provide important examples of and insights into those questions about purpose and legitimacy with which this book is concerned.

Politicians, journalists, lawyers, academics, activists, and migrants routinely query the justification of border control and immigration detention. Some favour the abolition of borders altogether. More commonly people express concerns about the restriction of certain populations. Critics address the conditions and length of time in detention (HL Deb 9 June 1978, vol 392 col 1674; D'Orey, 1984; Phelps, 2009), the involvement of the private sector (*The Times*, 1970; Bacon, 2005), the robustness of legal safeguards and due process (HC Deb 22 January 1969, vol 776 col 509; Fordham, Stefanelli, and Eser, 2013; Ashford, 1994; Woolf, 1988), the treatment of asylum seekers (HC Deb 2 August 1972, col 842; HL Deb 9 June 1978, vol 392 col 1677; Griffiths, 2013), race relations (Solomos, 1991; Bosworth and Kellezi, 2014; Jenkins, 1984), and practices of deportation (Brockway, 1978; Gibney, 2013; Brotherton and Barrios, 2013). Their concerns are not just practical but also discursive as they resist the divisive rhetoric about foreigners that all too easily takes hold.

Such views can be found over a long period of time. 'Can we think calmly', Lord Brockway demanded in the House of Lords in 1978,

> of what the deportation of persons long resident in this country means to them? Losing their jobs, giving up their homes, lifting their children, often born in this country, from their schools, seeking somehow for new security in countries with which they have lost familiarity, exiled, with perhaps nine months to wait before their distant appeal is heard.[3]

In the same discussion, Lord Avebury took aim at the uncertain length of duration, in a searing critique that seems remarkably familiar. 'People detained under the Immigration Act powers', he asserted,

> are unique among the prison population in that their future is entirely uncertain. Everybody else knows when he is next to appear in court or when he is to be released on completion of his sentence. The person detained under the Immigration Act powers has not the faintest idea when the Secretary of State will get around to considering his representations, if indeed he has been lucky enough to find anybody to make them on his behalf. The degree of uncertainty which is facing detainees in this position is undoubtedly a source of great distress and anxiety, and it is not surprising that some of them emerge from their ordeal suffering from severe mental ill health.[4]

In a House of Commons' debate on the administration of the 1968 Commonwealth Immigrants Act some years previously, the Labour member for Hackney Central, Clinton Davis, compared the growing restrictions over immigration to the Holocaust.

---

3. HL Deb 9 June 1978, vol 392 col 1674.
4. HL Deb 9 June 1978, vol 392 col 1677.

I cannot help likening the position to that which arose before the war. I am Jewish. A number of my relatives who were in Europe died in concentration camps. In those days a large number of people applied to be admitted to the United Kingdom, the United States and elsewhere but Governments adduced all kinds of reasons which, on the face of them, appeared to be sound and logical, though perhaps not very compassionate, for refusing admittance. . . As a result they died or were savagely tortured.[5]

Concerned particularly about groups of Kenyan and Ugandan citizens of Indian origin who had been denied entrance to the UK, Davis went on,

I am not suggesting that the position is totally analogous. There is not the direct physical persecution in the same way, but there is a form of persecution here. There is a form of intolerance, of relying upon rules and regulations and of ignoring the common humanity of the position. Nobody wants these people. Because nobody wants them, they are totally rejected and subjected to a form of persecution.[6]

The past does not simply reveal periods of greater (and lesser) compassion, but also a changing tempo of state intervention in which the British government gradually and then more rapidly began to deny entrance, remove, deport, and eventually, detain (Hansen, 2000; Wilsher, 2012; Wray, 2006). These developments occur alongside and are sometimes caused by changes in the nature of the populations who become subject to immigration control. As such, they signal the importance of context. The state tends to be reactive rather than proactive in immigration law, responding to events occurring beyond its shores as well as to those happening within. At the same time, however, each decision that is made to extend state power reflects existing, longer-term fears and views about the population in question.

A longer view demonstrates the enduring nature of increased powers of intervention. Once developed, the state rarely hands back its control. Even when powers were infrequently used, as in those allowing for the detention of undesirable aliens in the 1905 Aliens Act, they were not expunged.

Undermining any easy assumptions about the deliberate or systematic use of exceptional powers, however, parliamentary and archival documents also expose an enduring lack of planning where border control is concerned. It is often simply reactive. It is almost never principled, and, as

5. HC Deb 2 August 1972, vol 842 cols 859–60.
6. HC Deb 2 August 1972, vol 842 col 860.

a result, many acknowledge, hard to justify. Newspapers throughout the 1970s, for example, ran story after story on East African Asians seeking protection and residence in the UK as Colonial subjects with British passports.[7] Eventually the UK did resettle tens of thousands of this group, not before, however, expelling, detaining, and imprisoning many (Jenkins, 1984; Twaddle, 1974). A similar story took place in the late 1980s, when a large number of Tamils from Sri Lanka arrived. Corresponding to a period when prisons in England and Wales were severely over-crowded and disruptive, the unexpected arrival of Tamils meant that they were housed in a hastily rigged out floating detention centre on *MV Earl William* (see Figure 3), moored at Harwich alongside the quay (Ashford, 1994).

Chartered by the Conservative government from Sealink, the firm better known for its ferries to France, the *Earl William* was staffed by officers from Securicor. It was, Douglas Hurd, the Secretary of State for the Home Department, explained, 'A modern car ferry; sleeping accommodation is in four-berth cabins, each with integral sanitation'.[8] While the boat was able to hold 240 people, Hurd expected it to hold 'no more than 120'. Conditions, he assured parliament, were not too bad: 'The public rooms on the ship will provide adequate space for relaxation and visits by relatives, friends and lawyers in comfortable but not luxurious conditions'. Pressed into service in May 1987, the boat was abandoned by the end of October that year, soon after it broke away from its moorings during a storm on 16 October, and drifted across Harwich harbour with more than 40 Tamil asylum seekers aboard.

Just as the government routinely is taken by surprise at the number of people arriving, so, too, at certain points, politicians appear to be troubled by questions about their responsibilities towards those who wish to settle. In a memorandum to Cabinet in July 1965, for instance, the Lord President

7. On the first, see Patrick Brogen, 'An Asian odyssey that ended in a cul de sac', *The Times*, Friday 18 August 1970: 10 that describes the ordeal of a group of 21, 20 of whom, he writes, 'are called Patel, which complicates record-keeping. They are all Gujerati from Bombay and decided to set out together... They are mostly in their late teens or early twenties' and all had British passports. Refused entry to the UK when they attempted to come in from France, they were sent back to Boulogne after a night in Canterbury Prison. A few months later in the same newspaper, a similar case, involving three individuals can be found under the title of 'review of Asians' case after 3-week shuttle', *The Times*, 31 October 1970: 3. In this case, ten Kenyan Asians were shuttled back and forth between Europe and Africa when nobody would let them land, until, eventually, the UK government confined them in Ashford remand centre and Pentonville Prison.

8. HC Deb 1 May 1987, vol 115 cols 259–60.

Figure 3. *MV Earl William* moored in Harwich Harbour as a temporary deten-tion centre, 1987 (Photo credit: Ian Boyle <http://www.simplonpc.co.uk>).

of the Privy Council, Herbert Bowden, claimed that, 'Britain has always been reluctant to restrict the entry of people who hope to find greater opportunities within her shores',[9] before setting out in detail the govern-ment's concerns about the growing numbers of Commonwealth arrivals and plans for their restriction.

Finally, and often abutting concerns about border control, the historical development of immigration detention draws together the crucial nature of fears about race and national identity in policy development. Until more recent rhetorical developments, which have placed 'immigration' along-side 'asylum', or, even 'terrorism', immigration appeared in reports (Rose et al, 1969; Scarman, 1981; Parekh, 2000), legislation (see, for example, the 1965, 1968, and 1972 Race Relations Acts), government committees (Home Office, 1967; Race Relations Board, 1967), and royal commissions (Royal Commission, 1949), political (Foot, 1965), and academic literature (Paul, 1997; Gilroy, 2002; Solomos, 1991) as an adjunct to 'race'. In the House of Commons' debate on 2 August 1972 about the treatment of Commonwealth

9. 23 July 1965, *Commonwealth Immigration*, Memorandum to Cabinet by the Lord President of the Privy Council, CAB 129/122/9.

citizens mentioned above, for instance, David Lane, then Under-Secretary of State for the Home Department initially agreed with his opponents. 'Of course it is distressing to the individuals involved', he said, 'who as we know are United Kingdom passport holders in a special position within the entirety of would-be Commonwealth immigrants and to whom I acknowledge at once, this country has a special responsibility'. Nonetheless, he went on, 'Equally plainly, *a prerequisite of good race relations in Britain is control of immigration which is tight and is seen to be tight*'[10] (emphasis added).

History also reveals the economic nature of much migration and the border control it inspires. Long before academic debates over the connections between mass migration, post-Fordism (De Giorgi, 2010), and neo-liberalism (Melossi, 2013; Sitkin, 2013) or the popularization of the term 'economic migrant' to refer, disparagingly, to those who move in search of work, right-wing opponents to migration warned that, 'we cannot go on keeping open house for the paupers of all the world' (Jeyes, 1892: 191). On the left as well, Dario Melossi (2013) points out, foreign workers were inherently mistrusted, excluded from the native working classes and considered all too easily manipulated by capital.

Often these matters intersect. In an edited collection from the nineteenth century arguing for greater border controls, anti-Semitism merged seamlessly with a materialist analysis (White, 1892). The delightfully named Hubert Montague Crackanthorpe glowered, 'The Polish Jew drives the British workman out of the labour market just as a base currency drives a pure currency out of circulation' (Crackanthorpe, 1892: 59). Seventy years later, in a letter to *The Telegraph*, the former Under-Secretary of State at the Home Office, the Right Hon Dame Patricia Hornsby-Smith updated the connection, concerned no longer specifically with Jews, but with almost everyone else. 'For every Briton who wants to work abroad', she opined, 'there are a hundred Europeans and a thousand coloured people who, given the chance, would stream into Britain. We, therefore, must have immigration control' (Hornsby-Smith, 1968).

Immigration legislation

It is difficult, these days, at least in Britain, to imagine a world without strict mechanisms of border control. Yet, passports, visas, and immigration officials,

10. HC Deb 2 August 1972, vol 842 cols 862–3.

not to mention detention centres, are, to a large extent, twentieth-century inventions. To be sure, controls existed before. Early modern Europe operated with complex rules and expectations governing mobility (Weber and Bowling, 2007; Fahrmeir, 2000). Yet, for the most part, freedom of movement was, until the twentieth century, the preserve of the wealthy or the armed forces, controlled by a series of practices that are not strictly comparable to the bureaucratic mechanisms that characterize migration control today.

In most accounts of British immigration law, scholars date the beginning of the contemporary system of border control to the Aliens Act 1905 (Wray, 2006), even though earlier restrictions can be found in the 1793, 1815, and 1848 Alien Expulsion Acts (Wilsher, 2012; White, 1892) and in local parish practices (Weber and Bowling, 2007). The reason the 1905 Act is singled out is because it gave responsibility to the Home Secretary for all matters concerning immigration and nationality, thus centralizing control and establishing immigration officers at ports. It also differentiated between 'desirable' and 'undesirable' immigrants, the former of whom were allowed to settle, while the latter could be denied leave to enter. For the first time, British law required captains to declare the names and numbers of those in steerage class, and stipulated that individuals seeking to land had proof of financial capacity to support themselves. Specifically in terms of detention, it also gave the Home Secretary powers to deport (under an 'expulsion order') foreign citizens, who could be 'kept in custody' prior to their ejection.

Just as the 1905 Act introduced the practice of border control for (some) arrivals, the Aliens Restriction Act 1914, that was followed by the Aliens Restriction (Amendment) Act 1919, gave the Secretary of State emergency powers to deny entrance, detain, and deport. Whereas the 1905 Act concentrated on *arrivals*, the emergency legislation passed during the First World War sought to control foreign *residents*. Aliens were required to register with the police from 1914 and had to pay a fee. In return they received a certificate—an early form of ID card.[11] Although originally introduced as temporary measures in response to armed conflict, in a move prefiguring more recent reactions to terrorist events, such 'emergency' powers were continually renewed until they were incorporated into the Immigration Act 1971.

---

11. A sample of these cards from London spanning from 1918 until their abolition in 1957 can be found in the National Archives records of the Metropolitan Police in series MEPO 35.

Until the 1940s, broadly speaking, immigration legislation in Britain responded to external events not all of which directly involved the UK. After the Second World War, however, immigration control became more narrowly focused on the dissolution of the British Empire. While other global anxieties—notably the spread of Communism and the Cold War—were invoked in the constant renewal of the emergency powers, increasingly, legislation responded to Britain's changing relationship to places it had previously governed. Such laws also articulated a new, post-colonial, British national identity (Gilroy, 2002; Spencer, 2002).

Parliamentary debates, newspaper accounts, and government reports over these years, reveal a range of competing and contradictory demands to recognize on the one hand while restricting on the other, the rights of former imperial subjects (see eg Home Office, 1965; the National Committee for Commonwealth Immigrants, 1965–68). While the British Nationality Act 1948, which created the category of Citizenship of the UK and Colonies, included those born outside the territory, the Commonwealth Immigrants Act 1962 and the Commonwealth Immigrants Act 1968, narrowed access to British citizenship. The 'patrial' system, brought in under the 1968 Act, offered a right of abode only to those members of the Commonwealth who could boast a British father or grandfather, effectively linking the right to enter and reside with race, stripping such benefits from thousands of former subjects who had previously held them under the 1948 Act. The 1968 Act also expanded powers to deny entrance and restrict the right to enter for British subjects, creating a voucher system to try to 'manage' migration (Evans, 1972).

Such developments did not go unchallenged (Deakin, 1970; Jenkins, 1984). Considerable disquiet arose over the impact of immigration restrictions on citizens from all of the Commonwealth nations, not just the more favoured (whiter) ones of Australia, New Zealand, and Canada. Debates over the responsibility towards former imperial subjects came to a head in 1969 (Rose et al, 1969; Hansen, 2000). Following recommendations by the Committee on Immigration Appeals, generally referred to as the Wilson Committee (Home Office, 1967),[12] concerns grew over the rule of law and accountability in relation to Commonwealth citizens denied entry at the border, who were being returned to their country of origin without legal

---

12. The notes and papers of which, as well as the final report, are available in the National Archives in file LAB 8/3398.

recourse. 'It is very important that we have a system of appeal, and that justice is seen to be done, because of our status as a nation', proclaimed the Labour MP for Bolton West, Gordon Oakes. 'We hear a great deal today about Britain's prestige in the world', he went on,

> whether it is said to be declining or whatever else may be happening to it, but our prestige as a nation that believes in the rule of law and justice for all its citizens is still unchallenged throughout the world. Yet the very point where a Commonwealth citizen or alien sets foot on our shores has for 55 years been the point where the rules of justice have not applied, where he has had to be subject to an arbitrary decision by a civil servant with no right of appeal. That happens just when he has arrived at the place that he and his countrymen have been taught to regard as the mother of freedom and justice.[13]

In 1969, such concerns led to the Immigration Appeals Act that created the right for Commonwealth citizens to lodge in-country appeals when denied entry. Although rooted in concerns about the rule of law and accountability, this Act greatly expanded the Immigration Service and concomitant Tribunals and resulted in the first purpose-built Immigration Detention Centre outside an airport or prison, the Harmondsworth Detention Unit. These controls were consolidated and enhanced two years later by the Immigration Act 1971 that gave police powers to stop and search and ask for immigration documents, while also allowing for greater use of detention before deportation (Evans, 1972).

Despite such changes wrought to the status of Commonwealth citizens, the British Nationality Act 1948 stood unchanged until 1981 (Gardner, 1980). Amended many times since, the British Nationality Act 1981 made it more difficult to acquire British citizenship restricting *Jus Soli* to those children born on UK territory to permanent residents. For anyone else, nationality could only now be passed on if at least one parent was already a

---

13. HC Deb 22 January 1969, vol 776 col 509. Two months later when the Bill had its second reading in the House of Lords, more critical voices can be discerned, in those who did not wish to expand the right of appeal (see, for instance, Lord Brooke of Cumnor in the discussion of 'Immigration Appeals Bill', HL Deb 27 March 1969, vol 300 cols 1426–32). Nonetheless, the Bill was eventually carried. Concerns over justice, fairness, and due process, Lord Foot made clear, were persuasive. 'Do I regard the need for some appellate system, so that it may be seen to all the world and by the immigrant himself that he is getting a fair deal, that his case is being heard and that due consideration is being given to his particular circumstances, as overriding the difficulties which there are in occasionally transferring to a body of this kind questions which are the subject matter of discretion?', Lord Foot demanded. 'My answer to that question is "Yes"' (HL Deb 27 March 1969, vol 300 col 1434).

British citizen. For the first time, women could convey their citizenship to their children (Joppke, 1999; Weil, 2005).

Although often overlooked in recent accounts of immigration detention, the 1980s witnessed a continued restriction on immigration and an expansion of the power to deport residents, under the terms of the 1986 and 1988 Immigration Acts (Platt, 1991). During this decade, most detainees continued to be held in prison. In December 1983, one of them, Hardial Singh, appealed his post-sentence detention in Durham prison (*R v Governor of Durham Prison, ex parte Hardial Singh* [1984] 1 WLR 704). In his ruling dated the following year, then Justice Woolf made the first legal statement about the indefinite nature of detention. 'While the power given to the Secretary of State to detain individuals is not subject to an express time limit', Woolf determined,

> it does have limitations. The detainee can only be detained if he is subject to a deportation order, or is awaiting his removal. Further this period of waiting is limited to what can be deemed reasonably necessary for the Secretary of State to act to remove the detainee. If he is not acting with reasonable speed, then the Secretary of State must cease the detention (at 706).

Referred to as the 'Hardial Singh principles' this statement was the first attempt to determine the foundations of a time limit to detention in case law; a goal that has yet to be settled in UK law.

Outside Britain, the 1980s witnessed a steady stream of asylum seekers and migrants begin to escalate. It was also a decade of intense prison over-crowding. As the sum of asylum seekers held in prisons in England and Wales grew, the prison service and the immigration authorities began to concentrate them in specific prisons around London, starting with HMP Ashford, then HMP Latchmere and finally, in 1989, in HM Young Offenders Institute Haslar.[14]

---

14. On 10 March 1989, a particularly large group of men were resettled in Haslar from HMP Latchmere House. As Douglas Hogg, then Parliamentary Under Secretary of State at the Home Office, reported, out of a total population of 157 in Latchmere House, 94 men were being held under the Immigration Act (HC Deb 13 March 1989, vol 149 col 9). Moving them to Haslar, Hogg pointed out, reduced overcrowding and opened up more bed space in this site in Kingston-upon-Thames for remand prisoners who were otherwise being held in police cells in London. The move from Latchmere House, however, was not without its detractors, and was debated at some length in the House of Lords and the House of Commons. See eg HC Deb 13 March 1989, vol 149 cols 9–10 and the following month HL Deb 6 April 1989, vol 505 cols 1193–5.

During the 1990s the number of asylum seekers to Britain soared. This was also a decade when internal immigration enforcement toughened; 1993 was particularly significant on both counts. Joy Gardner, a Jamaican citizen, died during an attempt by the London Metropolitan Police to restrain her in an immigration raid to enforce her removal. It saw the passage of the Immigration and Asylum Appeals Act 1993 that allowed for the detention of asylum seekers during the consideration of their case while also giving them a right to appeal. This was also the year that Campsfield House Detention Centre opened outside Oxford. Three years later, the Asylum and Immigration Act 1996 further tightened control, consolidating the practice of immigration detention as a result. That year, Tinsley House, the first contemporary purpose-built detention centre designed and constructed by a private security company on behalf of the Home Office, opened adjacent to Gatwick airport.

In 1997, New Labour ended 18 years of Tory party rule. Although in opposition they had often spoken critically about the treatment of immigrants and asylum seekers, once elected, they oversaw a rapid expansion of powers to detain and deport foreign citizens, presiding over the largest expansion of the immigration detention to date (Aliverti, 2013). As they were to do in criminal justice, the Labour government legislated enthusiastically on matters of border control, passing seven Acts between 1999 and 2009 related to immigration matters: the Immigration and Asylum Act 1999, the Nationality, Immigration and Asylum Act 2002, the Asylum and Immigration (Treatment of Claimants, etc) Act 2004, the Immigration, Asylum and Nationality Act 2006, the UK Borders Act 2007, the Criminal Justice and Immigration Act 2008, and the Borders, Citizenship and Immigration Act 2009 (Bosworth and Guild, 2008; Bosworth, 2008; Zedner, 2010; Aliverti, 2012a).[15] They also changed immigration rules, published numerous consultation papers and, in general, talked about

15. The sum of laws introduced under Labour governing non-British citizens grows still further if we include those pertaining to terrorism, such as the Anti-Terrorism, Crime and Security Act 2001 and the Prevention of Terrorism Act 2005 both of which included special measures for foreign nationals. Until the ruling by the Law Lords on 16 December 2004, the detention of foreigners without trial in HM Belmarsh Prison in London under Part IV of the 2001 Act was an unlawful violation of their human rights (*A and Others v Secretary of State for the Home Department* [2004] UKHL 56). Foreign citizens (but not British ones) could also be held indefinitely and without trial in their own homes under control orders (Zedner, 2007a).

immigration and its control (Aliverti, 2013; Welch and Shuster, 2005a; 2005b).

After the terrorist events in New York City and Washington DC in September 2001, and the London bombings of July 2005, official and popular discourse on immigration in the UK shifted, linking issues of asylum to potential terror threats. Foreigners were no longer simply a danger to social order or race relations. They were potentially perilous to the very lives of British citizens. No wonder then, that over this short period, the Labour government opened three large new detention centres, expanding the custodial estate in former and current prisons as well.

The link between prison and detention resurfaced in 2006, when it became known that over the previous decade 1,000 ex-foreign national prisoners had not been considered for deportation according to immigration rules. An event that led to the downfall of the Home Secretary, Charles Clarke, this news also precipitated a new piece of legislation, the UK Borders Act 2007, and a new working relationship between the Home Office and the prison service (Kaufman, 2012; 2013). Since that time, any foreign national from outside the European Economic Area (EEA)[16] sentenced to 12 months or more in prison, or whose sentences over the past five years add up to 12 months, has been subject to mandatory deportation. EEA nationals are held to the same rules of expulsion if sentenced to 24 months. Any non-British national sentenced to prison may be considered for deportation. Some offenders have the deportation order included in their sentence by the judge or magistrate; others are given it while they are serving their criminal sentence when their case is considered by the Home Office (Bosworth, 2008; 2011b; Vine, 2011b; Kaufman, 2014).

To manage the increasing caseload posed by this population, in 2009 the UK Border Agency and the National Offender Management Service (NOMS) agreed on a system known as 'Hubs and Spokes'. Under this arrangement, individual prisons became designated as hubs. 'Spoke' prisons would channel their foreign prisoners to these 'hubs', which incorporated a set of embedded UK Border Agency staff to process their paperwork (Bosworth, 2011b; Vine, 2011; Kaufman, 2012; 2014). This practice launched a significant new symbolic role for the prison. While immigration officers had, for some time, been visiting penal institutions and foreign

---

16. The EEA includes all member states of the European Union (EU) plus Norway, Iceland, and Lichtenstein. In UK Immigration Law it also includes Switzerland.

nationals had been concentrated in the London prisons, by rolling out a national policy the government more closely bound the prison to border control and, in the process, shifted its purpose and effect. In addition to offering a secure environment to punish, deter, or reform, the prison has effectively become actively involved in identifying and creating citizens (Bosworth and Kaufman, 2011; Kaufman and Bosworth, 2013). The discards from this system, the 'non-citizens', are the product and the target of detention (Thwaites, 2014).

At the same time, the Labour government also sought to regulate those who came in search of work, introducing an Australian-style points system in 2008. Responding, in part, to an expanding EU, the points system has increasingly made it difficult for those outside the EEA to immigrate. The Labour government, under Tony Blair, introduced the study of citizenship into the national curriculum as well as into the naturalization process, and later, under the premiership of Gordon Brown, official ceremonies for new citizens.

Since coming to power in 2010, the Tory-led Coalition government has continued to make it difficult to immigrate and settle in the UK. As part of the Tory critique of the Labour initiated Human Rights Act 1998, the Home Secretary, Theresa May, has sought to deport foreign ex-prisoners more quickly. As Labour did before them, the Coalition government has targeted foreign offenders, the undocumented or over-stayers, as well as non-EEA and certain European 'legal migration'.[17] In response to electoral successes of the United Kingdom Independence Party (UKIP), elements within the Coalition government have begun to call increasingly loudly for an exit from the European Union or, at least, from some of its binding forms of governance, including the European Court of Human Rights.

While a brief summary of over a century of legislation cannot do more than skim the surface, some general themes emerge, which assist in understanding detention. First, as stated earlier, the law gives a clear sense of the expansionist logic of restricting unwanted immigrants. While Parliamentary debates reveal some disquiet with each new development, no government has been prepared to relinquish their power over foreigners. The titles of the Acts, and their content, also reveal subtle shifts and changes in the target of state control, from 'race' to 'terrorism', via immigration

---

17. See eg the Immigration Act 2014.

and asylum, the pool of the unwelcome and dangerous expands; each new category sitting alongside, rather than deposing, the last.

Secondly, running beside the expansionist logic, flowing from and upholding it, we see the emergence and consolidation of the immigration service, in all its iterations and names, as an identifiable 'professional' part of government. Despite enduring questions over specificities of their target, as well as the effects and efficiency of their methods, the legitimacy of immigration control itself becomes beyond question. While not all of the pieces of legislation mentioned above explicitly addressed detention, each of them provided the context in which detention emerged and has flourished.

Heathrow's 'cul-de-sac'

Harmondsworth detention unit opened in early 1970 on the site of the former 'road research laboratory' on Colnbrook By-Pass, in North West London.[18] Planning application documents from the Hillingdon Borough Council indicate it was conceived as, and agreed on the basis of being, a short-term solution brought about by the Immigration Appeals Act 1969. Prior to this piece of legislation, individuals held under Immigration Act powers were either housed in prisons or in a handful of rooms in major ports. The 'detention suite' in the Queen's Building at Heathrow (which was eventually replaced by a new short-term holding facility Cayley House, currently known as Lima 23) could hold up to 15 people for a maximum of five days (Ashford, 1994).

As Members of Parliament recognized, the Immigration Appeals Act 1969 would overstretch the immigration authority's capacity, not only to make decisions on individual rights to land, but, just as importantly, to house migrants while the appeals process was underway.[19] The same year Harmondsworth opened, *The Times* reported an 18-bed detention facility was also established in Dover Castle (Evans, 1970) (see Figure 4), a residential unit that existed alongside an immigration court until it

18. The subtitle of this section is taken from a December 1975 article in *The Guardian* written by Amrit Wilson (Wilson, 1975).
19. See eg the debate in the House of Lords at the second reading of the Immigration Appeals Bill referred to above (HL Deb 27 March 1969, vol 300 cols 1418–55).

Figure 4. Dover Immigration Detention Unit in the Officers' Mess, Dover Castle (Photo credit: MF Bosworth).

was closed in the late 1980s.[20] A third short-term unit opened in 1974 in the original Gatwick Terminal known as the 'Beehive', a site that, like Dover, was expanded over time and remained operational throughout the following decade.

Until 1993, when Campsfield House was converted from a YOI to an Immigration Detention Centre, Harmondsworth, Dover, and Gatwick constituted the total of Britain's Immigration Detention estate. Women, men, and children who could not be accommodated in these facilities were placed in prison, kept in police cells, hospitals, or released into the community.

20. Despite an extensive search at the National Archives, English Heritage, and within the Home Office itself, I have been unable to locate any written materials about this centre. A visit to the site in July 2013 revealed it to be extensive, with separate dormitories for women and men, a welfare office, a court room, and multiple showers and toilets. Photographs of the site can be found at the Border Criminologies website and on its Flickr account (see <http://bordercriminologies.law.ox.ac.uk/uk-early-detention-units/> and <http://www.flickr.com/photos/bordercriminologies/sets/72157636256208685/>).

The planning documents give some sense of the urgency of the establishment of Harmondsworth. Nearly one month before Royal Assent to the Act (16 May 1969), on 24 April 1969, the Ministry of Public Buildings and Works submitted a planning application to the Local Planning Authority. This application, for 'the use of existing single-storey office building and erection of two-storey building for detainee appellants, and for appeals and other purposes, at Ex-Road Research Laboratory, Colnbrook By-Pass, Harmondsworth',[21] was lodged under the emergency 'Circular 100 procedure', requiring an expedited process (see Figure 5). In a letter, dated 27 May 1969, a positive decision was grudgingly communicated by the town clerk, Mr George Hooper. 'The Council accepts that due to the urgency with which it is necessary for an appeal centre to be established, it has been necessary to select these premises for such a purpose, temporarily', Hooper acknowledged. 'However', he warned, 'the Council trusts that every effort will be made to provide suitable accommodation for this purpose on a permanent basis in a more appropriate location, possibly within the confines of the Airport'.[22]

It was not just the detention unit itself that the committee opposed, the clerk was at pains to make clear, but also the process by which the application had been made: 'The Council also regrets the necessity for the special urgency procedures being used in this case as it has not enabled as full consideration to be given to the matter as the Authority would have wished.' In what appears almost as an afterthought, he signs off, with one final admonition, 'The Council also hopes that adequate security precautions will be provided'.[23]

More than 40 years later, a closed immigration centre adjacent to Heathrow airport called Harmondsworth still exits, although it moved a short way from the original site, on which, in 2004, IRC Colnbrook opened. Considerably larger, and far more secure, Harmondsworth now houses 615 men, and includes a new wing built to Category B (High security) Prison standards. In its first iteration, it was described as having '40 beds, washrooms of both the Asian and European variety, a common room and dining room' (Evans, 1970: 3). Eight years later it still only had capacity for 72 (Strafford, 1978).

---

21. Hillingdon Council archives: L.B.H. T/P 8190B/6662.
22. Letter from Mr George Hooper to Ministry of Public Buildings and Works, dated 27 May 1969, held on microfiche at Hillingdon Council archives: L.B.H. T/P 8190B/6662.
23. Mr George Hooper, 1969 (n 22).

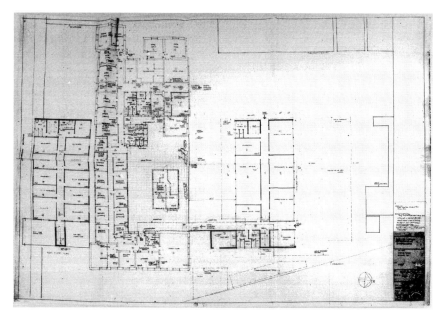

Figure 5. Plan of Harmondsworth Detention Unit (Photo credit: London Borough of Hillingdon).

A search for journalistic reports has unearthed a handful of accounts of Harmondsworth in its first decade. The most detailed of these appeared five years after it opened in an article in *The Guardian* newspaper, by Amrit Wilson—a member of the Joint Council for the Welfare of Immigrants (JCWI). Wilson offers a scathing account of the conditions and justification of Harmondsworth. Situated in 'a wasteland of motorways and outposts of the air terminals beyond Heathrow. The detention centre is one of the Government Buildings complex', he writes.

> To enter it you must ring a bell which sounds like a fire alarm. It summons the Securicor men who guard the building . . .
>
> Inside, there is a small visitors' room which was dirty both times I went there, a long narrow uncarpeted corridor with bedrooms on either side of it, a television lounge which is furnished in the drabbest manner, a 'recreation room' which contains nothing but a few wooden tables and chairs (though I was told playing cards are available), and a kitchen which detainees described as filthy. There is also a yard where one can sit and look through the wire netting at the appeals tribunal. That is how a lot of people spend their first days in Britain (Wilson, 1975: 12).

Three years later, Peter Strafford (1978: 3) of *The Times* took up the account, describing it laconically as 'one of the less cheerful places in London'. Nothing much seems to have changed. 'The buildings of the detention centre are part of a jumble of workshops and government offices, housing such bodies as the Civil Aviation Authority and the Post Office Computer', he observes. 'Inside, there are bare, drab but clean rooms with little more than the basic necessities, beds and lockers in the bedrooms; chairs, tables and a television set in the recreation rooms' (Strafford, 1978: 3).

The detainees, he finds, 'understandably enough' to be 'often bitter about being held there' and full of 'complaints about the food, that it was sometimes cold, and that vegetarians were often served the same rice dish every day for two weeks' (1978: 3). The detainees also criticize the Securicor staff for being rude. Nonetheless, Strafford concludes, 'it seemed clear that the basic complaint was not so much about the physical conditions at Harmondsworth as about the system of law that had landed the detainees there' (1978: 3).

Files from the National Archives reveal a protracted process that began in the late 1970s to redevelop Harmondsworth. Though attempts to enlarge the site were initially abandoned in 1981 'due to escalating costs',[24] by 1985 planning approval had been obtained to relocate and expand Harmondsworth under a DOE Circular 18/84 procedure. Initially planned for a site on Stockey Road, Hayes, Middlesex, formerly occupied by the Public Records Office, on the opposite side of the M4, eventually, 16 years later, Harmondsworth merely moved a few hundred metres down the road from its original site on the Colnbrook By-Pass. In the correspondence, growing concerns about security are evident, along with an expectation of a considerable growth in numbers of detainees. One letter, from HA Doherty, HM Inspector from Appeals Section Harmondsworth, dated 31 May 1988, gives extensive detail:

> The detention centre will offer 200 beds and all the accompanying facilities for housing 200 detainees; a gymnasium has been proposed in earlier discussions as an important adjunct to combatting boredom and is included in the analysis. The desirability of having a specified 'secure wing' for, say, 20 persons, has not been examined. If this wing is deemed to be a necessity it could form the hub of the other facilities and they could theoretically be used by

24. Letter from BL Shingleton in Home Office to D Vine, Property Services Agency, Gondolphus House dated 2 September 1981. CM 18/18, National Archives, London.

those detained in the wing; this would avoid duplication within the secure area. However, it may not be desirable to allow any free association of secure detainees in say the gym, or video room, with the other detainees; it follows then that some duplication would be necessary.[25]

There was some doubt at this stage over who would build or run the new centre. Rather than Securicor, Doherty makes it clear that

The estimates assume that the centre is Crown built and is IS [Immigration Service] managed; that is, it is not leased from or run by, a private contractor. Should the situation arise however, that a private contractor is in charge of the building then either there must be an element in the estimates for an IS manager, or accommodation officer to oversee the workings of the security firm and to ensure the fabric of the building, and, the needs of the detainees are cared for.[26]

In finalizing the plans, he goes on, 'the following should be kept in mind:

The desirability of having a secure wing or simply a few secure rooms merits debate.

Continuing to sleep 3 or 4 detainees to a room rather than offering single cubicles/rooms may be counterproductive; prison accommodation is going towards the privacy of single accommodation.

A garden or grassed exercise areas leads to upkeep and maintaining litter-free; a tarmac area does not create the same problems.

A Chapel rather than a prayer room seems appropriate in the light of efforts made by church representatives to keep detainees of various religious persuasions in touch with their faiths.[27]

In the appendix, further details emerge of plans for a crèche, a children's video room, a quiet writing/study room, a video room, day rooms, interview rooms, visitors rooms, holding rooms, visitors lobby, reception lobby, prayer room/chapel, bedrooms, laundry, drying room, baggage store, medical/dental room, kitchen, dining room, games room, gym, store, service area, and, finally, an exercise area 'with area for children (swings etc)'.[28]

Two years later, plans were still mired in minutiae. In a letter dated 24 April 1990, BA Wheeler, Chief Immigration Officer, HM Immigration

25. Letter from HA Doherty HM Inspector from Appeals Section Harmondsworth, dated 31 May 1988, signed Iris Russell (pp) to Mr Harris. Document number IS/88 41/25/1, in File CM 8 121/1. National Archives, London (HA Doherty, 1988).
26. HA Doherty, 1988 (n 25).
27. HA Doherty, 1988 (n 25).
28. HA Doherty, 1988 (n 25).

Office, Terminal 1 London (Heathrow) Airport, urges for better plumbing. 'At present', he writes,

> detainees in Harmondsworth do all their washing by hand, as washing machines have not been able to withstand the abuse they receive. It is therefore important that each laundry room [in the new facility] be fitted with two double sinks for this purpose. Spin dryers should be installed close to the sinks, to avoid too much drippage of water. Plumbing should be provided for two industrial washing machines per room.[29]

In his view too, attention needed to be paid to the toilets. Specifically, he wrote, there should be a balance of '1 Asian type WC to 4 European type WC'.[30]

Harmondsworth has shifted with the changing legal and political times. Following the passage of the Immigration Act 1971, the detained population began to include individuals from outside the Commonwealth. Although primarily used for recent arrivals, it could also hold longer-term residents in the UK found to be without documents or the right to remain. When concerns grew over the conditions in prison for foreigners held for immigration and asylum matters, it absorbed this population as well.

As the number subject to detention grew, inevitably the detention estate did too, with a slow but steady series of institutions joining Harmondsworth. The first of these was a short-term holding facility at Gatwick airport. Notwithstanding its occupancy until the 1990s, it is difficult to find accounts of this detention unit. Unlike Harmondsworth, it does not appear to have piqued the interest of local or national journalists. Nor have files been located in the local council. Instead, we are dependent on Parliamentary debates and a small selection of documents from the National Archives.[31]

Photocopies of hand-drawn plans reveal the Beehive as originally a small collection of rooms within the Gatwick terminal. Though primarily a short-term holding option, as plans to expand Harmondsworth faltered, pressures on the Beehive site grew, with the government forced to open new rooms and renovate others to accommodate additional women and men. Many of the letters are blunt, they need more space, but are unlikely

29. Letter from BA Wheeler Chief Immigration Officer, HM Immigration Office, Terminal 1 London (Heathrow) Airport to Mr D Matthewson, PSA, St Christopher House, dated 24 April 1990. In File CM 8 121/2, National Archives, London (BA Wheeler, 1990).
30. BA Wheeler, 1990 (n 29).
31. CM 18/18, National Archives, London.

to obtain it, Mr BL Shingleton writes on 3 June 1980, given 'the current financial and political background of this particular sphere of the Home Office'.[32] 18 months earlier, the same civil servant, when urging renovations in response to one of many damning fire safety reports, wrote to the property services agency,

> When considering the options presented by the Fire Officer it should perhaps be noted that the provision of detention accommodation is an essential operational requirement but also engenders an area of political sensitivity and I cannot foresee any possibility of the unit being closed to allow for a major works programme to be undertaken.[33]

Until the twenty-first century, most detainees were held in prison. Whereas some establishments, like Ashford and then Latchmere House and, from 1989, Haslar, were recognized as particular destinations for foreign nationals with separate landings set aside for 'Immigration Act detainees',[34] others, like HMP Pentonville (for men) and HMP Holloway (for women) were simply used for their administrative convenience in London. Hansard volumes throughout the 1980s from both Houses are full of requests for information about the numbers of immigrants detained in prison and their countries of origin. Often, the response, then, as now, is that such detail is unavailable. At times, however, figures pop up. On 31 March 1980, for instance, we are told by Lord Belstead, in response to a request from Lord Avebury, that out of a total prison population of 44,223, 190 men and 10 women were being held 'under the provisions of the Immigration Act 1971'.[35] Later that same year, on 30 September 1980, the same protagonists repeated their conversation. From that interaction we learn that 37 individuals were 'alleged illegal entrants'; 22 were 'people recommended for deportation by the courts without custodial sentence'; 40 were in prison 'recommended for deportation and custodial sentence discharged'; 30 had been 'detained under Section 3(5)(a) of the Immigration Act 1971' and eight were in prison 'detained under Section 3(5)(b) of the Immigration Act 1971'. Standing at a total of 135, it signified a decline in

---

32. CM 18/18 National Archives, London.
33. Letter from BL Shingleton in Home Office to Mr Grace in Property Services Agency in Home Office in response to fire letter from 5 December 1979. CM 18/18 National Archives, London.
34. See eg HC Deb 14 February 1986, vol 91 cols 567–8 for a discussion of the use of Ashford and Latchmere House.
35. HL Deb 16 May 1980, vol 409 col 539.

the average daily population of 192 during the first six months of that year from 1 January–30 June 1980.[36] Two years later, the sum had dropped again, to 102 on 11 February 1982. This time the document provides the nationalities and lists the 15 specific prisons in which the immigration detainees were held.[37]

In a House of Commons' debate in 1988, concerns were aired about the practice of imprisoning foreigners under Immigration Act powers, in response to the fate of one man, Mr Bahadur Singh, who died on a bus on his way home in the Punjab one day after his release from Barlinnie prison in Scotland. Held for six months, due to a breach of immigration laws for 'not having proper documentation', Singh had been arrested when he reported to the immigration authorities. In prison, Tom Clarke, MP for Monklands West, said, Singh suffered ongoing racial harassment and violence. 'The allegations are serious ones', Clarke pointed out,

> Mr Singh, a timid man, who spoke virtually no English, was beaten up in his cell by five white inmates carrying metal bars and kitchen knives; that he was attacked while he mixed with other prisoners; he had hot tea and soup thrown at him and was struck by a metal tray in the dining room; that racial slogans and threats were daubed on his cell door; and that the wardens specifically responsible for that part of the prison pretended not to notice any of this.[38]

Taking aim at the relationship between immigration control and criminal justice, Clarke wanted to know, 'Why do we lock up illegal immigrants beside violent criminals in our toughest jails?' More broadly, he noted, Singh's experiences raised questions about race and ethnicity. 'What special arrangements exist in our prisons for religious worship by minorities?' he demanded. 'What proportion of our prison officers come from ethnic minorities . . . how sensitively are cultural questions tackled by prison administrators?'[39]

While mindful that 'the members of the ethnic community who find themselves for whatever reason detained in Scottish prisons, should have no fear of persecution', the Parliamentary Under-Secretary for Scotland, Lord James Douglas-Hamilton, was unmoved by Clarke's concerns. Deflecting the

36. HL Deb 20 October 1980, vol 413 cols 1749–50.
37. HC Deb 17 February 1982, vol 18 cols 126–9.
38. HC Deb 8 July 1988, vol 136 cols 1375–84.
39. HC Deb 8 July 1988, vol 136 cols 1375–84.

immigration matter—as one concerning 'my right hon. Friend the Home Secretary', he assured Clarke that Mr Singh's case had been adequately investigated. 'It is open to any inmate to discuss with prison staff any difficulties which he or she may be experiencing. They will always take steps to ensure his safety'.[40]

In contrast to Douglas-Hamilton's confidence in the penal system, first-hand accounts from detainees reveal enduring fears and concerns about being held in prison (Wansell, 1973; Barbed Wire Britain, 2002; see also Ellis, 1998; Shackman, 2002). One man, whose name is not provided, portrays the alarm he felt when first moved from a detention unit to HMP Haslar:

> On 14 October I was picked up in a transit van with four others and taken to HM Prison Haslar in Gosport, about 80 miles from London. My dreams and hopes were shattered as contact with relations and my solicitor were no longer easy and communication on the telephone was more costly. The rumours about a remote prison were very frightening; they said it was a new establishment, a sort of slave-labour camp, where detainees could stay and work for the rest of their lives in isolation (detainee cited in Ashford, 1994: 59).

Indeed, although Haslar turned out not to be as terrifying as he had feared, the detainee remained critical. Work paid very little and men found it impossible to take up educational opportunities on offer 'because no one knew the exact date of their release or deportation. One could start an intensive today and tomorrow could be released or deported. Above all, no one had peace of mind to study' (Ashford, 1994: 60). Most problematically, the men found it hard to obtain information about their case. 'All I could do was sit and wait', he concluded (Ashford, 1994: 60).

Two new groups appear in the Hansard debates about detention in the 1990s: asylum seekers and Iraqis or 'residents of Arabic and Palestinian origin' confined as a result of the first Gulf War. On 24 January 1991, Labour MP David Blunkett, then in opposition, asked the Secretary of State for the Home Department 'on what statutory authority' and 'on what basis' the latter were 'being arrested or detained'.[41] The response from Mr Peter Lloyd was clear:

> By virtue of section 3(5)(b) of the Immigration Act 1971 orders of intention to deport have been served on a number of Iraqi and other nationals on my

---

40. HC Deb 8 July 1988, vol 136 cols 1375–84.
41. HC Deb 24 January 1991, vol 184 col 300.

right hon. Friend's personal direction that their deportation would be conducive to the public good for reasons of national security.[42]

Later that year, in response to a question from Labour MP Alistair Darling, Mr Lloyd, reported that 'since 1990 there has been an increase in asylum applicants detained at Harmondsworth'.[43] Whereas the numbers of Iraqis detained and deported were limited by the duration of the Gulf conflict, the flow of asylum seekers was harder to staunch. As the nation's prisons filled to bursting, the government looked for a solution elsewhere to hold them.

Campsfield House and Tinsley House, both of which were opened in the 1990s, revealed two possible means of expanding the detention estate. Haslar had simply incorporated foreign citizens within a prison, holding them in a specific section of an operating prison. In contrast, Campsfield House,[44] previously a YOI, was entirely 're-roled' in 1993, becoming a privately run detention centre for women and men, 'managed', as Charles Weadle Under-Secretary of State and Conservative MP for Bexhill and Battle, put it on 17 March 1994, 'on behalf of the Immigration Service by Group 4 Total Security Ltd under a total management contract'.[45] Two years later, Tinsley House, took the involvement of the private sector further in an early example of a private finance initiative (PFI). Although not 'fully funded through the private finance initiative', Timothy Kirkthorpe, the Conservative MP for Leeds and Tory Whip explained, 'the cost of the building works . . . [was] borne by the private sector', and 'the running of the facility . . . the subject of a separate contract [with Wackenhut]'.[46]

While part of the same ideological framework that, in the 1990s led the government to privatize some prisons, the involvement of custodial companies in delivering immigration detention met with significantly less resistance or public outcry (Bacon, 2005). Indeed, unlike prisons there has

---

42. HC Deb 24 January 1991, vol 184 col 300.
43. HC Deb 14 October 1991, vol 196 cols 17–24.
44. Campsfield House proved to be a lightning rod for political campaigners, from the start, as the campaign to close it began when it opened (Hayter, 1998; Kimble, 1998; <http://closecampsfield.wordpress.com/home/>). Located near to the University of Oxford, Campsfield House has been the object of Masters and doctoral studies, as well as small pieces of research into various aspects of its living conditions (Griffiths, 2014; Bacon, 2005; Bercher, Clements, and McMurray, 2000; Muzaffar, Haque, and Sugden, 1998). It was also rocked by detainee resistance almost from the start, witnessing a series of riots, food refusals, and escapes throughout the 1990s (HMIP, 1994; Hayter, 1998).
45. HC Deb 17 March 1994, vol 239 col 780.
46. HC Deb 4 June 1996, vol 278 cols 330–1.

never been any great desire on behalf of the government to run their own immigration detention centres. While some are run by the public sector, in the form of the prison service, all are governed through contract subject to the logic of contestability and finance.

In 1994, the Home Secretary formally invited the Chief Inspector of Prisons, then Lord Ramsbotham, to inspect Campsfield House.[47] 'Campsfield House is not a prison', Rambotham noted, 'and so does not fall within our statutory areas for inspection' (HMIP, 1994: 1). The problem was not just a procedural one but also conceptual, he went on:

> We have had, therefore, to consider the basis on which the inspection could be properly and carefully conducted. . . Holding detainees, the majority of whom have not gone through a court procedure or committed a criminal offence, should be clearly distinguished from prison. We found that the lack of definition led to contradiction in policy and practice, particularly in the area of security and control. A clear statement of purpose should be developed on which consistence policy and practice can be built (HMIP, 1994: 1).

In their first official account, HMIP were cautiously positive. Five years later, by which time they had been given responsibility to inspect all detention centres under the terms of the Immigration and Asylum Act 1999, they were more alarmed (HMIP, 2002). At this stage, they found Campsfield House to be dangerous, with detainees reporting sexual harassment. They also noted the lack of facilities, poor quality food and medical care (HMIP, 2002: 10–12). Reminding their readers that, 'an immigration removal centre is not a prison. Detainees have not been charged with a criminal offence nor are they detained through normal judicial processes' (HMIP, 2002: 4) the system still appeared to be without a clear statement of purpose. Such findings led, in 2004, to the creation of a specialist team within HMIP devoted to the detention estate.

From detention to 'pre-departure' accommodation

In 2001, British immigration detention centres fell under a new statutory instrument, the Detention Centre Rules. Closely modelled on the Prison

---

47. The decision to invite HMIP to inspect detention centres was announced in the House of Commons on 5 May 1994. See HC Deb 5 May 1994, vol 242 col 623.

Rules 1999,[48] this document lies behind the basic parameters of daily life inside. It is supplemented by various Detention Service Orders[49] and by the 2003 *Detention Services Operation Standards Manual* (Home Office, 2003).[50]

That same year, detention centres were renamed Immigration Removal Centres by the Labour government to signify more clearly their purpose. Such places, their new title suggested, were not meant to hold anyone for very long, but rather were designed to provide short-term secure housing prior to administrative removal or deportation. In addition to rebranding these facilities, the Labour government engaged in an active building and conversion programme opening seven removal centres between 2000 and 2009 (Dover, Lindholme, Oakington, Dungavel, Yarl's Wood, Colnbrook, and Brook House), as well as obtaining planning permission for two additional institutions that, as yet, have not been built.[51] They also oversaw a rebuild and significant expansion of IRC Harmondsworth and opened a number of new short-term holding facilities.

The Coalition government, which took power in 2010, has continued, albeit at a slower pace, to open new IRCs. At the same time, countering some of the expansionist logic of the system, the government has also restricted, although not entirely ended, the use of detention for children. While IRC Yarl's Wood stopped admitting families with children under the age of 18 in December 2010, some months later, following extensive renovations, a small family unit in IRC Tinsley House quietly reopened. Later that same year, a former children's home near Gatwick airport was converted into the Cedars Unit, offering secure 'pre-departure accommodation' centre for families (Bhui, 2013a: HMIP, 2012a).

In March 2011, HMP Morton Hall was converted from a women's prison to a men's IRC as a replacement for IRC Oakington that, despite originally

---

48. Which updated the Prison Rules 1952, created by section 47 of the Prison Act 1952.
49. One example is DSO 08/2012 'Mobile phones and cameras in immigration removal centres', which 'sets out UK Border Agency's policy on the possession of mobile phones (and cameras) by detainees, staff, visitors, legal advisers and external medical practitioners in immigration removal centres, short-term holding facilities and the pre-departure accommodation' (Home Office, 2012). Another example is DSO 06/2008 concerning suicide prevention (Home Office, 2008). All DSOs may be found on the Home Office website: <http://www.ukba.homeoffice.gov.uk/sitecontent/documents/policyandlaw/detention-services-orders/>.
50. Further guidance on how to treat those in detention can also be found in HM Prison Inspectorate's *Immigration Detention Expectations* that describes in some detail minimum standards of care and custody in a human rights framework (HMIP, 2007a). This document is explicitly modelled on the Inspectorate's *Prison Expectations* (HMIP, 2008).
51. Adjacent to Yarl's Wood and in a site near HMP Bullingdon, outside Bicester.

being designated a temporary solution, had finally closed in November 2010 after a decade in operation. Two years later, at the end of 2013, the government announced it was re-roling HMP The Verne into a new men's IRC that would open in Spring 2014.[52] As a result of these decisions, the prison service has become once again a key provider of immigration detention spaces, albeit within a privatized, contractual system. Subject to the same rules of contestability and governance, they compete alongside private custodial firms for the right to detain foreign citizens.

In these developments, we see how the private impulse so crucial for establishing the system (Bacon, 2005), has expanded the administrative and the penal state. Indeed, in detention, the distinctions between these sectors are often blurry, as the custodial companies employ former state and private prison governors, and the Home Office does as well. Given these links, the role of the prison and its position as the comparator has become ever more deeply entrenched (Bosworth, 2007a).

Conclusion

Much has changed since Harmondsworth opened. Most obviously, the immigration detention system is significantly larger. The reasons given for detention are also far broader. As a designated fast-track site,[53] Harmondsworth still contains some recent arrivals whose claims are being assessed, though today they identify as asylum seekers rather than as visitors or prospective workers. It also holds ex-prisoners, visa-overstayers, the undocumented, and those whose asylum claim has been rejected (see Figure 6).

The immigration system itself, armed with its tribunals, judges, and caseworkers, has also grown in size, in response to numerous pieces of immigration and asylum legislation (Wilsher, 2012; Thomas, 2011). Matters

52. In March 2014, plans to reclassify HMP The Verne as an IRC were put on hold until September 2014, even as the first immigration detainees arrived. Maintaining it as a prison establishment enables greater flexibility for the government, allowing for dual use. Once it is re-roled entirely into an IRC it will no longer be able to hold men serving criminal sentences.

53. For a small number of individuals, removal centres enable the state to ascertain people's identity or to rule on their asylum claim. Since March 2000 the UK has operated a fast-track asylum process. The first processing centre was Oakington, which has since closed. From 2003 a detained fast-track process began at Harmondsworth for men and, in 2005, at Yarl's Wood for women. Men on the fast track may also be held in Colnbrook and Campsfield House. Yarl's Wood and Harmondsworth both include an Asylum and Immigration

Figure 6. Exterior of IRC Harmondsworth, 2014 (Photo credit: MF Bosworth).

that used to be considered purely administrative—overstaying or working without a visa—have been criminalized (Aliverti, 2013). Such developments, captured by the unlovely term 'crimmigration' (Stumpf, 2006),[54] have increased the population subject to detention while further entrenching the relationship between detention and imprisonment. They have also, as subsequent chapters will argue, shaped detainees' sense of self and how others view them.

Some key elements, however, have remained constant. As Harmondsworth was in 1970, most detention centres today are contracted out to the private sector. Indeed, the same company—then called Securicor, now known as G4S—still runs a number of them. So, too, the lingering effects of Empire remain visible in the disproportionate numbers of Commonwealth citizens held under Immigration Act powers. Though

Tribunal adjacent to the detention accommodation, where such cases are heard and determined, usually within a matter of weeks. (For more details, see Refugee Council 2007.)

54. Though originating in the US, examples of 'crimmigration' have been identified across numerous jurisdictions, including Australia and the EU more broadly. (See eg Stumpf, 2006; Chacon, 2012; Vasquez, 2011; Welch, 2012; Spena, 2013; João Guia, van de Woude, and van Der Leun, 2012; Aas, 2011; Aliverti, 2012a; 2012b; 2013.)

the population in detention is drawn from all over the world, those from former British colonies make up the majority (Bosworth, 2012; Kaufman and Bosworth, 2013).[55] Other issues, too, remain in place. Just as they did in the 1960s, politicians continue to claim a generous national identity, while simultaneously making it increasingly difficult for large portions of the world to enter legally or to remain. The 'island' character of Britain remains sacrosanct, binding its residents together, while providing a natural barrier to those who would penetrate it.

At the same time, concerns continue about the responsibilities owed to the vulnerable. Like Lord Avebury, nearly 40 years ago, critics still argue that it 'is absolutely intolerable that a person comes here as a refugee from a country where he is definitely under threat of persecution . . . yet he remains in prison for such a long time as to cause him to suffer grave mental distress leading to illness from which he may take a very long while to recover'.[56] Just as concerns linger over the detention of asylum seekers, so, too, earlier fears about: 'The good name of Britain, our relations with other members of the Commonwealth and, above all, justice and common humanity',[57] remain unresolved.

Then as now, removal centres raise difficult questions about belonging in an age of diversity, about confinement during a period of mass mobility and about the limits of the nation state. Unwilling to hand back its powers over foreign nationals, the British state has created a system which propels itself forward, despite evidence of its inefficiency and in the face of considerable suffering. Under what circumstances, if any, could detention be challenged? What kind of state is being created by exclusion? In order to address these questions we need to understand these centres better. To do that, we need to look inside them.

---

55. In December 2013, for instance, the largest population in detention was from Pakistan followed by India, Bangladesh, Nigeria, and Afghanistan.
56. HL Deb 9 June 1978, vol 392 col 1678.
57. 23 July 1965, Commonwealth Immigration Memorandum, p 31.

2

Understanding immigration detention

I will never forget the face of the Afghani boy who is being deported today. I felt the same as I did with Tina the day she left for the first time. Somehow I feel responsible (Fieldnotes, Tinsley House, April 2011).

I am struggling to see how I can connect with the humanity of the men if I'm afraid of them and the officers (Fieldnotes, Brook House, March 2011).

Sometimes all the days feel the same, but they are different. There is the continuous sense of panic to get people to talk to me all the time though (Fieldnotes, Tinsley House, March 2011).

Academics have written surprisingly little about everyday life in immigration removal centres. Details can be gleaned from parliamentary debates, governmental (HMIP, 2013; 2012a; 2012b), and non-governmental organizations (Phelps, 2009; BID, 2013; Girma et al, 2014), and the occasional media report (McVeigh, 2011; O'Hagan, 2012). Researchers also interview former detainees in the community (Griffiths, 2012; Klein and Williams, 2012). First-hand accounts can be found on websites, particularly those critical of detention.[1] For the most part, however, academic debate over the purpose, justification, impact, and nature of detention (and its corollary, deportation) has developed independently from sustained engagement with the lived experience of those within these institutions (although see Fischer, 2013a; 2013b; Hall, 2010; 2012; Bosworth, 2012; Bhui, 2013a; 2013b; Fili, 2013).

1. See eg <http://closecampsfield.wordpress.com>; <http://www.biduk.org/137/detainees-stories/overview.html>.

Doubtless, theoretical inquiry can be rich. However, when nearly all the available scholarly debate is based on secondary materials, questions must arise, not only about accuracy, but also about interpretation. Can we really grasp the nature of these institutions without going inside? What can an interior view contribute to our understanding? What might it lend to our critique? How might it challenge the theoretical framework we have come to rely on when talking about border control?

Most obviously, going inside illuminates parts of detention that we simply cannot otherwise see, filling in gaps in our knowledge. It challenges easy assumptions about the exercise of power, its effect, effectiveness, and legitimacy, by considering how such matters are made concrete in everyday interactions and experiences. In so doing, fieldwork reveals the salience in these institutions of identity rather than regime, estrangement rather than enforcement, inconsistencies, uncertainties, and ambivalence.

In contrast to the language of many theoretical accounts of border control, this book does not depict a 'Camp' operating under a state of exception (Agamben, 1998; 2004). Nor do modes of governance work seamlessly to control (Foucault, 1991). Detainees, while exceedingly vulnerable, have not been reduced to 'bare life', outside the law, existing only as sacrifice. They continue to act, to feel, to talk, looking and sometimes finding sympathy, empathy, and recognition. Despite handing them over to the private sector, and aiming to eject them, the state has not (yet?) abandoned them (Johansen, 2013).

To be sure, the allure of Foucault and Agamben is clear. Detainees themselves, struggling for a vocabulary with which to describe their experience, fall back on comparisons with other, more familiar, examples of penal excess. They often feel utterly powerless. Innocent, from Rwanda, for instance, held for many years in detention, shouted to me as I was walking around IRC Colnbrook: 'This is 100% Guantanamo Bay here, this is Britain's Guantanamo' (Rwanda, CB). Elsewhere, in the lower security removal centre Campsfield House, Sanjeewa from Sri Lanka painted a similarly bleak picture of the dehumanization he was experiencing: 'They treat us like dogs', he complained. 'This is like mental torture. They do not beat us or hurt us but they wear us down' (Sri Lanka, CH).

Yet, as Alison Mountz has observed in her work on off-shore detention, 'the intimacy of exclusion requires analytical tools beyond those available in Agamben's writing' (Mountz, 2011b: 382). So, too, Katja Aas (2011) has demonstrated the need to update Foucault's notions of biopolitics and governmentality under conditions of mass mobility and the shifting nature of the sovereign state. Such concepts can feel far removed from people's daily lives. First-hand accounts remind us of our shared humanity and, in so doing, provide an important counter to the powerful rhetoric of securitization and criminalization that characterizes border control (Bhui, 2013b). Testimonies are moving. They reveal similarities and shared aspirations as well as differences of opinion. They are messy and confusing. They might also provide the basis for more creative thinking. Staff and detainees express considerable confusion and ambivalence about IRCs, reflecting the overall uncertainty about such places and their purpose. Listening to them raises profound questions about the logic of border control, bringing home its costs and its ambiguities.

Preparation, access, and trust

It took 12 months to obtain permission to do this project. I had been writing for some years on legal changes to border control in the US and in the UK (Bosworth, 2007a; 2007b; Bosworth, 2008; Bosworth and Guild, 2008) but, like many scholars in the field, I had never been inside a detention centre. I was warned that the UK Border Agency, as it was then known, as well as the private companies, were unlikely to facilitate independent academic research and so I sought advice. As a criminologist, I turned to the institution I knew better—the prison service—meeting a former prison governor who had participated in a review of the causes of a major disturbance in an IRC.

This man was direct. I needed to conceive and pitch my project as more than just an 'academic' study. What could I do for the UK Border Agency? Why *should* they let me in? A pure ethnography, he counselled, would be unpersuasive. I needed to design a project that would be more 'useful'.

Utility is a subjective term. In the social sciences and in policy terms, it usually signals a quantitative bent. New public management is in the thrall of the Excel spreadsheet, with staff meetings organized around monthly or weekly statistical reports. Surveys, charts, diagrams have become familiar currency in a system required constantly to monitor itself. Under these circumstances, qualitative methods are increasingly considered unreliable and without rigour; just someone's 'opinion'.

The purported opposition between qualitative and quantitative methodologies is, for the most part, easily dispatched. Quantitative instruments rely on qualitative strategies. Observation, interviews, informal discussions, focus groups, secondary literature, and theoretical frameworks underpin them. Questions cannot spring fully formed from nothing.

A demand for utility raises other, pertinent issues for criminologists. Particularly in morally contested sites like immigration detention centres, where people suffer and often feel disempowered, is it right to work 'with' the state? What are some of the risks in doing so? What would be the costs of refusal?

Although we spend considerable time learning how to garner the trust of vulnerable groups, criminologists pay rather less attention in our training and research preparation to doing the same with gatekeepers (Bosworth, Hoyle, and Dempsey, 2011).[2] In most publications how entry was obtained is rarely addressed and the account of the project proceeds as though it never were a problem. Such silence glosses over the significant difficulties many researchers endure, and can simplify complex and contested parts of the project. It obscures the potentially compromising effect of working with gatekeepers, while conveniently ignoring any debt we might owe them. It also overlooks our own role in shaping the field, people's access to it, and what is discussed.

Sometimes we downplay our duty to gatekeepers in order to protect them from internal retribution. In restricted sites like IRCs, which the government remains anxious about opening up for academic scrutiny, it is right to be cautious. Other factors may be rather less heroic. As many critics of criminology have pointed out (Foucault, 1991; Cohen, 1988; Christie, 1977; Hannah-Moffat, 2010), it is difficult to find faults and retain research access. Nobody wants to admit to toning down their assessment or failing to raise particular issues, yet when research access can so easily dry up, it is sometimes difficult to be frank.

Criminologists have, for many years, argued with one another over the dangers of becoming an agent of the state (Christie, 1977; Cohen, 1988; Loader and Sparks, 2010; Sherman, 2009; Bosworth and Hoyle, 2011). Michel Foucault (1991) famously singled out criminology as a lost cause,

---

2. An exception to this claim concerns those who interview policy makers, judges or politicians, who gain trust of those with power (see eg Annison, 2014; Loader, 2006).

potentially radical but enslaved by its epistemology and ties to the government. Nils Christie (1977) also notably suggested criminologists ought to close down their centres of study rather than risk expanding the penal state. In their view, an uncritical methodology based on a positivist epistemology had compromised the whole field.

I have considerable sympathy with the view of both of these men. I, too, value the independence of academic research and I do not think we should be in the habit of doing the government's job for them let alone that of private enterprise, particularly when we find their actions are so often troubling. Equally, however, I think criminologists should and can contribute to policy debates. This duty is magnified when the policy in question is contested. Those same ties to criminal justice agencies and the state that worry Foucault and Christie, have helped criminologists negotiate access to other penal institutions.[3] As migration control becomes more deeply intertwined with criminal justice policy and practice, criminologists may be particularly well-suited to study it as we call upon existing bodies of literature on incarceration and policing.

In any case, just as quantitative instruments rely on qualitative methods, academic scholarship only proceeds through interactions with the object of its study. Without empirical research—which requires some kind of cooperation with gatekeepers—we would be limited indeed in what we could say. There is no easy way around the fact that in order to understand detention we must go inside removal centres and, to do that, we have to find a way of working together with those who run them.

In light of all of these matters, and in response to the advice from the former prison governor, I settled on a mixed-methodology. Following lengthy periods of fieldwork, I would design a survey to capture the quality of life in detention. Whereas the qualitative component might only interest

---

3. Criminologists, who depend heavily on the state to facilitate their projects, have identified a general retraction of research access, in a range of criminal justice arenas around the world (see eg Simon, 2000; Bosworth et al, 2005; Wacquant, 2008). Writing in Canada, criminologist Kelly Hannah-Moffat (2011) argued that governments are increasingly unwilling to allow critical researchers access to criminal justice sites, either setting up their own in-house research teams, or working solely with particular groups of trusted individuals who rarely raise a fuss. For Hannah-Moffat, scholars are offered an impossible choice: to silence themselves or to be excluded. I am fortunate to be located in Britain, which has a longstanding and robust relationship between the prison service and the academy. Here prison ethnography remains strong, and in policing, parole and youth justice as well the government maintains close working ties with scholars. Why then not on matters concerning immigration control?

an academic audience, the survey would address policy concerns. Where possible, I would combine elements from both.

In choosing this route I was guided by Alison Liebling's research in prison (Liebling, 2004). In 2004, Liebling published an influential study of English prisons that differentiated among them in terms of their 'moral performance'. Some prisons, she argued, work 'better' than others. Usually, these prisons feel safer and prisoners and staff in them get along more harmoniously. Unlike traditional prison sociology, Liebling did not just conduct an ethnography. Instead, based on a combination of focus groups, observations, and interviews, she designed a survey to measure prisoner (and staff) perceptions of theoretical concepts including justice, fairness, and legitimacy.

Her survey, known as the 'Measure of the Quality of Prison Life', or, more commonly the MQPL, was, in short order, adopted by the prison service and is now routinely administered by them across the penal estate. Primarily an internal review mechanism, it is used to differentiate among similar institutions. Though not without its critics, who raise questions about the feasibility and ethics of managing prisons by metrics (Carlen, 2005), its supporters argue that it not only accurately distinguishes between institutions but also that it integrates prisoner viewpoints into management decisions (Liebling, Arnold, and Straub, 2011; Liebling and Crewe, 2012). There is also a MQPL for prison staff (Crewe, Liebling, and Hulley, 2011).

Mindful of Foucault and Christie's criticisms of criminology, as well as the dangers of interpolating penal power through statistics, it seemed to me that there was scope to develop a similar survey tool for detention. Notwithstanding the homogenizing language of measurement in an environment steeped in coercion and inequality, the MQPL has embedded an expectation that prisons need to take into account prisoner viewpoints. Such an approach was not evident in detention. Perhaps a similar tool in that location might illuminate detainees' experiences and concerns, I proposed. Beginning with detailed observation and informal interviews, I decided to design a 'Measure of the Quality of Life in Detention', the MQLD, a copy of which can be found in the Appendix (for more detail, see Bosworth and Kellezi, 2013).

Once I had settled on a methodology, the former prison governor generously introduced me to two ex-colleagues: an outgoing Centre manager, and the CEO of a private security firm running two facilities. The latter, subject to permission from the Home Office, volunteered one of his company's centres for the pilot study. The former, after a genial meeting,[4] offered to contact the head of detention services on my behalf and recommend the research project. A few weeks later this senior civil servant agreed to meet me. Shortly thereafter I was invited to present my research plans to a meeting of all the centre managers and to relevant Home Office personnel.

Given the politicized nature of immigration detention, all parties were understandably concerned about my intentions. 'We don't want to tell you what to say', Harry put it in our very first meeting, 'but we don't want your research to embarrass us' (Home Office). Their concerns however, abutted their aspiration for understanding. While I encountered some explicit suspicion towards and derision of 'liberal' and 'naïve' academics, most senior staff members in the Home Office and the private companies were, if anything, alarmingly optimistic about the potential of the project, speaking of its potential 'huge value for detainees' (SMT, CB). 'If we had proper information about problems', Lindsey, at Campsfield House earnestly told me, 'we could fix them' (SMT, CH).

Like these senior staff, a number of detainees hoped that an account of life inside might change people's minds about the government's migration policies. I was urged to tell people outside what it was 'really like' in detention. The problem, Tahir angrily asserted, was that 'people don't see nothing. The citizens out there don't know what is going on' (Sudan, CH). If only they knew more, he thought, they would demand change. While Tahir agreed to be interviewed, his preferred solution to describing life in detention lay not in academic writing, but in the power of film. 'Madam, only one thing will help us', he claimed. 'One thing that would help every single man here. If we could be allowed yeah, and helped to make a documentary about detention centres . . . If we could make a documentary, and interviews camera wise in this place, I swear to God, then you will see how many people they release, they will see what happens . . .' (Sudan, CH). In contrast, Asa believed my position at the University of Oxford was key. 'If you don't tell the truth you will let me down, the people out there and yourself', he warned. 'When I talk to you I talk to your institution and you as the representative. It is a strong institution and I expect great things to come out of it' (Kenya, TH).

---

4. In which I inadvertently broke institutional rules by bringing my mobile phone into the facility, taking a call from my husband about when to collect the children from school.

Others wanted to tell me their story, no matter what the effect. 'His mouth is full of it', Aufa explained on his friend's behalf: 'He needs to talk' (Pakistan, BH). Still others, however, were mistrustful, unsure of my academic credentials and, unlike Asa, of my home institution. 'You know, all those politicians—they went to Oxford', Saqib teased. 'What are you doing up there? I hope you didn't teach them!' (Pakistan, CB). Usually, suspicion made people upset. 'Why are you here?' Jamil challenged me, 'Who let you in? Maybe you're from UKBA and everything I tell you, you will go and tell them. I know how the system works. Why should I talk to you?' (Uganda, BH). Others struggled to see the benefit of an academic study. 'You do nothing!' Deb yelled at me, 'you don't help. You just ask people about their experiences. But you do nothing for us' (Nigeria, YW). 'Who will read your book?' many demanded. 'What's in it for me?' (Various, all centres).

Although prison sociologists tend to concentrate on either prisoners or staff, fearing interaction with one group will erode their ability to build working relationships with the other, I did not find equivalent barriers in detention. This did not mean everyone was happy for me to be there. Slade did not mince words: 'If it was up to me I wouldn't let you in here' (SMT, BH). Others were just uninterested: 'Here's this woman, look after her and let her do whatever it is that she does', Reina breezily announced when she dropped me off at the housing unit (DCO, BH). When I forgot to wear my homemade identification in Yarl's Wood—a copy of my University of Oxford business card inside a plastic folder pinned to my blouse—I was written up on an SIR, a 'Security Incident Report', by a Detention Custody Manager (DCM) whom I was trying to arrange to interview.

I too, was not immune from self-doubt, and neither were the two research officers, Blerina Kellezi and Gavin Slade, who worked alongside me at some of the centres. 'I continue to feel incredibly pressured by this study and unsure of myself', I confessed after four months at Campsfield House (Fieldnotes, February 2010). All the fieldwork diaries are filled with questions about the purpose of the study, its potential, and its emotional toll. Each of us reported depression, anxiety, uncertainty, sadness, anger, and guilt. 'Did not feel like going in at all. Quite a bit of anxiety', Blerina noted about a three-day stint in Brook House in June 2011, while Gavin, reflecting on his relationship to the detainees as 'a white English boy', wrote: 'I do get tinges of shame at times . . . especially given the [Colonial] history. It is proving emotional' (Fieldnotes, April 2012).

Such hopes and fears frame this project, acting as a spur and, at times, as a burden. I worried about the effect of seeming too critical, at the same time as I was often frustrated about the ineffectiveness of critique more generally. Notwithstanding the scarcity of academic accounts, the Home Office and the private contractors do not lack evidence about the damaging effect of detention (HMIP and ICIBI, 2012; Phelps, 2009; BID, 2013). Rather, they are either unable or unwilling to make the sweeping changes necessary, even though many staff are personally concerned with the impact of current policies and practices.

Much of what I witnessed and was told about detention was negative. Some of it was shocking. Detainees and staff spoke frequently of depression, frustration, sorrow, fear, and anger. They were, for the most part, unhappy, and detention centres were, without exception, vexing places. At the same time, however, many staff members sought to alleviate the anxieties of those whom they hold. Detainees also found some relief and levels of support in these places, in the religious services, in the friendships they forged, in some of the classes they attended.

Detention centres are, nonetheless, deeply troubling. They cause considerable suffering, notwithstanding attempts at all levels to avoid it. These places urgently need sustained critique. Yet any such critical account must be responsive to the political horizons and framework within which these places operate. The challenge, in short, is immense: how to make sense of what I found and how to do so in such a way that is useful and persuasive.

The research sites

I began this project in IRC Campsfield House. When I was doing my research it was managed by GEO on behalf of UKBA, although shortly after I left, the contract came up for renewal, and the Home Office awarded it to Mitie. Campsfield House is located at the end of a quiet country lane, over the road from the Oxford Airport and next door to an HM Prison Service training venue for control and restraint (C&R).[5] Surrounded by a metal fence edged in razor wire, internally it looks more like a hospital or a

---

5. When the training sessions are underway, the noise radiating from the C&R centre is quite alarming as staff members shout and hit loudly within. The first time I heard the racket I thought there was a riot, and could not understand the insouciance of the staff around me.

school than a prison, corridors encircling a lawn in one part and a bitumen courtyard in another. The men are free to walk around the main site until quite late at night, after which time they must stay on their housing unit until morning. In 2013, the site was comprehensively rebuilt by Mitie (see Figure 7). Just before completion, the main housing block was destroyed by a fire, lit by a man facing removal to Afghanistan.

Staff members enter the main site through the 'SMT Corridor' walking over from the gatehouse. I followed the same route, always accompanied by a Detention Custody Officer (DCO), and only admitted after I had left my wallet and car keys in a locker, received a visitor's badge, and had my self and my papers lightly searched ('patted down') by a female officer. The corridor into the facility doubled as the 'legal corridor', where the men met solicitors and Home Office staff. The stench from this corridor—of sweat, fear, and anxiety—was often overwhelming.

I spent much of my time in Campsfield House in the library (see Figure 8), sitting quietly at the back of the room, responding to men who approached me, trying to gauge what was going on. Detainees had been informed about the project and I held some focus groups to advertise it

Figure 7. View of staff entry to IRC Campsfield House (Photo credit: MF Bosworth).

Figure 8. Library in IRC Campsfield House (Photo credit: S Turnbull).

more widely. However, it was a slow process. 'Very awkward, cautious curiosity from men. Library totally silent. Am waiting, waiting, waiting' (Fieldnotes, January 2010).

I also spoke to staff and detainees in the welfare office and in the temporary structure that, at the time, housed the art room and the ESOL classroom. Near the end of my fieldwork I passed some weeks in the induction unit, watching detainees arrive and leave, sometimes booked out for medical appointments, at other times released on bail or given temporary admission. I attended detainee meetings in the visits hall and ate lunch with staff and detainees in the dining room. I did not enter the main housing units other than on a guided tour and nor did I spend time in the gym. I was shown the segregation block when nobody was present, and spoke briefly to staff in the healthcare unit. I sat in some of the outside areas chatting to staff and men while they smoked. Finally, I also spent quite a lot of time on the SMT corridor interviewing staff, and in the cramped (and not particularly clean) staff room.

As in most of the IRCs, there was not all that much for the men to do in Campsfield House. There was a reasonably well-stocked library containing books from a wide range of languages. Yet I rarely saw anybody read them; instead men sat for hours poring over newspapers and/or using the computer terminals to access the internet. At the time, the library contained three desktop computers in the reading room and ten more in a separate room. Beyond the library, towards the housing units there was a small games room containing X-Box and other consoles. Around the corner a large sitting room was equipped with a big screen for watching films and Sky Sports. This room, on Fridays, was used as a mosque. Passing through it you reached the visits room, which was accessed separately by those who came in to see the detainees. A vestibule between these two spaces contains vending machines and an observation area for the DCOs.[6]

The detainees at Campsfield House were served lunch together in a dining hall, lining up in loose but distinct national groups; the Chinese together, the Vietnamese as well, Indians and Pakistanis congregated, as did Jamaicans and Nigerians, alongside smaller groups from a range of African countries. The men ate in rapid shifts outnumbering the space available, while the officers and other staff generally dined before them. Unlike the other centres, staff in Campsfield House were entitled to free meals during their shift, an aspect of their pay and conditions that many of them emphasized in interviews.

While I was conducting research in Campsfield House, I was invited by the Centre Manager at Colnbrook to pilot the project there as well. In material terms, Colnbrook, which opened in 2004, was very different. Designed and built by Serco to Category B prison security standards, it was a daunting and confusing establishment. A traditional 'H-block', behind its plain façade it is multi-storeyed, with the living units separated from the 'regimes corridor' (see Figure 9) and staff administration.

There are four 'courtyards', one of which has been laid to grass, and another of which houses the centre 'garden', that includes a shed, built by some staff and detainees, a collection of planters, picnic tables, some trees, chairs, a Buddha statue, a beehive, and, for a while, rabbits (see Figure 10). The remaining two outdoor areas are paved in concrete. The living units look like standard prison wings, complete with suicide netting, metal

---

6. Following the extensive renovations carried out in 2013 and 2014, much of this internal layout at Campsfield House has changed. However, the main kinds of areas—a big screen room, mosque, activities—remain present, just configured differently.

Figure 9. Exterior IRC Colnbrook (Photo credit: MF Bosworth).

Figure 10. Picnic tables in IRC Colnbrook garden (Photo credit: MF Bosworth).

doors, metal staircases, and shower blocks with half size doors enabling the staff to see who is within.[7]

Colnbrook has two segregation units.[8] At the time of my research it also had a small 'enhanced' unit, located above the visits hall and accessed through a separate door, for those considered well behaved. This area was much quieter and calmer than the other wings, and included a dining area, a pool table, a large screen television, and games consoles. This proved to be a useful place to meet detainees and chat to them informally. Since I left, it has been converted into a short-stay unit for up to 27 women.

Staff members entered Colnbrook through the gatehouse, handing in their 'tallies' before passing through secure glass doors to receive their keys. This space was filled with Serco branded posters and a television on a loop describing the goals and vision of the company: '[we aim] to be one of the top 750 listed companies in the world by 2010', it intoned. 'We foster an entrepreneurial culture. We enable our people to excel. We deliver our promises. We build trust and respect. Look professional, be professional' (Fieldnotes, May 2010). There were signs listing rules and useful phone numbers, recent issues in health and safety and incidents of violence. Posters reminded everyone that they could expect to be randomly searched at any time. I entered this way as well and would sit awaiting collection by a staff member. I was never searched.

The door leading out of the gatehouse takes staff into a 'sterile area' overlooking the main facility, from which you can see one of the concrete exercise yards and its barbed wire fence, as well as the outside of the visits room and the enhanced unit. To the left, Harmondsworth is readily visible behind rows of razor wire, and on the right, the dilapidated exterior façade of an airport hotel (see Figure 11). Entry into the main residential part of Colnbrook is controlled from a distance by staff in the gatehouse who respond to the electric buzzer.

Many of the internal corridors at Colnbrook had been brightly and beautifully decorated by detainees. The paintings, which at the time were

---

7. In addition to the regular IRC, Colnbrook includes a Short-Term Holding Facility (STHF) where people can be held for up to a week, in cramped two-person cells, for 23 hours a day. My request to include this section in my research was denied.
8. In IRCs detainees may be held for a short period (usually only up to 24 hours) in segregation on either R40 ('Removal from Association') or R42 ('Temporary Confinement') (The Detention Centre Rules, 2001). According to the survey, few detainees understood the difference between R40 or R42 (Bosworth and Kellezi, 2012).

Figure 11. Sterile area in IRC Colnbrook overlooking IRC Harmondsworth (Photo credit: S Turnbull).

designed by one man in particular, included architectural gems from around the world, flowers, birds, aphorisms, famous women and men (see Figure 12). The rest of the building was painted institutional beige by a team of paid detainees who worked continuously. Once they finished, they started again. Just like a nineteenth-century prison, the work was without end. Unlike Campsfield House, the corridors in Colnbrook predominantly smelled of paint.

The same company that ran Colnbrook (Serco),[9] at the time also managed IRC Yarl's Wood—the nation's only predominantly female establishment, and my third site.[10] Yarl's Wood is located at the far end of a long road that leads up to a former Ministry of Defence site in Clapham, Bedfordshire. It opened in November 2001 at twice its eventual size, and was designed to hold as many men as women. Within months, however, the men destroyed their section, burning it to the ground. Surrounded by

---

9. In March 2014, the contracts for Colnbrook and Harmondsworth were jointly awarded to Mitie, to run under the supervision of a single Senior Management Team.
10. Much of the following description of Yarl's Wood below has been taken from my account with Blerina Kellezi of race relations in Yarl's Wood. See Bosworth and Kellezi, 2014.

Figure 12. Corridors in IRC Colnbrook decorated by detainees (Photo credit: MF Bosworth).

green rolling hills and quaint villages, Yarl's Wood is not easily accessible without a car, since it is situated nearly 20 minutes drive from the nearest train station (see Figure 13).[11]

The current building holds 450 detainees in four residential wings and a segregation block all of which, given the women's ultimate enforced 'flight', are ironically named after birds: Dove, Avocet, Crane, Bunting, Hummingbird, and Kingfisher. Until January 2011, when families were relocated to Tinsley House and then to the Cedars Unit near Gatwick airport,[12] such groups were placed on the Crane wing.[13] When they arrived women were placed on the induction unit in Bunting.[14] Kingfisher was (and remains) the segregation block.

11. The centre runs a free coach service to and from Bedford train station most afternoons to help those making social visits. Lawyers or other advocates who can visit in the morning have to make their own way there.
12. Although a small number of children were detained in Yarl's Wood during my research I did not interview any of them.
13. These days Crane has become the induction unit for single women. A new wing referred to as Hummingbird houses married couples and families with adult children.
14. Bunting is now a short-term holding facility for men.

Figure 13. Exterior of IRC Yarl's Wood (Photo credit: S Turnbull).

   In the two regular housing units of Yarl's Wood, women were grouped in pairs in small rooms that included a separate shower and toilet area. On Bunting, the rooms were single occupancy, whereas on Crane families of four could be placed in adjacent rooms with interlocking doors. Most of the rooms, other than those in Kingfisher, overlooked grassy outdoor association areas. They were furnished sparsely, with two beds, wardrobes, and notice boards, as well as a desk. A small television set with an integrated VCR player was bolted to the wall. With their brightly coloured curtains and shabby furniture they resembled student halls of residence as much as prison wings. Yet, each housing unit is connected to the main part of the institution by an iron gate, which can only be opened by a staff member.

   For much of the day women in Yarl's Wood were free to wander around the building, carrying the key to their room with them. However, they were never allowed into any other residential unit than their own. They were locked in their housing block for lunch and dinner, and, following an evening period of general association, had to remain there from 9 pm to 9 am. Each unit has its own dining room and a number of small lounge areas containing sofas from Ikea, a television, and some books.

Those who leave the residential area during association time can mingle with others in the main area of the institution where there is a large indoor gym, a doctor's surgery, a library, a hairdressing salon, a small indoor cinema, a 'cultural kitchen', and a number of designated religious areas including a church, a mosque, and a Hindu/Sikh temple. Some detainees congregated on the 'activities corridor' that included an art and craft area and an IT room equipped with computers from which they emailed friends and family outside the centre.[15] Others sat in small 'association' rooms, chatting to one another or calling friends and relatives on their mobile phones.

The 'cultural kitchen', which had recently opened, could be booked for a whole day by six women at a time. They were provided with raw ingredients and allowed to cook lunch and dinner under the supervision of a DCO.[16] The room was decorated to resemble a middle-class British family house, complete with dining table, sofa, large screen television, and a CD player. The Ikea tableware was brightly coloured and the kitchen implements and electric goods homely; these were not institutional items, but ones picked out at the local superstore, including a mid-range quality kettle, microwave, oven, and blender. The women were allowed to bring in their own DVDs and CDs and quite often everyone ended up dancing after the meal finished. They were not allowed to share the food they made with any women other than those in the room, although custodial staff members routinely dropped by to sample it.

In Yarl's Wood, for the first time in my research career, I was issued keys. Unlike Campsfield House and Colnbrook, where the uniformed members of staff and the Senior Management Team had kept a fairly close eye on me, employees at Yarl's Wood, for the most part, were quite happy for me to be left to my own devices. With keys I was free to walk around, able to spend time on the housing unit and speak to women in the privacy of their rooms. I was assisted in the fieldwork in Yarl's Wood by a research officer, Blerina Kellezi.[17]

---

15. Many of these spaces were duplicated on the family unit, reflecting the historical segregation of the two populations. When Yarl's Wood still held children they were always kept wholly apart from the single women other than in the visiting hall. Since the project ended, the layout has changed in order to make better use of that space.

16. When I began my research the DCO would collect cash from the women and buy specialist ingredients for them from local shops. This practice, however, was eventually abandoned when the DCO complained to the centre manager about how much of her time it was taking. From that point detainees were able to select from items used in the institution's own kitchen.

17. Unless pertinent, I do not differentiate between my fieldwork diaries and Blerina's nor designate who conducted which interview. Elsewhere, Blerina and I have written together about the research project (Bosworth and Kellezi, 2013; Bosworth and Kellezi, 2014).

The next two locations for the research were IRCs Tinsley House and Brook House. Together referred to as the Gatwick IRCs, these institutions are as different to one another as are Campsfield House and Colnbrook, despite, at the time, being run by the same Senior Management Team from G4S and situated only a few hundred metres apart alongside the Gatwick runway. Tinsley House is bright and sunny, with wide corridors that, as ever, wrap around a small (and, at least while we were present, unused) grassy courtyard (see Figure 14).

At Tinsley House we were issued with ID cards that gave access to all parts of the building, although since we primarily stayed in the main parts we rarely needed to use them. The welfare office and healthcare centre were close to the staff entrance, along with the laundry and the housing units. Either by passing through the residential units or by walking across the outdoor area staff and men enter the main part of the facility which includes the library, computer room, dining hall, two separate big screen television areas, the art room, and the multi-faith room. Opened only part of the day, one end of the ground floor housed a gym. Offices for the onsite Home Office staff as well as the 'legal corridor' were situated upstairs on the other side (see Figure 15).

Figure 14. Courtyard in IRC Tinsley House (Photo credit: G4S).

Figure 15. Exterior IRC Tinsley House (Photo credit: G4S).

Blerina conducted much of the fieldwork in Tinsley House. Moving freely around the centre she spoke to men in the library, in the recreation rooms, classrooms, and in the dining hall. She sat with some in the holding room as they awaited their airport bus. She played pool, watched TV, and helped men fill out forms, answering, sometimes, their questions about her marital status, her plans for children, my role in the project, and her opinions about border control.

While Blerina concentrated on Tinsley House, I spent time in the neighbouring, high security, Brook House (see Figure 16). Before entering Brook House I had heard about it from former residents and staff. The view appeared to be that it was a troubled institution, or at least had only recently emerged from a disordered period, and that it held the most 'dangerous' detainees.[18] Staff, elsewhere, warned me to be careful. 'I call it Broken House. . .' Allen,

18. In their announced visit in 2010, for example, HMIP were unusually harsh: 'we were disturbed to find one of the least safe immigration detention facilities we have inspected, with deeply frustrated detainees and demoralized staff, some of whom lacked the necessary confidence to manage those in their care. At the time of the inspection, Brook House was an unsafe place' (HMIP, 2010b: 5).

Figure 16. Exterior of IRC Brook House (Photo credit: Home Office).

then an officer at Tinsley informed me ominously. On my first day, my anxiety palpable, I note anxiously that,

> Everyone in UKBA has been telling me that Brook House has been 'settling down', but the DCM showing me around told me that on the weekend there were 5 assaults on staff, including one man having his nose broken, another staff member being bitten and I think someone else might have had their arm broken. Doesn't sound too good to me (Fieldnotes, February 2011).

Built, like Colnbrook, to a Category B prison design, Brook House certainly felt oppressive. 'It's, the atmosphere . . .', Allen pointed out.

> Somebody'll get in, they'll say 'It's alright, it's not prison, it's only a detention centre.' You go through one, two, three, four, five, six, seven, eight—eight doors—before you actually get in a wing. And you walk in the wing, suicide netting. You get, you get high before you get up to the first landing 'cos of all the cannabis, you know. And it's, yeah, you can't hear yourself think for the boogie boxes, so yeah it's . . . For someone who's just, hasn't, hasn't done a crime, just over-stayer, get into that environment—frightening (DCO, TH).

The building looms over everyone, from the dark, low ceilings of the entry corridor, to the noisy housing units. Its walls stand unadorned by detainee art and it was also built without a gymnasium. Instead, each unit includes a small room with exercise equipment. Men in Brook House are housed on separate wings onto which they are locked at various times of the day. The wings, as at Colnbrook, are arranged over three levels with anti-suicide netting strung between the two upper floors. There is no natural light or air in the centre at all, and the windows are glazed to prevent views outside (see Figure 17).

At the time of the research, Brook House was in the process of converting one of the housing units (B-Unit) into a 'basic regime' unit, designed to hold men in two-person cells all day long whom G4S deemed 'un-compliant' as well as new arrivals and those who were leaving. This strategy, I was told, would help G4S maintain order on the main units. In further evidence of their faith in incentives, Brook House had also recently

Figure 17. Interior of housing block in IRC Brook House (Photo credit: Home Office).

rebranded D unit as an 'enhanced' unit, although most of the 'enhancement', which was to include games consoles, and a big screen television, had yet to occur. Instead, while I was there they replaced all the steel doors with more secure varieties.

Brook House was the only institution where I turned down the offer of keys due to concerns about my personal security. As a consequence, I was restricted in where I could go. Unlike other centres, the design of the building prevented people from milling around and mixing informally. The activities corridor, usually a good place to be based, was run according to a strict timetable that did not allow for much more than general observation. The 'cultural kitchen' was organized differently as well; rather than a group of men cooking together, one man worked alone under the close watch of a staff member, preparing a meal for three friends who would be escorted in and out.

Having to be ferried around by staff was awkward and inefficient. After a 90-minute drive from Oxford, I often had to wait for an hour in the gate house for someone to collect me. Unlike Campsfield House where I was subject to a fairly cursory pat-down, in Brook House security was far more intrusive. 'On way in I was thoroughly searched, including, for the first time, in my mouth and behind my ears, in the cuffs of my trousers and in my shoes. This really annoyed me' (Fieldnotes, April 2011). Once inside, however, staff surveillance was far more haphazard. On one occasion I was taken to the staff lunch room where I was summarily abandoned by a DCO who had better things to do. While someone unlocked the lift for me, I found it led to an empty corridor. Without the lift key I had no choice but to get out. Luckily a Home Office staff member showed up and, without asking me who I was, let me into the Senior Management area.

After a break in the fieldwork of some months, IRC Morton Hall, run by HM Prison Service, was added as the final site. Interviews here were conducted by a third member of the research team, Gavin Slade, over a concentrated period of one month, during which he was present in the institution five days a week. Although I visited Morton Hall earlier in the project to set up this part of it, meeting with staff members and exploring the site, I did not do any of the detainee interviews myself.

Morton Hall was, until March 2011, a women's prison. Located in rural Lincolnshire, Morton Hall underwent a security upgrade when it was converted into an IRC. Previously an 'open' prison, built in a leafy green campus, it had been equipped with minimal barriers. These days the greenery remains but a high wire fence has sprung up, and locks and bars have been added to the doors and windows. Flowerbeds were destroyed and some trees removed in anticipation of the new arrivals. There are five residential units and an induction unit in Morton Hall, each of which is named after a famous woman: [Mary] Seacole, Torr,[19] [Elizabeth] Fry, [Queen Elizabeth II] Windsor, [Helen] Sharman, and [Amy] Johnson. The layout of each unit varies slightly. Fry and Windsor are older units with two-storey high wings. Their ceilings are low, and little light enters the corridors. Officers are hidden away in a small bureau. Fry and Windsor were designated as the units for holding the most high-risk detainees. Torr, Sharman, and Johnson in contrast are newer, laid out on one level, have higher ceilings, more windows and the staff in them located in an open plan lobby at the front of the buildings (see Figure 18).

Reflecting its recent past, as well as a concerted effort on the part of the prison service to offer a more detailed regime than most IRCs, Morton Hall had kept some of its industrial workshops as well as a greater emphasis on education. Detainees spent a lot of time in the 'hub' where there was a shop and computers. The diversity unit included a small library with daily newspapers in different languages and fax machines.

When Gavin conducted his interviews, Morton Hall had recently acquired its second Centre Manager and was undergoing some changes in staffing, drawing in younger male officers from nearby Ashwell Prison. Unlike longer-term employees of Morton Hall, these officers had limited experience working with foreign nationals. Whatever their employment background, most Morton Hall staff were white British citizens who lived locally.

Given the layout of Morton Hall, and in a bid to reduce his impact on staffing and to remain autonomous, Gavin drew keys. As Blerina and I had in the other establishments, he visited all parts of the centre, observing everyday activities, chatting informally to staff and men as well as recording formal interviews. Similar to our experience in Yarl's Wood, Gavin passed considerable time in the housing units, conducting formal and informal interviews in the men's rooms.

19. A local aristocratic family who owned the original, long demolished, stately home from which the IRC takes its name.

Figure 18. Windsor Unit IRC Morton Hall (Photo credit: HM Prison Service).

The participants

Over 20 months and six establishments, we spent around 2,400 hours in the field, the equivalent of three days in detention per week. During this period we spoke to many people. Yet, how, and more importantly, whether we were able to quantify the research participants proved to be far from straightforward. On the one hand, all members of the research group kept detailed fieldwork diaries, in which we recorded the formal and informal conversations and interviews we conducted. In addition to these diaries, where possible we digitally recorded interviews all of which were then transcribed verbatim.

On the basis of these records it is possible to enumerate the number of detainees and staff who participated in the research. While such figures give a sense of the scope and ambition of the project, they reveal nothing of the nature of our interactions. It would be wrong to imagine that all the interviews were the same. Some were no more than brief conversations, in passing in a corridor or over the table in the art and craft room.

Others lasted many hours. Some interviews were conducted in pairs, others as focus groups. Most were done one-to-one. Some began with the survey but switched into a less formal conversation. Others simply stopped abruptly when participants answered their phone, or became agitated or bored. Some women and men eschewed a formal discussion, but agreed to complete the survey in the privacy of their room. We often spoke to the same people on a number of occasions. A few contributors interacted with more than one member of the team at different locations. Interviewed by me in Colnbrook, they met Gavin in Morton Hall; I encountered them in Brook House after they had spoken to Blerina in Tinsley House.

Even when we sought to direct conversation—for instance by administering the MQLD survey—women and men did not always cooperate. Conservations and more formal interviews were interrupted by roll call, lunch, or activities. While some resumed later, others did not.

In any case, notwithstanding the survey, this study was, quite deliberately, not a purely quantitative one. The dominant methodology was ethnographic and exploratory. We relied on informal techniques like observation, casual conversation, as much as on structured interviews and questionnaire administration, enduring awkward silences, confusion, and discomfort in our attempts to bear witness and to understand.

We had to work hard to garner the trust of our participants. The vast majority of the detained population in all six establishments were highly anxious or depressed (Bosworth and Kellezi, 2013). Under these circumstances it is not surprising that many were sceptical about chatting to university researchers. While some spoke of the emotional benefits of sharing their stories, others were deeply worried. Still others were simply unconvinced of the utility of doing so. Sometimes the cause of their wariness was unexpected. I am an Australian citizen. During the research I became British as well. In Yarl's Wood, Blerina was told that some women in the prison were warning others, 'Don't talk to Mary—she's going back to Australia to open a new detention centre'. Serco, who were running Yarl's Wood at the time, had recently been awarded the contract in Australia to manage all their detention centres. All of a sudden, my nationality seemed awkwardly timed and suspicious. Similarly, my status as a 'criminologist', although apparently reassuring to the Home Office and the private contractors, was viewed with misgiving by some detainees. 'Why criminology?' they demanded, 'We are not criminals' (Various, all centres).

We encountered difficulties in communication and organization. While most detainees speak some English, their level of fluency varies, rendering some interviews hard to decipher. My foreign language skills are limited to French and Italian, while Blerina speaks Italian, Albanian, and some Spanish and Gavin can communicate in Russian, Georgian, and Greek. We used all of these languages. I also employed interpreters in Dari, Mandarin, and Spanish, and had some documents translated into Punjabi. Bringing in additional members of the research team was not always possible. Detainees sometimes offered to translate. However, this too was not always a successful strategy. Not only did it raise ethical questions about confidentiality, but those interpreting usually found it hard to avoid intervening. 'Interview with Bangladeshi man who didn't speak very good English. I spoke to him with help from a friend of his who translated. The friend often disagreed with how the first man answered my questions, and so didn't tell me what he said' (Fieldnotes, Campsfield House, November 2009). Finally, while some centre managers offered me the use of the 'Language Line', detainees did not trust the official interpreters who staffed that service and so I decided not to use it. I feared it would create further barriers in an already difficult environment, and, if the detainees were right, might not be reliable.

In addition to communication barriers, detainees who had previously agreed to be interviewed sometimes failed to turn up, either because they had been released, removed or deported, or perhaps had simply forgotten or changed their mind. Staff at the gatehouse occasionally refused entrance, pleading ignorance about my project. 'Am meant to be at Brook House', I wrote in an irritated entry in my fieldwork diary, 'but staff at gatehouse said not a single member of SMT there or UKBA. So nobody knew who I was. Came to Tinsley House where also suddenly more difficult about access . . . have been waiting over an hour' (Fieldnotes, April 2011). Days were also cut short by illness, personal demands at home, and my teaching responsibilities.

In order to familiarize ourselves with the institution and to try to generate relationships with staff and detainees, each member of the research team spent considerable portions of their days in detention 'hanging around', sitting alongside detainees eating lunch, working in the library, or making items in the arts and craft room. We watched them sing with volunteers from Music in Detention, play arcade games in the summer fete, and have their hair done either in the salon or outside their cells in the housing unit. We sat alongside them in the legal corridor as they waited for their appointments with the onsite Home Office staff or their lawyer. At Tinsley House, Blerina sometimes stayed late, remaining with detainees before they were marshalled onto planes. At Yarl's Wood she caught the bus with women who had been released into the community, occasionally offering them small sums of money or information. As the senior member of the research team I was invited to a range of staff meetings concerning suicide, self-harm, security, cultural, and religious matters. At Yarl's Wood the women taught me how to make pork dumplings and Chicken Jollof. In the cultural kitchen I watched Nigerian soap operas and was teased about my inability to dance. In the men's institutions all the researchers passed the time watching cricket and football. Men in Brook House tried to teach me card games, while in Yarl's Wood the women instructed me on the intricacies of paper folding, much to the delight of my children who keep the paper flowers in their bedroom.

Such interactions, and others like them, characterize daily life in detention. They do not always, however, generate 'interviews' and, as a result, risk being omitted in a bid to construct a narrative. Other experiences are also hard to integrate: the noise, the smell, the excessive air-conditioning, the heat, the sound of people crying. At Campsfield House, the Centre Director at the time had a bathroom deodorizer in his room, puffing cloying citrus scent into the air, even though the Senior Management Team corridor was safely separate from the men on the legal corridor, from whom the smell of anxiety leached powerfully. Whenever I returned home from Campsfield House I immediately showered and changed my clothes, anxious to be rid of it.

Though Campsfield House was the most extreme in its pungency, the odour of anxiety permeated all the buildings to some degree. At times this stench was exacerbated. In Colnbrook a man in solitary confinement engaged in a 'dirty protest', his urine pooling on the ground outside his cell as I walked past while the smell of faeces seeped out. Also in Colnbrook on the first day I visited, a strong smell of marijuana seeped down the hall, much to the embarrassment of my staff guide who clearly hoped I did not recognize it, whispering to another officer to perform a room check.

The sound of detention is also memorable. Most obviously the spaces pulse with different languages. Then there are the frequent interruptions of mobile phones. The relative peace and harmony of Yarl's Wood, in its isolated commercial estate, was often broken by alarms, when emotions in the dining room boiled over and women fought with one another. On one occasion a 'freeze all movements' occurred while I was sitting alone in a common area, and I witnessed a woman being forcibly taken to the segregation unit, kicking and screaming. The Gatwick IRCs are built so close to the airport runway that, despite the double-glazed windows, the rumble of lift-off is clearly audible. When I was shown around the segregation unit at Brook House, two men were simultaneously kicking their doors and ringing the alarm bell. One, I recorded in my fieldwork diary was 'pissing through the door'. The DCO on duty I noted, assured me, unconvincingly, 'you get used to it' (Fieldnotes, February 2011).

The composition of the detainee population and their appearance are also worth describing. Very few of the women and men in detention were white. Most were young, although in each detention centre we encountered some elderly people. Not only is detention literally a corporal experience—bodies are locked up—but people's demands for release are also often grounded in their physical attributes. Men, in all centres, often displayed their bodies to interviewers, showing us scars, telling us stories. Women's bodies were more varied. Some were covered up, others were put on display; some of the detainees were pregnant, others miscarried.

Detainees are allowed to wear their own clothes and keep in their room a certain amount of personal belongings. They wear a range of outfits. Some are clad in bulky tracksuits provided by the centre. Many wear IRC-issued flip flops. Others are more smartly dressed. Clothes reveal religious and ethnic identities; some of the women covered their hair with a hijab,[20] or their body with a jilbab,[21] others (men and women) wore a shalwar khameez.[22] Some of the Muslim men wore a taqiyah[23] and, on Fridays, a number wore gowns to prayer. African and Afro-Caribbean women often sported elaborate, and ever changing, braids. The shop at Yarl's Wood sold hair extensions and women braided hair in the hairdressing salon as well as in their rooms and in shared areas. At Brook House, a Pakistani man employed as a barber painstakingly shaved and styled the hair of a number of his friends, while they were draped in bin liners to protect their clothes.

20. A head scarf that leaves the face visible.
21. A long, loose-fitting gown, worn with a head scarf that leaves the face visible.
22. A tunic and trousers.
23. A short, rounded cap.

The diversity of the population was remarkable. Sometimes, the sheer difference, in language, culture, ethnicity, between me and those whom I was observing and interviewing felt impermeable; at those moments IRCs seemed no less than a deliberate (albeit impotent) bulwark against the developing world. At other times, the familiarity of detainees shone through. Men and women spoke in strong British accents. Many had lived in the UK for the same length of time as I had, others for far longer. Most spoke of recognizable aspirations, experiences and desires, longing for family, security, meaningful employment, and education. At those moments, the purpose and nature of IRCs seemed less clear. Were they, perhaps, a secure airport lounge? A zone of transition? A deliberate attempt to police, shape, or control the internal border and make-up of the country in which I too was a migrant?

Some of the detainees struggled with the diversity of the population. In Yarl's Wood, to a far greater extent than in the men's facilities we visited, there were frequent disputes between Chinese nationals, Jamaicans, and Nigerians. Racist comments, in English and Mandarin, were common currency between these three groups, leading at times to physical violence. Further distinctions, albeit less overt, were apparent among different national populations and between different religions (Bosworth and Kellezi, 2014). As Effa, from the Cameroon put it, 'there is a lot of tribalism in here'. In my fieldwork diary from Campsfield House, I describe the visual effect of such arrangements in the lunch hall:

> They came in in ethnic waves; the Chinese nationals first, taking up an entire half of the room, then, as they finished, all the various African nations replaced them one by one. As we left the room, I realized the other half was taken up with the Arabs and Asians . . . it was very, very loud and lots of different languages.

I conclude, somewhat inarticulately, 'Once again, struck by how it's NOT prison' (Fieldnotes, February 2010).

Making sense of detention

After two years in the field, working with two research officers and employing a number of ad hoc research assistants to help administer the survey, I was left with a mountain of material. The surveys were easily dispatched, entered into SPSS and analysed accordingly. Data from them formed the basis for two reports for the Home Office and private contractors as well as series of quantitative articles and conference papers (Bosworth and Kellezi, 2012; Bosworth, Kellezi, and Slade, 2012; Bosworth and Kellezi, 2013). The qualitative material, however, was more troublesome.

All interviews were fully transcribed along with fieldwork diaries, producing thousands of pages of text. With the help of Blerina, I attributed pseudonyms to the participants, creating Excel files of basic demographic data for each participant. To ensure all names only appeared once, we used online resources for expectant parents, starting with three letter names in English. Where possible we have allocated culturally appropriate names, to correspond to their nationalities.

Before entering the field, I had planned to analyse the transcripts using the qualitative data analysis package, NVivo. I gradually abandoned this idea as the method seemed ill-fitted to the project. Blerina made a first run through of the interviews from Yarl's Wood, uploading them into NVivo and creating a series of 'nodes'. Given the volume of material, however, it rapidly became clear that to enter it all into NVivo would not only be extremely time consuming, but, more importantly, risked forcing the material into an unnatural taxonomy. The only other alternative would be to create an unwieldy array of tiny categories.

It may be that someone more experienced with NVivo than I could have made it work more effectively. However, I resisted it for other reasons fearing that the rise of qualitative data programs is little more than an attempt to respond to old positivist concerns over the 'subjective' nature of qualitative research. Ultimately, I opted for a more anthropological approach, carefully reading and then re-reading the interviews, descriptions, brief conversations and field notes, sometimes listening to the recordings again as well. I used a combination of what might be loosely called coding strategies, identifying themes by cutting and pasting (or highlighting in the text) quotes and descriptions under conceptual subheadings that included: masculinity, femininity, legitimacy, prison, staff satisfaction, relationships, immigration, fear, uncertainty, recognition. Such categories were kept deliberately broad, and were largely used to identify general patterns, forcing me back time and again to the transcripts themselves.

In taking a more intuitive and less systematic approach to the material, I felt better able to respond to unexpected issues that arose, and also less constrained by needing to fit things together. Evidently, this technique raises the risk that I may overlook some important elements. Thousands of pages of notes are difficult to remember. However, ethnographies do not purport to find a single truth, but rather to seek understanding. There can always be more than one perspective. In any case, the project was exploratory. For long periods I was unsure about what to make of what I was witnessing. A more flexible method of analysis retains some of that tension.

Conclusion

Custodial institutions are notoriously difficult spaces to access and in which to conduct research. As this chapter has demonstrated, in removal centres, such challenges are amplified. From communication to finding an appropriate space to interview, staying in touch with a population unsure of the duration of their detention, to understanding across culture and gender, barriers were legion. Sometimes, they felt petty. 'Arrived, no arrangements made. Put in library, not ideal, need to ask for other space', my fieldnotes tersely report (Fieldnotes, Campsfield House, November 2009). At other times, they were more fundamental. As female researchers, in institutions for men, Blerina and I sometimes struggled to find a suitable place to conduct interviews. We could not venture into the men's rooms for fear of raising questions about the nature of our relationship with the participants, and the only other available spaces, in the 'legal corridor', ran the risk of making men think we were lawyers or working for the Home Office.

Even frequent informal public interactions with male detainees sometimes had unintended consequences. In Tinsley House, after one man addressed Blerina in an email as 'babe', I was called in to answer questions from the Home Office regional manager. Was Blerina engaging in an inappropriate relationship, he wanted to know?[24] All electronic

24. In fact, only a few men flirted with us. Those who did tended to be younger and were often long-term British residents and/or ex-prisoners. Some explicitly told Blerina that her lack of children at the time rendered her not entirely 'off the market'. With me, they mainly expressed surprise about my age, often assuming I was a student. On one occasion I took pity on a young man who gradually realized he had been chatting up someone old enough to be his mother. In his case I reduced my actual age by five years to minimize his embarrassment!

communication is monitored, and since the man had written in English they had understood what he had said.

Finally, the levels of distress among the detainees were often unbearable to witness. 'After I had long chat with Farzad, I left Tinsley House crying. Tried to relax in the toilet before I left so the officers would not see. The Afghani stories are pure desperation. I am not sure I can take this for much longer' (Fieldnotes, April 2011). On a number of occasions I left the centre abruptly, having reached the limits of my capacity to soak up other people's misery. While the research was ongoing and for months after it ended, I suffered from insomnia, bad dreams, palpitations, breathlessness, tears, and dizziness. It took about one year to be able to read the fieldnotes and transcripts without a sense of rising anxiety, sick to my stomach.

These aspects form another context to this project, raising questions of their own about understanding. Is it possible to understand across language or culture (Spivak, 1998; 2000)? What about race and gender? What is the effect of trauma, suspicion, or hostility? Given the lack of equivalent academic research in the field, on what basis might I judge my interpretation of participants' accounts?

They also raise questions about traditional criminological frames of analysis. Drawing on my previous experience of prison research, I had expected detainees to be concerned with the minutiae of daily life inside; relationships, food, work. This project, however, unlike the traditions of prison sociology found little analytic purchase in sociological notions of 'total institutions', with their neatly differentiated 'inside' and 'outside' (Goffman, 1968).

Power, in detention, is not so easy to delineate. Rather than dwelling on the nature of their custodial experience, individuals spoke at length about their immigration case, the reason for their detention and their fears of return. Some brought their dossiers to us, eager to share copies of newspaper clippings relative to their case as well as letters from or to the Home Office, their lawyers, NGOs, their relatives, no matter how personal. These dog-eared bundles sometimes included certificates of qualification or participation which were proudly brandished as 'proof' of their achievements, commitment, good character. All, they suggested, evidence for why they should be allowed to stay.

Such resistance to concentrating on the conditions of detention was not limited to detainees, but also characterized staff. Although they were more prepared to talk about the nitty gritty of pay and conditions, they too puzzled about the purpose of their job and the reasons for such places. Over the project I came to see that all the aspects which felt so confounding and made the research so difficult, the diversity, the regime, the disconnect between highly securitized spaces and the allegedly transient (non-criminal) population they held, embodied the confusion surrounding border control in general. As the following chapters will demonstrate in greater detail, IRCs have no clear, inherent purpose or legitimacy. They are institutions defined by competing aspirations that, when we pay closer attention to them, often seem to bear little relationship to reality. Exploring life inside such places, does not necessarily explain their external purpose and legitimacy. For that we need a more complex frame of analysis. It is to that task that I will now turn.

3

Recognition and belonging in an age of deportation

Since I have been here I have not developed as a person. I have developed as an animal (Mansour, BOC, TH).

I am a prisoner (Tina, Taiwan, YW).
Lesa (DCO) (very sternly): No, you are not. You are a resident.
I feel like a prisoner (Tina).
You are not. You. Are. A. Resident! (Lesa, DCO).
But there are walls here. I am trapped (Tina).

Britain, along with other Western neo-liberal states, has spent considerable effort over the past decade in marking out (some) foreign nationals as dangerous, unwelcome, and excludable. Eliding different categories of foreigner, starting with the 'bogus asylum seeker', before moving to the terrorist and the foreign offender, various British governments have pitted these rhetorical figures against the British citizen, shoring up a narrative of national identity in a period of mass mobility (Bosworth and Guild, 2008; Wilsher, 2012; Young, 2003a).

Detention centres have played an important role in this narrative and its execution. Secure facilities enable the state to gather documentation to admit or expel new arrivals while cordoning off those who may be removed or deported. IRCs identify detainees in more symbolic ways as well. Held in institutions closely resembling prisons and staffed by uniformed officers carrying keys, detainees are implicitly (and sometimes explicitly[1]) cast, like prisoners, as dangerous and undeserving. Predictable racialized

---

1. Daily Mail Reporter (2011). '"Undesirable and dangerous" immigrant criminals cannot be deported from Britain, say Euro judges' *Daily Mail Online*, 28 June 2011.

interpretations of specific nationalities also play an important role in defining them as strange and unwelcome.

Unlike prisons, IRCs, do not aim to reintegrate. Their inhabitants are deportable, expendable, and unwelcome (De Genova and Peultz, 2010; De Genova, 2002), strangers no matter how long they have lived in Britain (Ahmed, 2000). 'I look at it this way', Aufa remarked, 'specially them laws, they bring it in for terrorist. For terrorist . . . yeah, everything'. Resident in the UK for over 30 years, Aufa felt keenly the effect of the new immigration laws. 'They're using on everyone', he argued. 'Stop and search, you can look, photography, you can put it this way. They bring it for the terrorist and you know, they're using on everyone. They want to use to send someone from other countries. That's why they bring this law in. They want to send them to their home countries' (Pakistan, BH).

Part of the problem detainees like Aufa face is that a key part of their identity has already been determined by their confinement, over-riding other aspects of their sense of self. For many this identification is hard to bear. 'I don't know who I am!' Hali cried. Resident in the UK for 15 years, she no longer knew where she belonged. 'I'm just someone in detention. I don't feel myself. I don't know who I am anymore' (Nigeria, YW). Identity, Hali's sorrow reminds us, is a matter of affect and the law (Butler, 1990; 1997; 2005). Legal categories shape lived experience.

Most bridle against the stigma of the 'detainee' label, aware that if they are to avert deportation or removal, they must convince the Home Office that their identification is incorrect. As other aspects of their identity fade in relation to their legal status in the environment of a detention centre, detainees find it increasingly difficult to be heard or recognized. Yet, notwithstanding their precarious status (Butler, 2004), many persist in identity-based claims, crafting alternative subject positions, from which they might not only seek legal remedy (for instance in proving their grounds for asylum), but also through which they understand their experience. Staff, too, are often unsure of what a 'Detention Custody Officer' is, or should be. In making sense of their custodial role, they turn to those whom they guard, differentiating among them in order to understand.

In so doing, albeit with limited effect, both groups subvert the logic of an institution set up to segregate individuals purely on the basis of their citizenship. While subsequent chapters focus on the gap between people's sense of self and the identity attributed to them by the state, this one examines the relationship and dissonance between the official identification of detainees and their sense of self. Identity, their accounts reveal, is irreducibly relational, and cannot be fully contained by the walls of a detention centre. As a mode and site of governance, it is simultaneously painful and precarious, the source of much uncertainty and distress.

Identity and identification

Under conditions of globalization identification can be complicated. Consequently, while the majority of detainees are held for less than two months, some remain in custody for considerable periods as aspects of their identity-based claims are disputed. Some barriers relate to the everyday logistics of communicating with other sovereign states who may deny citizenship claims. Even when they accept the individual's nationality, certain countries simply take a very long time to issue official travel documents. On occasion the Home Office loses paperwork (HMIP and ICIBI, 2012). Detainees themselves may hold up the process, refusing to identify themselves to the British authorities. They may assert a false identity, declaring they are Chinese nationals when they are Malaysian, Kosovars rather than Albanian, Romanian instead of Moldovan. Some hide or have their documents destroyed. These and other barriers reflect how difficult it is to fit people's identities into single categories.

While a simply binary opposition between citizen/non-citizen animates and justifies most border control measures, not just detention, it does not map everybody's lives readily. Until they received a deportation order, for example, some of those who had lived in the UK since childhood either did not appreciate that they were not citizens, or had not realized that they could be treated differently from others with British passports. Once the implications of their nationality became evident, some engage in what Peter Isin and George Nielsen (2008) have labelled 'acts of citizenship', laying claim to an equivalent kind of membership—as a hard worker, mother, or tax-payer—unrecognizable in law, but grounded in familiar moral hierarchies. A few, like Ziggy born in Jamaica, simply denied the law altogether, claiming British citizenship in the absence of a passport, by virtue of long-term residence and cultural affinity. 'I am a British citizen', he insisted. 'I just don't have a passport. I did primary school, middle school, high school. I am British' (Jamaica, BH).

Others refuted the salience of nationality. 'My life is not in Brazil', Emilia proclaimed (Brazil, YW). Still others, like Abdoul-Haziz, were simply baffled by the paradox of world events. Agitated and highly distressed he yelled repeatedly: 'The British, they are there, fighting in Libya. Why can't they help me? I'm Libyan!' (Libya, BH).

Darko, who acceded his lack of British nationality, acknowledged that 'It doesn't matter what you feel, it's up to the government to decide who is British and who isn't' (Serbia, MH). Yet he struggled to grasp why that one aspect of their identity overshadowed the rest. For all of these people, citizenship was simply one axis of their identity, an element among many, and rarely the most important, of their sense of self. As grounds for detention and deportation it was, therefore, difficult to accept.

Detainees and staff disputed many axes of subjectivity in IRCs. As the quotes at the beginning of this chapter attest, women and men commonly asserted that their confinement negated their most fundamental identity, that of a human. They had become no more than animals. 'They take us around like cows, like sheep!' Kissa expostulated. 'At least sheep know whom to follow, but we are just take here and there. Why do they have this place? They keep women in here for a long time and they deport them anyway' (Uganda, YW). Some denied that they were detainees at all, claiming instead to be prisoners, slaves, victims of kidnapping, or torture. 'I don't want to live life in the world where detention by the UK-sponsored kidnapper is thought to be my solution', Ridoy spat (Bangladesh, MH), while Kissa demanded, 'What's the point of being a slave here? You are a slave' (Uganda, YW). Still others rejected such appellations 'I'm not a prisoner!' Innocent shouted at me one day. 'I'm a citizen, just like you' (Rwanda, CB). 'I'm no kill people. Just having illegally work', another man sadly observed (Unknown nationality, CH).

Kazi, from Pakistan, focused his attention on the inherent stigma of being locked up, stating plaintively, 'I belong to very good family. I never handcuffed before' (Pakistan, MH). When discussing her night in a police cell en route to Yarl's Wood from the airport, Aatifa used similar language. 'I am from a very respectable family in Pakistan', she cried out indignantly, 'I had never been to a place like that before' (Pakistan, YW). Yet, as Ayesha recognized, such assertions counted for little. 'I'm educated', she declared, 'but you put me here like we are just stupid like monkeys. What we doing here? I'm just eating and sleeping and just thinking: "What happen next, what happen next?"' (Pakistan, YW).

Others were bewildered by what they felt was a sudden emphasis on their 'racial' identity. Prior to his detention, Richard, explained, he had occupied many roles as father, worker, and a member of the wider community. At Morton Hall, however, 'it's all different. It's all different', he sighed. 'Ethnic, ethnic group B2. You feel that, "oh my . . . I'm African. I'm in a foreign land"' (Zimbabwe, MH). Meg, in Yarl's Wood took a similar view, angrily demanding, 'Why we always have to be prisoners? Black people have been prisoners since creation' (Jamaica, YW).

Women and men challenged their detainee identity in other ways as well. In Tinsley House, Boseda, an elderly Nigerian man always wore formal attire, strolling calmly up and down the corridors with a friend. 'We get up everyday and dress up like we are going to the office', he reported, 'and then walk up and down these corridors. That is because there is very little left for us to have self-respect in here, and dressing up, clean and elegant is the one way we can maintain self-respect and is something that makes me happy' (Nigeria, TH). In Yarl's Wood, Aatifa also stood out, heavily made-up, clothed in colourful, richly embroidered garments, her elegant dress was better suited to a party or a dance, than yet another day behind bars. Instead of imitating a worker, this woman who had fled a violent, arranged marriage in the UK, only to be beaten by her brother in Pakistan and forced to return, asserted grimly, 'I dress up and enjoy myself as much as I can here because I know when I go back, that my life is over' (Pakistan, YW). Also in Yarl's Wood, Gena caused consternation emblazoning a T-shirt in art and craft class with the slogan '100% British!' (India, YW). When asked about the design, Gena made it clear that rather than a statement of fact, these words were an aspiration. 'I have full confidence in my own case', she explained. 'I tell everybody I am British. Everybody calls me British, even the officers. Then I dance, I sing, I just cheer up everyone, because that's life. I get kisses and hugs from everybody. It's wonderful to be loved' (Bosworth, 2012).

Detainees used their bodies in other ways to challenge their detainee identity. Adopting a strategy that is also common in prison (Sabo, 2001; Crewe, 2009), women and men worked on their physique, lifting weights and spending every available moment in the gym. Others participated in so-called 'dirty protests', self-harm or food refusal. In Tinsley House two Iranian men sewed their lips shut.

In these examples, women and men enacted a presentation of self that stretched beyond the walls of the IRC, challenging the logic of exclusion inherent in their enclosure. However ineffective in terms of immigration law, their identity-claims revealed important lines of connection with familiar goals and aspirations, characteristics which detention custody staff and some onsite Home Office workers found disorienting. As such, their testimonies exposed multiple layers of membership, guarding against simplistic interpretations of their subjectivity.

To be sure, identity is not just symbolic. Women and men contested their status as detainees for more practical reasons as well. Only by finding an alternative subject position could they challenge their detention itself. Those filing fresh claims for asylum sought to prove their sexuality, or membership of a particular religious or ethnic group. Parents demanded protection of their 'right to family life' under Article 8 of the European Convention on Human Rights,[2] hoping to persuade the Home Office or their immigration judge of the salience of their parental identity. Those who were younger than 18 years, struggled to prove their age.

In their competing claims, detainees were at a significant disadvantage. Not only had most of them exhausted their legal avenues for redress, but, in any case, certain aspects of their identity were hard to prove. 'Someone my age in Malawi should be married', Nia disclosed. 'But I don't have a man in me' (Malawi, YW). Fearful of returning to Malawi, where section 137A of the penal code criminalizes 'indecent practices among females', she was unsure how to demonstrate her sexual orientation to the Home Office.[3] Unlike Azadeh, in flight from relatives in Iran who had discovered her sexuality, but with a partner and brother resident in Europe able to support her claim for asylum, Nia was attempting to navigate the British asylum system on her own.[4] She did not even want the women at Yarl's Wood to know, 'I can't tell them about who I am because they are African and they will judge me. So I just am alone' (Malawi, YW).

For others, while their identity was not in question, its meaning was disputed. A number of men, for example, complained that the Home Office refused to recognize the significance of their family commitments,

2. A protection that is increasingly difficult to achieve, particularly for those with a criminal conviction.
3. In 2010, following the imprisonment of a gay male couple, considerable international attention was directed to Malawi's criminalization of homosexuality and lesbian relationships. Since November 2012, the anti-gay laws have officially been suspended, though, at the time of writing, still on the books (Mujuzi, 2011; Mapondera and Smith, 2012).
4. And indeed, while Nia lingered in detention, Azadeh was granted refugee status and released within a week.

a bureaucratic response that not only prevented their wider, legal claims but, on a personal level effectively erased their identity as fathers. I was warned by custodial staff on a number of occasions to disbelieve men's accounts of their love for their children. Instead, in a scornful and distinctly racialized account, staff assured me, men like these were only interested in having sex with their 'baby-mamas'. 'The men are not as close with their kids as the women', a wing officer at Morton Hall opined, 'Of course they talk about it, but actually they aren't that bothered about not being with them' (DCO, MH).

Unsurprisingly, this denial was often hard to bear. The men worried about the impact of their enforced absence on their loved ones. 'I know what it is like to grow up without a father', De'ron warned. 'My mother struggled to raise 9 children; she was mother and father to us. So they want my children to grow up without a father?' (Jamaica, TH). Others feared that their children would follow in their footsteps. 'Who is hoping to look after my children?' Mac demanded angrily. 'Do they want them to make the same mistakes I made and up in prison or on benefits? I don't want them on benefits. I want to look after them' (Nigeria, TH).

Most men did not want to leave their children behind because they loved them. 'My kids, my kids have been put into care', Adashe wept. 'Now I ain't going to have access to my kids for good . . . How am I supposed to live without my kids? I mean I thought that was the whole idea of having, of life. You know what I'm saying? To have your kids and to work and look after your kids. But then if I can't have my kids, what kind of life do I have now?' (Zimbabwe, MH).

Like De'ron, Clinton wanted to honour his parental responsibilities. As with Mac he feared the outcome if he did not: 'I want to raise them right and teach them right things about life', he proclaimed. 'If I don't, my kids will end up in gangs and then in prison.' Yet, such potential threat to the British state, it became clear, was not his main concern. Instead, in a change of tone, he started to describe his daughter, sounding just like any other proud father. 'I have a beautiful daughter. She is only 6 but she is so clever. She is the best in her school and has a lot of certificates for being clever. She can read and write very well. She can spell her name and my name . . . Who is going to take care of my children?' (Jamaica, BH).

To be sure, not all fathers lived with their children. Even those who did, valued other aspects of their identity as well. Sometimes these matters were hard to reconcile. Adan, a young Iraqi Kurd who had resided in the UK for four years, described the conflict between his mother's expectations of him as a son and his own desire to be a father. On the one hand, like the other men, he was loath to leave his child behind. 'I have my son here so I can't go back', he declared. 'I can't let my son grow up without a father' (Iraq, TH). On the other hand, he reported, his Iraqi family was urging him to return: 'My mother said, "son, don't stay there. You are wasting your life and my life by staying in detention". I can go back home', he acknowledged, but only at great personal cost; 'my son is here' (Iraq, TH).

Women complained of similar matters. For them, detention acted as a formidable practical barrier as well as a symbolic one, effacing or at least minimizing their maternal identities.[5] 'It is unfair that mothers are in detention', Alba complained. 'As a mum I am not a danger to society. They should let me out' (DRC, YW).

Like those in prison (Bosworth, 1999: Women in Prison, 2013), women in detention often struggled to find family members to take care of their children. Some of their children were living with relatives in the community. Others had been taken into care, awaiting reunification with their mothers at the airport (BID, 2013). Still others were sent back to relatives in their mother's country of origin. A few women had seen their parental rights terminated. Their children were either in the process of being adopted or were in long-term foster care. Others had lost access to their children prior to their detention, when they fled an abusive husband; a bleak reminder of the limited legal rights women possess in many parts of the world (Hudson, Bowen, and Nielsen, 2011; UN Women, 2011). Many had left sons and daughters behind with relatives in their country of origin, seeking out economic opportunities in the UK and sending home remittances to pay for their education and housing. Not all of the women knew where their children were. If the children had been removed by the British state, either into care or to be adopted, women often claimed not to understand what was happening. In each situation, they found it difficult to be recognized as a mother.

---

5. Whereas there has been considerable outcry in the UK against the detention of children (BID, 2013), and, more recently, concerns voiced about the detention of pregnant women (Medical Justice, 2013), very little attention has been paid to the mothers' needs and experiences as women. Instead, in both cases, attention has focused on the effects of detention on children. As with debates in the US over reproductive rights, such inattention to the women's experiences, even from within critical organizations, however unintentionally, objectifies the mothers concerned (Flavin, 2010).

Such diversity in the cause and nature of their separation from their sons and daughters made it painful for women to discuss their family life with one another. They also complicated a simple account of their subjectivity. On the one hand, for those who were previously living with their children in the UK, detention itself was the problem. In one fiery interview, for instance, May, a long-term British resident from Jamaica, who had recently been stripped of her indefinite leave to remain and was facing removal, complained about the negative impact of her detention on her son and daughter, aged 10 and 17. Previously well behaved, the son had recently been excluded from school, while the daughter's marks were slipping. Witnessing their pain from a distance was more than May could bear. 'What is the relationship of a mother with her children?' she angrily demanded. 'Whose children are these? Do they know how tied a mother is to her children? ... Every child needs a mother at home with them!' (Jamaica, YW).

Whereas for May, detention was preventing her fulfilling her role and identity as a mother, how might we understand the relationship between detention and identity for those women who had already lost touch with their children, or who were being denied access to them not just by the fact of their confinement but by their estranged husbands? Those who had abandoned children when they fled domestic abuse, or whose sons and daughters had been taken from them by their husband or his family, found it particularly painful to articulate a sense of themselves as mothers. For Abbo, who had escaped a violent and unhappy marriage, leaving her one-year-old daughter behind, matters were compounded by the British government's rejection of her asylum claim, a decision, which, she pointed out, denied her identity as a mother all over again. 'What do they [the Home Office] think? What do they think would cause someone to leave behind their child?' she demanded. 'Do they think someone would do that unless they had a real reason?' (Uganda, YW).

Unusually, despite having left her husband, Abbo had stayed in touch with her daughter, speaking to her regularly on the telephone. In this she resembled other mothers who had moved to Britain to work. Such women, like Camila (Brazil) and Pam (Nigeria), had often lived in the UK for many years without immigration status. Camila who was employed as a nanny before her arrest, had sent remittances to Brazil for nearly six years, supporting her daughter, mother, as well as her unwell sister. Pam's income had paid for the care of a mentally-ill adult daughter. Despite taking on the putatively 'masculine' role of breadwinners, such women had not shed their 'feminine' duty of care. Instead, they had been forced to fulfil both roles, effectively acting as mother and father to their children, although unable to do either face-to-face (Hondagneu-Sotelo and Avila, 1997; Parreñas, 2010; Ehrenreich and Hochschild, 2003; Hewett, 2009).

Finally, women whose children had been placed in foster care complained about difficulties in arranging visits and their fears of losing access to their children permanently. The intersection of family law with immigration matters, sometimes shaped also by criminal law if they had served a prison sentence, made it very difficult for these women to realize their identities as mothers. Ava from the Cameroon, who spoke little English, simply did not appear to grasp what had happened. Although her sons had been removed from her care prior to detention due to allegations of abuse, she persisted in believing that they would be returned to her. The last time she saw their 'carer', Ava described indignantly that the woman had told her 'these are not your children, they are mine!' Somehow, despite having completed the family court process prior to her detention, she had not understood that, indeed, the boys were never coming home.[6]

Notwithstanding the barriers, many women and men strove to resist, or at least to make do, asserting constitutive aspects of their identities even as they were losing their capacity to enact them. One man, whose fatherhood had been denied as it was just beginning when he was detained the very night his wife went into labour, sought a way to engage with his family outside. 'Sorry, I have to find Internet', Jim apologized when asked to participate in the research. 'They arrested me yesterday when my wife was in labour. Can you imagine? They brought me here and she has since given birth to a boy. I am looking for Internet so that I can see the photos of the baby' (Unknown nationality, TH). Although unusual, in terms of being arrested during his wife's labour, he was not the only man I interviewed whose wife had given birth during his period of detention. Others had been detained in the final stages of their partner's pregnancy and had yet to meet their baby.

---

6. This piece of information was communicated to me by the administrative assistant of her family lawyer when Ava put me on the phone to try to determine what was going on. Despite introducing myself quite clearly as a researcher with no personal or legal relationship to Ava, I was readily informed by the legal employee that her case had been terminated some months ago and that her children were to be adopted. 'All Ava needs to know', the woman added 'is that they are in foster care'.

Those with children in the UK spoke of telephone calls at bedtime, parenting from a distance. Men in art and craft class produced jewellery for their wives and girlfriends, while women in Yarl's Wood made cards and other trinkets for friends, relatives, and children, using centre activities to fulfil their gendered responsibilities outside and, on occasion, to acquire new skills that might enable a new role and identity upon return or release. One woman, who had told her daughter that she was working away, arranged for her mother to buy toys for her child and leave them on the table, saying 'mummy visited while you were at school' (unknown nationality, YW). In each case, through such everyday actions, they reminded themselves and others that they were more than just detainees. Although bound by the walls of the institution, their sense of self extended far beyond.

As feminists have long pointed out, for white women motherhood has always been an important barometer for good citizenship (Pateman, 1992; Hill-Collins, 2000). Likewise, fatherhood and worker are key legitimating subject positions for white men (Connell, 2005). For those in detention, however, the otherwise positive value attributes to gendered identities such as these were compromised by their lack of citizenship. Under these circumstances, detainee bids to be recognized as subjects of value were more easily brushed aside.

Staff and identity

Detainees were not the only figures in IRCs grappling with questions of their identity. A number of custody officers and Home Office staff also felt unsure of whom they were holding or why such people were there. Such questions about detainees led many to wonder about their own identity and purpose.

Some refused to acknowledge the salience of detention at all in such matters. 'I mean they're normal human beings', Stan asserted. 'Know what I mean? Just cos they're in here, doesn't mean to say you got to talk to them any different or whatever' (DCO, YW). The Pastor at Yarl's Wood agreed, emphasizing the talents of those he had met at the centre. 'We have some real gifted people that come through these places. Doctors and people with PhDs and, you know, Masters and all sorts'. A number were, at least sometimes, sympathetic, acknowledging the difficult lives many of those in their care had led. 'Some of what these guys have had to deal with', Jeanine told me, 'is terrible. I don't know what I'd do if I was in their shoes' (DCM, CB).

At the same time, however, officers were often cynical. At Yarl's Wood, where otherwise many staff expressed considerable compassion for the detainees, Luna dismissed the women's stories as 'an auction of misery. Those with the most win' (SMT, YW). In a strikingly gendered trope, this senior member of staff scorned the female detainee identity as inherently duplicitous. The women, she made clear, were manipulative and difficult, exaggerating their problems in a bid for sympathy.[7]

Definitions of detainees were apparent in the terminology staff used. At Yarl's Wood and Colnbrook, officers were encouraged to refer to detainees as 'residents'. Mostly, at least in my earshot, they did, although on occasion they stumbled. When asked whether he felt 'valued' in his job, for instance, Todd replied, 'For the girls, yeah. Well, residents that is. I shouldn't call them girls. For the residents, yeah' (DCO, YW). Whereas Alex Hall (2012) found staff at an IRC that had recently been converted from a prison continued to refer to detainees as 'Cons', most of the officers at Morton Hall avoided this label. More generally, however, in each centre, staff often referred to those who had been to prison as 'foreign national prisoners', or more succinctly as 'FNPs', as though they were still serving a sentence.

In Morton Hall, one officer, who had worked for the prison service for 24 years, found it difficult to reconcile the detainees' status with the custodial environment in which they had been placed. 'At the end of the day', Jonathan pointed out, 'these guys are deemed to be innocent, not committed any crimes, same as civilians. But', he stumbled on, 'they're in detention. They're held in a secure environment'. This custodial environment, Jonathan recognized, cast them as dangerous and guilty of something, although he was unsure of exactly what. Struggling to reconcile this paradox, he stuttered, 'I don't, I don't actually, I don't look at them as criminals, but . . . they have committed, they have done wrong, because they're in the

---

7. In common with the other IRCs, the staff area at Yarl's Wood prominently displayed photographs of detainees labelled as 'development nominals'. For these women, who were identified as potential security threats, their identities were further stigmatized and their trustworthiness maligned by concerns over their putative dangerousness. During my research project, most of those on the noticeboard under this heading at Yarl's Wood were particularly outspoken. Some had been reported in the national media and had also participated in a recent food refusal and disturbance.

country without [pausing] A lot. Not all of them. A lot of them are here because they shouldn't be' (DCO, MH).

In making sense of detainees staff divided them into groups organized according to a range of intersecting factors, the most important of which were criminal record, length of residency, nationality, and gender. At Campsfield House, for instance, Peter, a detention custody manager who had previously worked in a private prison, saw a clear distinction between ex-prisoners and the rest. 'I was always tell people, you don't need to worry about the ex-FNPs', he claimed with a knowing laugh. 'It's the rest who are the problem. We don't know what they've done' (DCM, CH).[8] Lina was rather less sure about the relative virtues of ex-prisoners, although, like Peter she clearly saw them as a specific 'type' of detainee. 'You can't pick out from looking who have been in prison', she noted, 'but after a while you know. They might be slightly more in your face. Know their rights. But I have no problems with them', she assured me.[9] Others, like Allen at Tinsley House, were more explicitly negative, differentiating 'foreign national prisoners', whom he characterized as, 'rapists', 'kiddie fiddlers', and 'murderers', from the rest who had 'just forgotten to update their visa or whatever' (DCO, TH). Foreign ex-prisoners were, in his view, forever dangerous and undeserving. 'I know they've been to prison', he acknowledged, 'and prison's a way of rehabilitating someone, but the fact that they've done something like that, surely can't be acceptable' (DCO, TH). Their identity was fixed.

In all centres, staff differentiated between long-term UK residents and more recent arrivals. Sometimes, as with Lina's account of ex-prisoners, the main issue appeared to be one of control. Long-term residents were easier to manage. 'I think generally if someone's been living in the country quite a few years', Arvil argued, 'doesn't matter what nationality they are, they tend to be a lot easier to comply with, than maybe somebody who hasn't' (DCO, TH). Others, however, found long-term residents confounding, often uneasy about deporting people who had spent almost their whole life in Britain. 'People that have been here like twenty years and got a wife and kids here and you know, done . . . well they've obviously

---

8. In this example, Peter echoed the view expressed by Hall's participants that detainees 'could be anyone' (Hall, 2010).

9. In fact, as another staff member pointed out to me early on in the research process, ex-prisoners often identity themselves by referring to staff as 'Miss', 'Sir' or 'Gov', deploying prisoner argot.

done something but, you know, they're being sent back. And there ain't really nothing they can do about it', Stevie commented. 'That is hard . . . to think you know, they got a wife and five kids here. He's been at school here. He's got a National Insurance card' (DCO, BH). As he went on, it became apparent that Stevie found this man familiar not just culturally, but also in class terms. 'You know, he talks like us. Well maybe not like you!' Stevie laughed, 'He talks like me, you know? And they're being deported. But, such is life' (DCO, BH). Bound to some detainees by a local accent, a shared level of education and class position, Steve's conscience was pricked.

Often staff distinguished between detainees on the basis of nationality, deploying a range of familiar, racialized, generalizations. Although always careful not to articulate overt prejudice, they usually used one nationality as a foil for another, comparing them in order to explain which group was easier to manage. 'A nationality doesn't deem how aggressive they are', Bob began, 'but there's definite traits inside that come across . . . So for example Nigerians are really, really loud guys. That's how they talk, argue, shout, whatever. But . . . a Malaysian . . . is quite chilled out, relaxed, quite, you know, passive' (DCO, CH). In a particularly detailed example, Lela offered an explanation for why 'Some of the African nations are quieter than others. I mean, Nigerian women tend to be fairly forthright (laughs) tend to leave you in no doubt as to exactly how they're thinking or feeling', she proclaimed. 'Whereas, you find the likes of the Cameroonians are a lot more patient and probably less high maintenance as well. And then from little tiny countries like Lesotho and that, you barely know they're there. And the Côte d'Ivoire ladies are, I don't know, there's a softer, they're just slightly softer' (DCM, YW).

Finally, staff singled out specific detainees for praise. Usually, this view was limited to individual women or men with whom they had struck up a friendship. At Colnbrook, for instance, a series of officers spoke warmly of David whom they were trying to help find accommodation in Uganda. The staff, who judged him to be personable and remorseful, considered him as an exception to the rest, deserving of their compassion. Likewise, in Yarl's Wood, despite being unable to communicate with her, Leah took a young Chinese woman, Hui-Ying under her wing, 'I'd take her home with me if I could' (DCO, YW). In that case, Leah's compassion was generated by a combination of factors including Hui-Ying's youth, her multiple attempts at self-harm and the length of time she had been detained while the British and Chinese authorities failed to resolve her case.

Whatever strategy they used, it became clear that staff members' perception of detainees, whether as individuals, or more commonly as a group, played an important role in their opinions and interpretation of their own job, its purpose and legitimacy. How they viewed those in their care, in other words, was integral to staff views of their career. For some, acknowledging their shared humanity was painful. 'I hated this job for the first year', Lily admitted. 'Hated it. I felt so bad for the women. I mean they're humans just like us, aren't they?' (DCO, YW). For others, the attributes they shared with detainees made their job interesting and worthwhile. 'When you actually get to see them [detainees], meet them and everything, you know', Ammon claimed.

> 99.9 per cent of them are nice people, you know. They're just unfortunate. You can have, you know, a good laugh with them. You know, as well, I was quite surprised. It's quite, sounds quite bad, but I was quite surprised how many of them actually spoke English. I mean some of them can actually speak better English than me. You know, a lot of very intelligent people as well. I was pleasantly surprised at that, you know (DCO, TH).

Staff views about detainees also shaped their sense of self. Many employees at Morton Hall were anxious about who they were now they were no longer in charge of prisoners (Bosworth and Slade, 2014). Some, like Diane, responded to their status confusion by relying more heavily on a symbolic articulation of their professional identity. 'As long as I'm in this uniform, this is a prison officer uniform, with the Queen's thing on and I'm a prison officer', she stated firmly. 'And if somebody said to me "You've got to change your uniform, become a custody officer" it'd be like "See you then! Going to go find a real prison to work in". At least you know where you are with them' (DCO, MH). Outside the prison service, however, staff found it more difficult to identify the nature of their corporate identity. At Colnbrook, where the Home Office staff emphasized the risks and dangers of the detainees, they characterized themselves as community guardians. 'We are protecting the community', Cynthia asserted defiantly. 'People tell us we're bad and holding them unlawfully but we are protecting the community' (Home Office, CB). In contrast, Todd, a detention custody officer at Yarl's Wood, defined himself as a 'Care worker'. 'Although the badge says detention custody officer', he said,

> It's more like a care worker to be honest. A social worker . . . Citizen's Advice Bureau. 'Can you help me? Do you know . . . ?' Yes. Not a prison officer certainly. No. We've got keys, but ain't that many doors to open now . . . No,

I don't feel like a prison officer, or any custodial officer if you like. It's like a care worker . . . we are care workers. That's the way I see it. And we just provide a safe environment for our ladies (DCO, YW).

Compounding matters, many of the staff had transnational ties of their own. There were, especially in Colnbrook, a number of first generation British citizens working for the Home Office and for the private custodial firms, whose parents had immigrated during earlier periods of labour shortage, or as asylum seekers. Others had been migrants themselves, acquiring British citizenship through naturalization. Some, reflecting the freedom of movement within the EU haled from Poland, Spain, or Italy. A number were married to foreigners, while still others had personal and professional ties in countries of origin outside their immediate family. One man had actually been detained himself, in the US, when he had travelled to Mexico without his British passport some years previously. These people, like those they locked up, existed within global networks of family, friends, travel, and desire. Many, taking advantage of low cost airlines, travelled on holiday towards the very destinations that some of those whom they were guarding were seeking to avoid.

Such matters generated considerable ambivalence among officers, a point to which I will return. For the present, however, they direct our attention to the relational nature of life in detention and to the familiarity of many of those detained and their aspirations. For, notwithstanding Luna's position that 'we are not here to form relationships with these women. That is not our job' (SMT, YW), in the intimate setting of a custodial institution, relationships are difficult to avoid. The institution is designed to sever ties. By incarcerating those deemed unable to stay, it isolates them, confirming their identification as unwelcome. Yet, identity is irreducibly relational. Bars and locked doors cannot entirely define those within. Even under conditions of great coercion and uncertainty, people find points of commonality, coming to know themselves by recognizing others (Fraser, 2007a; Ahmed, 2000).

The familiarity of strangers

In their identity-based claims, the men and women in removal centres revealed themselves to be familiar and their ambitions to be commonplace. Drawn to the UK for affective reasons as well as for economic or security

ones, detainees were not, in other words, and despite formidable differences in language, culture, dress, and religion, so difficult to recognize.
Many, like Adan, were enthusiastic nationalists. 'I love being in Britain',
he announced. 'It is the best country in the world.' His eagerness, it turned
out, flowed from everyday matters: work, education, personal relationships, and leisure. 'I can find a job very easily', he said,

> I was working in a car wash. I have done different jobs, I even went to school
> and learned to read and write. In Rotherham, I learned English, and the
> job centre send me to 6-month training. I have never been to school in my
> country . . . I like the people here. They respect you. There is no respect back
> home. They respect you when they talk to you, there is no swearing, and they
> listen to you. I enjoy my job. I enjoy going out clubbing' (Iraq, TH).

People's goals and aspirations were usually gendered. 'I am 30. I want
a life', Gabir asserted. 'I will go back and try to do something. Get a job.
Buy a house. Get a wife. I want a life' (Algeria, BH). Gabir had aspired to
greater social freedom, at least for a time, away from the prying eyes of his
extended family and their expectations. However, having been imprisoned
and then detained he subsequently sought refuge in those very gendered
aspirations, goals as familiar in Britain as they would be in Algeria: a job, a
house, and a wife.

Mpoza, another ex-prisoner, felt the same. 'I have wasted a lot of time
and opportunities to have a family', he said sadly. 'I want to have a family
when I get out of here. First thing I will start looking for a wife' (Uganda,
TH). A long-term detainee, Mpoza had, for a number of years refused to
produce the identity documents necessary for his deportation. Such resistance, sat at some distance from his conservative family values. 'In the UK',
he complained sounding like the same kind of social conservative who
would deny him entry, 'everyone gets divorced. There is no respect for the
family. Here it is worst than in other European countries. I have a big family. My parents choose each other and are only together. I want a big family'
(Uganda, TH).

When considered through this lens, women's aspirations also seemed
hardly revolutionary. 'I've never seen snow in my life', Laili reported as she
recounted her decision to travel to Europe. 'I've never been to any of the
Europe country. So the first one was Paris, and the second is the UK. I have
friends here. So I say, "well, everything is, it seems so different". And I,
you know, I took all my saving, yeah. And I was here. I say, "oh, I want to

spend time here"' (Malaysia, YW). As an unmarried daughter, in Malaysia Laili had to look after her aging parents. England offered her an alternative future, where she could explore her desires on her own terms. 'Life has been so stressed', she said,

> you know, with responsibility and with families and all this. I say, 'I'm thirty-six, so I want a life'. I want to be, yeah, free from work and all these thing. Then I'm so happy that I never have an English boyfriend before. And I say, yeah, I mean I never have a white Christmas. Everything was like, 'well, all my dreams came true'. Yes, fulfilled, yeah (Malaysia YW).

Yet, the women's gendered aspirations were often difficult to reconcile with their national and cultural identities. Laili felt guilty that she was letting her parents down. Others had more urgent problems, revealing in their reasons for flight, or their desire to stay in the UK, and their hopes or fears for the future, a direct link between gender, autonomy, and safety. 'We don't want to stay to get things from the government for free', Aatifa stated impatiently. 'We just want the safety. The UKBA they don't believe us because so many Pakistani women have the same story. They think they can't all be true. They don't care. If the UK government began caring about Pakistani women they'd have no room left' (Pakistan, YW).

Jennet agreed. 'I want my own room', she murmured. 'I would wake up in the morning and drink my coffee and quickly go to school or college and after come in and go to working and, and one week, two times . . . I will learn dancing! I like dance, very like it. And it's like that I want, not too much, just this' (Turkmenistan, YW). Jennet's aspirations, like Gabir's, seem unexceptional. Yet, a room of her own, the ability to study, a job, and some dancing were all precisely the reasons she had left Turkmenistan and would be denied to her upon return. 'My problem, is my father and that's it. Hitting . . . all the time hitting, all the time like you're a bitch. In my country', she claimed sadly, 'what my father does is normal. The police won't help . . .' (Turkmenistan, YW).

Gender was not the only resource that women and men used for making sense of detention, and it was not the only aspect of their identity destabilized by their confinement. Some, particularly those from former British colonies, were part of an extended family group in which all other members had been naturalized. 'I came as a child [when I was four years old]', Ridoy explained, 'with my family, with my parents. I didn't ask to come here . . . I've got family. I've got kids. I've got parents living here. I've got friends. I grew up here. I went to school. I went to college' (Bangladesh, MH).

Aufa, born in Pakistan, told a similar story. 'I'm the only one [who didn't get citizenship]. My dad was British. He was here in 1958 and my mum, everybody got it. But when I applied, because I have criminal record in 1988 right, and they refuse, and they told me to apply again.' Unfortunately, Aufa went on, 'But I never bothered. Because . . . I wasn't thinking about is a British passport is important. Now I think how important is. Because I've been in trouble before, never mentioned it. That's what happen, I just got caught and there's a new law out from 2007' (Pakistan, BH).

In Aufa's account, his identity—as a convicted long-term legal resident— changed in meaning and effect between 1988 and 2007. Whereas when he was younger, his criminal activity merely prevented the acquisition of the same kind of passport as his extended family, after 2007 it became grounds for his banishment. All of a sudden, his family ties and residency, along with any plans he might have forged, were irrelevant, superseded by his nationality.

Even those whose UK residency had been relatively brief expressed familiar views. Bao-Yu, for instance, had modest goals. A former factory worker from China, she wanted more from her life. In China, she had worked seven days a week. Living in a dormitory and sending money to her parents to raise her daughter, she been unhappy. 'I want to change my life', she said. 'So, have a better life. Was in China very hard. So, and also can give more education my daughter, yeah . . . She has no chance in life without education' (China, YW).

Bao-Yu's aspirations were, at least in part, economic. She shared such hopes with many others. Poverty, Hali made clear, is stultifying. 'Because my parents are poor I couldn't help myself', she described. '[I moved] just from one country to another, from one country to another, trying to find a way to stand, to become a human being' (Nigeria, YW).

Until immigration officers came to her door one morning with an arrest warrant, England had borne out Bao-Yu's hopes. She had attained some economic security, made new friends and fallen in love with a man who said he would marry her. She felt settled, approving of all things British from 'the way that English women look like', to the food and the land-scape. 'Oh, England', she sighed. 'I love the English culture, like, I like the English garden and then the . . . people have a very private life. And I like English National Trust . . . Beautiful place. Yeah. I couldn't find that sort of place in China' (China, YW). Hali resident for 15 years was being forced back to the poverty of her life in Nigeria. Her autonomy and Bao-Yu's desires comprehensively denied.

Some of those who moved to Britain as adults had been taught at school to aspire to British mores and values. 'Back home', Abd bitterly exclaimed, 'they say that if you live in London you are happy. They dream about London as if it would give you most happiness' (Pakistan, TH). In this vein, too, citizens of former Britain colonies complained about double standards. 'When the British went around the world', Mpoza pointed out, 'they did not apply for visas or residents permits. They just went in and took what they wanted' (Uganda, TH). Clarence agreed, complaining that 'the British went around the world stealing everything, and they are still stealing from us' (Unknown nationality, MH). Even those without colonial ties interpreted matters similarly. 'Oh my God!' Iola laughed,

> I have a theory that people are actually judging based on their own qualities. If a thief, I am gonna always think that someone coming is stealing from me, you know, if I'm thief, you know . . . so England, because all through the history they have been going around and taking other people's imperial politics, they think that if they let foreigners in that, foreigners will do the same with them. That's the answer. Oh my God, thank you! (Serbia, YW).

In these accounts, removal centres might be better understood as another postscript to empire, housing those who have been multiply dispossessed; a restatement of the power of the metropole under conditions of mobility (Spivak, 1999). Yet, post-colonial relations are not simply matters of oppression. Nor were post-colonial aspirations merely economic. Instead, Adah explained, they shaped people's desires. 'When I was a child', she said, 'I always told my mother I wanted to marry an Englishman. . . you know, I love England!' (Nigeria, YW). Brought up in a middle-class Nigerian family, she had read English novels at school, from which she had learned to associate English men and the country itself with chivalry and honour. Despite describing unsatisfactory personal experiences of romantic love in Britain, she remained adamant, 'English men treat English women better than African men' (Nigeria, YW). Seok-Teng, who had been living with a much older English man, agreed, 'English women are Queen' (Malaysia, YW).

Indeed, many women were explicit. Traditional gender norms in their country of origin were oppressive. 'If I were born again I would not be born as an Asian woman', Sarasi moaned. 'Or if I was born in Asia I want to be born as a man. Women there are kept at the feet of man' (Sri Lanka, YW). Fleeing a violent husband, the future looked bleak, her past unbearable. Aida from Nigeria took a similar view, emphasizing the intersection between her economic precarity and the risk of sexual coercion. 'There is no future for me in Nigeria', she stated flatly. 'As long as you are a young woman there is no future for you. If I can't find work there, men will come after me and I will have to get money from them' (Nigeria, YW).

In fact, many of the women in Yarl's Wood had also been victimized by British men. One, who had been 'helped' to leave her country of origin by a British tourist, arrived in the UK only to find he demanded sex in return and kept her confined in his apartment. She eventually escaped when he left the door unlocked, stopping a woman on the street for assistance. That woman advised her to contact the Home Office who immediately placed her in detention. Others, who had sought legal protections against domestic violence, reporting it to the police, had found the promised state assistance to be lacking, either trumped by their lack of immigration status, or simply insufficient.

Whatever their perspective, whether discussing the UK or their home country, a clear connection became evident between gender, agency, and autonomy. Incarcerating people on the basis of their national identity and expelling them from the country, inevitably affects their capacity to define a self in the world. Global gender and economic inequalities, seemingly far removed from British shores, are imbricated in the bodies of those detained. Present in our territory and embedded in our laws, they are both an outcome and a cause of detention itself.

Conclusion

Although mechanisms of identification are commonplace across a range of social institutions and central to contemporary methods of government (Schinkel, 2011), being confined and deported or removed on the basis of identity (rather than, for instance, criminal activity) is neither easy to explain nor to endure. Incarceration in an IRC is particularly painful and confusing for those whose sense of self does not equate with their formal identification by the British state. 'Really and truly I been brought up here', Tahir avowed. 'I been bred in this country. Like, I went to infants, primary school, secondary school, colleges, university. De Montford University. My whole family are here. My girlfriend, my missus, everyone. My whole life is in United Kingdom. What I am doing under these roofs?' (Sudan, CH).

IRCs materially and metaphorically excise such figures from the community, erasing their subjectivity and refusing them the benefits of shared group membership. In so doing, they enable what Stuart Hall (2001: 218) refers to as 'colonial amnesia', effectively denying Britain's role in establishing paths of migration by enclosing and then expelling those who do not fit its legal requirements. Yet, IRCs do not work seamlessly. Although, from a distance, it may be hard to recognize those within, their putative unfamiliarity compounded by incarceration in prison-like facilities, inside IRCs issues of identity and belonging are actively negotiated. Basic confusion exists about the detained population, at all levels.

Unlike prisons, which they so closely resemble, detention centres do not produce recognizable subjects. 'It's not like they're real offenders', Alice pointed out, 'it's just you know, they might have worked without a passport or something' (Home Office). Whereas the goal and originating purpose of prison is to 'make sense of' (punish, reform, deter) offenders, IRCs have the opposite effect, rendering those within unfamiliar. Detainees, their confinement attests, are not like 'us'. They are foreign, bound for and belonging elsewhere. Their foreignness cannot be changed, no matter how long they have lived in Britain. They are always, already, different and unknowable, potentially a threat.

While wealth and education protect some, the majority of migrants and many of their descendants remain a priori suspect. In Sara Ahmed's (2000) terms, they are always already 'strangers', no matter how familiar they may be. From difference and suspicion, it is a short step to exclusion. Unable to recognize them, we find it hard to care about such people. When we are moved, it is often to subjugate them further. In these practices we witness evidence of Judith Butler's observation that 'part of the very problem of contemporary political life is that not everyone counts as a subject' (Butler, 2009: 31).

Such non-subjects, whom Butler refers to in typically opaque prose as 'ungrievable', are particularly precarious, existing outside our usual ethical and normative frames and expectations, as well as sometimes outside the law. 'I am nobody from nowhere', Adah noted sadly. 'You know, no-one's gonna help me' (Nigeria, YW). As Merveille bitterly put it, 'We are people who have been forgotten' (DRC, CB). Yet, notwithstanding their undeniably vulnerable status, Adah, Merveille, and others resisted their detention, seeking legal remedy, striving in all sorts of ways to bring themselves into view. 'I'm sick of being invisible', Adah concluded (Nigeria, YW).[10]

In their testimonies, the purpose of detention as well as its challenges, starts to emerge. They are designed to identify their inhabitants as excludable. Only once such identification is fixed can the state remove them. Yet such designation is both practically and emotionally difficult to do. In seeking to oppose their identification, detainees face many hurdles. They must map out an alternative identity in the face of numerous barriers from the confines of the building in which they are housed, to the intersection of class, race, and gender. Not everyone succeeds. Not everyone even tries. However, as subsequent chapters will argue, identity is a slippery concept and not always an effective terrain on which to govern.

---

10. Her ambitions were not realized, as Adah was eventually removed. She and I remain in contact as she sets about starting a new life in Lagos.

4
Everyday life in detention

I went to Arts and Crafts, where it was Leah's (DCO) surprise birthday party thrown mainly by Chinese women but also by others. Leah cried. The Chinese women sang songs, especially Hui-Ying who has been there for two years and last time I was around was on [suicide] constant watch. . . Leah took the women on an impromptu conga line around the centre, saying in a loud voice 'This is the biggest display of conditioning I've seen in my six years at Yarl's Wood—and the answer is no!' to which Tina replied 'I'm going to kill the manager and I want a puppy and a pig. Is that alright?' Leah—'Yes! It's yours' (Fieldnotes, July 2010).

The difficult thing is to pass the time. Let it pass. It goes slowly (Darko, Serbia, MH).

Having explored how IRCs attempt to 'fix' the identity of (certain) foreigners as deportable and unwanted, noting the variety of ways in which staff and detainees subvert that logic, this chapter turns to the rhythms of daily life in the centres themselves. Drawing on staff and detainee testimonies, as well as from fieldnotes, it concentrates on daily life. What is there to do in detention? How do people pass the time? With whom do they associate?

Such simple questions are difficult to answer since there is considerable variation in the centres and in people's reactions to them. Certain establishments foster a compassionate environment. Institutions differ also in the nature of their regime. Life within them is usually shaped by the material environment, as higher-security institutions operate a more restricted regime than lower-security ones. Yet the buildings do not entirely determine experience. While there were physical similarities between Colnbrook and Brook House, their timetable and institutional culture were distinct. Similarly, although Tinsley House, Campsfield House, and Yarl's Wood operated a system of 'free flow' in which, during the day, detainees could access most parts of the building, there were important differences among them.

Morton Hall widely spread out and open, situated within extensive lawns and gardens, initially appeared distinct. 'If you ignored the prison fence', the fieldnotes record, 'it was similar to a council estate, but with well appointed lawns instead of a "rec". I was half expecting to see a "no ball games" sign on the unit walls and perhaps some graffiti and a skateboard ramp . . . The grounds were quite nice and even have little Graeco-Roman statues on the lawns' (Fieldnotes, April 2012). Yet, for its confined population, the landscaping was of little consequence. Wherever they were held, detainees were concerned most of all with their immigration case.

This aspect of detention, in which the attention of staff and detainees is often trained elsewhere, gives it a particular liminal and unsettled character. Many detainees are so preoccupied about their future that they are unable to engage in classes or activities. For staff, the unpredictability of the immigration system undermines attempts to create a meaningful regime. It can also be used to justify doing little. By placing staff and detainee accounts about how they pass the time in this wider context, this chapter revisits key assumptions in the academic literature about the relationship between the internal life of a custodial institution and its external justification and purpose, in a bid to make sense of an institution whose goals simultaneously transcend the individual sites of brick and mortar and are inscribed within them (Sykes, 1958; Liebling, 2004; Sparks, Bottoms, and Hay, 1996; Crewe, 2011). To what extent can an analysis of what detention centres are like explain what they are for? (Crewe, 2009; Bosworth, 2013).

From arrival to departure

Detainees usually arrive at an IRC in an armoured van. Once they have passed through the heavy gates at the entrance, they head to reception, accompanied by a uniformed member of staff carrying keys. The uniform varies across the centres. Officers at Yarl's Wood had recently replaced their white collared shirts with pink and blue checked ones in a bid to 'soften' their appearance and to reduce their resemblance to law enforcement agents. The women associated white shirts, a number told me, with the police in their home countries. Changing their uniform, they hoped, would set the women at ease. DCOs at Morton Hall, in contrast, wore standard prison uniform, despite complaints from detainees.[1]

In reception, custodial staff administer rudimentary screening instruments, leaving more detailed health needs and risk assessments (including documentation of evidence of torture)[2] for the induction unit and healthcare team.[3] When detainees leave the IRC, they retrace their steps, exiting through reception. In contrast to prisons, where, other than in exceptional cases movements must occur during daylight hours and on weekdays in order to minimize the disruption to the individual being shifted, this part of the centre is open 24 hours a day. Detainees frequently arrive during the night.

Reception spaces differ in design and decoration. In Yarl's Wood the walls of the waiting rooms, ranging along one side opposite the staff work area, were painted with cheerful outdoor scenes and motifs. There were snacks available in a refrigerator at the back of the room, and those waiting could catch a glimpse of the storage area behind the officers' desk. In Campsfield House, reception included separate rooms for arrivals and departures. Officers sat behind a crowded desk, on which detainees' files sat alongside computer terminals, telephones, a fax machine, and a photocopier. Behind them overstuffed cupboards bulged with papers and other items.

Staff reported that working in this part of the centre could be challenging. Turnover is rapid and unpredictable. Reception holds a list of expected arrivals and departures, as well as the names and details of those leaving the premises for medical, legal, or other reasons. On the one hand, their job might be considered simply a matter of 'booking in, booking out', Ashby acknowledged (DCO, TH). Yet such a view, he claimed, overlooked the complexities of staffing the entry and exit point. 'I'm responsible for money', he pointed out. 'I'm responsible for property. I'm responsible for people. I'm responsible for correct paperwork' (DCO, TH). Such duties were difficult to execute when paperwork and property did not always accompany the new arrivals. 'If they come from a prison', Scot clarified, 'nine times

---

1. Unlike officers in the privately run centres, prison service staff in IRCs are also permitted to carry batons.
2. Evidence suggests that so-called Rule 35 is not always appropriately administered (HMIP and ICIBI, 2012; HMIP, 2012b; Medical Justice, 2012).
3. Detention centre rules stipulate that detainees should be seen by a member of the healthcare team within 24 hours of arrival. This task is usually performed by a nurse.

out of ten their prison file will come with them, so we've got the history of what they were like in prison. If they haven't come from prison, all we've got is the piece of paper from UKBA with a very brief history of them on it' (SMT, YW).

In any case, there is more to reception than paperwork. People often arrive upset and confused, sometimes unaware they were to be detained, uncertain of what lay ahead. Some may be anxious about the whereabouts of their property, children, or partners. Many will never have been in a detention centre before. Still others are traumatized by their voyage to or within the UK, perhaps hidden in the back of a lorry, taken into custody unexpectedly while 'signing on' as an asylum seeker, arrested at work or at home, held for days in a police cell. Language barriers and health needs make matters more vexing still. Such factors, Judy noted, render reception 'a hostile area. It's the first port of call when they're put in detention', she explained,

> so that's the first place they see. So we are the faces they see as detaining them there. And then we're also the people that are there sending them out, handing them to these escorts to go. Some of them want to go, but not a lot of them do. And they're getting sent back and it's us that are basically handing them across to these guys to take them, forcibly or not forcibly. So it's quite hard for us to get that rapport going. Because when they first come in they could be tearful, they could be upset, they could be angry. There's so many different emotions that they've got. And then once you've calmed them down, within a few weeks you're back there again because you're sending them again. So it's trying to get that happy medium when you're booking them in (DCO, CH).

In Colnbrook, the officers on reception were assisted by detainee 'Buddies'. Based on prison 'Listeners', who receive extensive training from the Samaritans, 'Buddies' at Colnbrook were meant to offer a sympathetic ear to new arrivals. They attended group training sessions with a psychologist in order to be appointed, and thereafter had regular 'debriefing' sessions with one particular officer. Working alongside the custody officers, Buddies answered questions and allayed fears. They could also assist with interpreting. Many took the opportunity to pass on nuggets of institutional lore. 'I tell them', David asserted, 'don't add problems to your problems. It's not officers' fault. It's paperwork. It's immigration. It's Home Office . . . They blame officers, but it's not officers. They're just doing their jobs.' Pausing, for reflection, David noted with a frown, 'So me doing this job helps the officers' (Uganda, CB).

Such work did not come without cost. It was, inevitably, emotionally demanding, an aspect which those already anxious about their own immigration cases, often found taxing. 'People suddenly spill out their life', Leonce grimaced, 'and you have to go and get tissues' (Colnbrook, DRC/Belgium). There were less obvious challenges as well, in encounters with individuals who were not anxious. 'Europeans', David noted with some frustration, 'are just held here one night. They have options. That was a reality check' (Uganda, CB).

In addition to screening new arrivals and offering them basic information about the centre, staff in reception must maintain a log of detainees' possessions, retaining banned or excess items in bags in the property section. Some centres issue mobile phones, others allow detainees to keep their own so long as they do not include a camera, still others replace the SIM card. Detainees who are destitute, or who have been brought in without their property[4] will be issued with clothing, usually some combination of ill-fitting tracksuits, flip flops, and a selection of items donated by charities.

Just as they would be in prison, once they have been 'processed' in reception, new arrivals are usually placed in an 'induction unit'. In Tinsley House, however, which had no separate housing area for new arrivals, men were allocated to rooms on the normal housing unit and simply put through an orientation process. As with reception, the content and nature of this introduction ranged from centre to centre. Usually the process included some kind of tour of the facility, as well as a meeting with the onsite immigration officers. It was typically at this point that detainees were screened by healthcare, notified about the local visitor group, and given a list of immigration lawyers to contact.

Unlike the prison service, which formally acknowledges the vulnerability of those who have just arrived, by placing these identified as particularly sensitive in 'first-night' cells where they receive more information and help, Colnbrook and Brook House hold new detainees in far more restricted conditions than are subsequently available in the main units. A number of men reported their time in the short-term holding unit in Colnbrook as the most unpleasant part of their custodial experience. 'That place is like hell!' Aziz exclaimed. 'Sometimes you're in there for a week. People treat their

---

4. Difficulties in retrieving property from their accommodation or from police stations are legion and take up a considerable part of the welfare officer's attention in each IRC.

dogs better than they treat us!' (Pakistan, CB). 'I was in Colnbrook for one night', Mac recalled,

> There were no curtains in the window and there were women in the rooms above opposite our windows and they could see us so we could not get changed. There was no curtain in the toilet or bath so I could not go to the toilet because my roommate could see me naked or in the toilet. So I did neither when I was there. The TV was very loud and there was no remote. I asked for the remote and they did not have one. They said all they could do is switch off the whole electricity for the room until the next morning. I said no, so TV was on, loud all night and I did not sleep (Nigeria, TH).

Routinely criticized by HMIP (2010a; 2013), the conditions in Colnbrook's STHF also worried some staff.[5] Others, however, believed that it served an important role: 'The purpose of the STHF', Mishal bluntly asserted, 'is to ensure that when men come over to the longer-term units they are happy to be there and more obedient' (DCM, CB) (see Figures 19 and 20).

In contrast to the segregation practised in Brook House and Colnbrook, Yarl's Wood and Campsfield House allowed detainees on entry to mingle with the mainstream population during the day, only locking them into the induction unit at night. Conditions on the induction unit were also better than elsewhere in the facility, with single rooms at Yarl's Wood and detainee Buddies in operation at Campsfield House. In both places new arrivals were monitored. 'We keep them in there [the short stay unit] hopefully for twenty-four hours to observe them', Christopher explained,

> from wherever they come from, whether it be prison, picked off from a police station, all sorts. And we keep them in there for twenty-four hours. Not contain them in there, but they stay in the unit for twenty-four hours. They're given association, and then they come back. We just monitor them about to make sure they're okay. Because usually if, it's when they're on their own they go into depression, and we're there to hopefully help them out, so . . . And then once we're satisfied with them we pass them onto the blocks (DCO, CH).

Yarl's Wood adopted a similar approach. The women on the induction unit, Lela explained, 'tend to be very tearful, very needy on there because

---

5. An independent academic study of life in STHFs remains to be done. Instead we must rely on regular HMIP (2010a) and IMB (2012) reports on conditions in such places, as well as on individual reminiscences about them.

Figure 19. Short-Term Holding Facility Corridor in IRC Colnbrook (Photo credit: MF Bosworth).

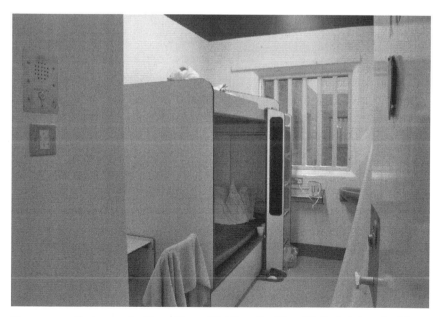

Figure 20. Bedroom in Short-Term Holding Facility, IRC Colnbrook (Photo credit: MF Bosworth).

bless them, they've usually just been picked or could have just been shipped over from a prison'. In cases of severe distress, she said,

> we'll try and find another person from their country if possible or that we know they share a language with and put them in touch with each other, you know, take them along or get the person from the other unit. And we have been known to take them actually on to Bunting [the induction unit] and say, 'This is so and so' and, you know, they, they really do depend upon each other cos they're all in the same boat (DCM, YW).

In addition to encouraging detainee contact, officers on Bunting ran a computer-based multi-language induction course, explaining the layout of the centre and the daily regime. They also handed out basic hygiene items including sanitary towels, detergent, tweezers, nail clippers, and scissors.[6]

Once detainees are judged ready, officers in the IRC allocate them to beds on a housing unit. Different centres varied in their strategies for making this decision. Adopting terminology and technique from the prison service, in 2009 Colnbrook developed a 'room share and risk assessment' tool, allocating men to shared rooms based on a series of questions about their views on religion and race as well as staff perceptions of their risk of suicide or self-harm. Campsfield House was far less formal. I saw induction staff show the men a board on which the available rooms were listed alongside the name and nationality of their occupants, and ask them to choose with whom they would prefer to share. While staff there were happy to group people according to national origin and reported no problems with their system, officers in Yarl's Wood, where women could also elect to share a room with someone of the same religion or citizenship, were a little more cautious due to perceived tensions between different groups.

Decisions about room allocation affect everyday life in detention. Even though in many centres detainees can mingle during the day, they are rarely allowed onto a housing unit other than the one on which their room is located. Given the limited regime in each centre and the small number of staff, such restrictions meant that the relationship with a roommate could define a person's experience of confinement.

Some were content. Brenda, at Yarl's Wood, for example, built a close friendship with her roommate. However, she was aware that she had no

---

6. Some women complained about the presence of male officers on Bunting and in the general housing offices, finding it embarrassing to ask them for sanitary towels or tampons.

control over her living space and was afraid about who would come after her friend was removed. 'Some people are not clean', she commented, 'or they have a lot of problems'. If you are 'in a bad mood, having a bad room-mate is horrible' (Uganda, YW). Pam ended up swapping rooms after 'not getting on with my roommate'. Although they were both Nigerian, their shared nationality had not helped. 'We don't speak the same language', she pointed out, 'and are culturally very different'. More prosaically, her room-mate was often 'on the phone at 1 and 2 in the morning', interrupting her rest (Nigeria, YW).

According to Adah, who was on suicide watch and had been for most of her time in detention, when she was first confined in Scotland, it was her roommate in Dungavel who had helped her adjust. 'I gave up on church and praying', Adah recalled. 'It looked to me that my prayers not answered. I never ate either. So they put me in shared room and the other woman helped me' (Nigeria, YW). It was this woman, rather than a member of staff, who intervened.

> She said to me: 'immigration won't care, it's your body; it's your life'. My cellmate went to the pastor for help. He came and saw me; spoke to me for some time and read the bible for me. He told me that I don't have to give up on myself and God hasn't given up on me. So next Sunday I went back to church. It helps (Nigeria, YW).

Just as the room allocation process varies across institutions, so, too, do the rooms themselves, in terms of their design and their capacity. At Yarl's Wood almost everyone[7] shared with just one other person. At Campsfield House, in contrast, rooms ranged from single occupancy to multi-bed dormitories, while in Tinsley House men shared with up to three others. In the three other men's establishments they usually bunked in pairs (see Figure 21).

Men in Colnbrook, Brook House, and Morton Hall, challenged the institutional terminology for their living quarters and their roommates. 'It's a cell not a room!' Charles hissed. 'It's got bars on the windows, what room has that?' (Nigeria, MH). 'It's quite hard', sharing a living space with a stranger, Edem reported, 'but sometimes you get the cell mate who you

---

7. During the research period one woman had been housed in a single room on the induction unit for over a year. Her post-traumatic stress symptoms were so severe that she could not share a room with anyone else. She regularly endured terrifying nightmares and urinated in her bed. Whereas a few men in Colnbrook reported similar problems, they were housed in shared rooms.

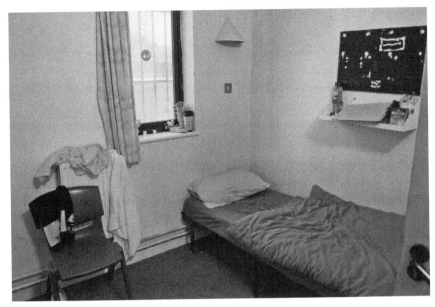

Figure 21. Bedroom in Yellow Block, IRC Campsfield House (Photo credit: S Turnbull).

can talk to' (Togo, CB). Compounding matters in Colnbrook and Brook House, the men had no access to fresh air or natural light within the centres. 'The windows give us no oxygen', Haq protested. 'There is no fresh air. My skin feels different, itchy. I need Vitamin D from the sun' (Iraq, CB).

It was not just in the sleeping areas that Colnbrook and Brook House aped the prison but in the organization of their housing units, which were designated as 'standard', and 'enhanced', and, in the case of Brook House, 'basic' as well. Such terms are derived directly from prisons in England and Wales, which, since 1995 have been governed by the 'incentives and earned privileges' (IEP) scheme, according to which prisoners may obtain greater freedoms in return for compliant behaviour. All prisoners begin on 'standard' level, but may be demoted to 'basic' or raised to 'enhanced' depending on the outcome of regular assessments by their personal officer.

While IRCs experimented with a version of this system, only Colnbrook and Brook House applied it with much differentiation; indeed, during the project, most others abandoned it altogether, and since the research ended all have done so.[8] Part of the problem, staff observed, was that detainees and

---

8. Figures provided by Morton Hall for the month of April 2012, for example, show only eight out of 386 men on standard, with the rest on enhanced.

staff found it hard to understand the system.[9] Given the local constraints, detainees also had little to lose. 'I would [not] have a clue whether these people are on enhanced or basic', Ben admitted.[10] 'So that system just doesn't work and I don't think they're even told about that now. They used to be told that when they were on basic they weren't allowed to attend certain things but now I think people have said "Look, how are we supposed to know?" So now they just attend everything' (DCO, CH).[11]

In contrast to Campsfield House, those on the enhanced units in Brook House and Colnbrook were offered better living conditions than the rest of the population. At Colnbrook, for instance, the enhanced unit was much smaller and quieter than the accommodation elsewhere in the centre. Situated in a space above the visits hall it looked a lot less like a prison than the rest of the establishment. The common area was furnished with sofas, rugs and a large screen television. There was also a fish tank, and men had access to games consoles, table football, and a pool table.[12] The enhanced unit (D-Wing) at Brook House was a regular multi-level housing unit, kitted out with more comfortable furniture and equipment including a 'wide screen to watch movies, leather sofas, three (big) plasma screens with PS2, Wii and one other kind of console' (Fieldnotes, March 2011). There were plans to install a 50-inch screen television on the top floor to enable the men to watch Sky Sports.

In these spaces, interactions between staff and detainees and among detainees could be calmer and more relaxed. The spaces themselves were considerably quieter. Detainees on enhanced also received a little more money, £1 a day instead of 71p for those on the standard units. In Colnbrook, men on the enhanced unit tended to spend more time out of their rooms, sitting on the sofas and watching television together. There and in Brook House they also played the games consoles and pool with each other and with the staff. Yet, such informality was limited, belied,

9. This view was reinforced by the MQLD, where detainees failed to understand which IEP level they were on (Bosworth and Kellezi, 2012a; Bosworth and Kellezi, 2013).

10. In fact, Campsfield House did not have basic.

11. At this point, concerned perhaps that I might imagine that Campsfield House was too lenient, Ben's colleague Chris hurriedly interjected, 'don't get me wrong, we still issue them the strikes, it's just they don't get bumped up or marked down on the privilege scheme' (DCO, CH).

12. As noted previously, since the research ended, the enhanced unit has been converted into a short-stay unit for women.

and often undermined by the highly 'securitized' environment in which the enhanced wings were situated. As one staff member commented in Colnbrook, deploying strikingly similar terminology to that used by Haq on the regular housing unit, 'It's like being in a prison we have no fresh air or natural light' (DCO, CB). No matter in which unit they were located, staff and detainees at Brook House and at Colnbrook complained about being under constant supervision.

> During lunch the male Asian officer challenged one of the detainees to an X-Box game (shooting); he was playing it with him and refused to answer the phone.[13] The female officer made a point of saying that 'I hope they got that on camera', pointing to the CCTV in the corner. The officers are clearly obsessed about the cameras, and use them to monitor me as well as the men. They also are aware that they themselves are being watched constantly (Fieldnotes, March 2010).

When asked about the IEP system, detainees were often disparaging, even as they sought access to the improved conditions. 'They call it enhanced', Edem scoffed. 'Don't know how they work it out really. I'm not really interested in whatever the group is. I think that is political. People want to keep their job, they create some kind of situation they can make themselves look good on top of the boss who's watching them from far away. Somebody's making money, somebody's company' (Togo, CB). As in prison, staff in Colnbrook and Brook House strategically deployed room allocation on the enhanced units as a method of governance. Men could be returned to the regular units for fighting, possessing contraband or, in the case of Sami, for 'aggressive and manipulative behaviour' (Lebanon, CB).[14] They could also be shifted back to the main housing units if the onsite immigration officers found them to be non-compliant with their immigration case.

In centres without enhanced units, detainees and staff still differentiated between sections of the institution. Often their views were based on perceptions of compliance. At Yarl's Wood, for instance, one of the housing units was considered more rowdy than the other, a perception related to the institutional view of Jamaican and Nigerian women. At Morton Hall,

13. In this particular example both the staff member and the detainee had created buxom, nearly naked, white, female avatars, adding an additional level of complexity to the negotiation of identities inherent in any interaction between staff and detainees in an IRC.
14. A long-term detainee, who told me he was a former member of Hezbollah, Sami was fighting his deportation to Lebanon on the basis of family ties, having been resident in the UK for decades. He was a controversial character, well known also in other IRCs.

the residential areas varied in their atmosphere and population, once again cleaving to apparently racialized stereotypes in which the housing block considered to be the 'roughest', Fry unit, held mainly ex-offenders predominantly of African origin. A lengthy fieldnote captures the range and effect of Morton Hall's interior organization:

> The units around Fry and Windsor where I enter the compound are slightly more menacing, holding as they do, the 'high risks'. There is clearly a strategy in splitting up the ethnicities—Black Africans on Fry; Chinese in Windsor; Pakistani and Indian on Johnson and Sharman; Bangladeshi in Torr. By far my favourite unit is Johnson where I get lots of positive feedback whenever I go there and the atmosphere is noticeably better. The design and light in the newer non-high risk buildings (Johnson, Sharman and Torr) is much more conducive to openness among the detainees. Something about Fry and Windsor is oppressive. You can wander into Johnson the staff office is small, on the right, with a reception desk out front, there's a TV on and some leather seats with a glass roof letting in light. I notice in the mornings The Jeremy Kyle Show playing on the TV. Another devious strategy by UKBA to break the will of the detainees and make them want to head home? Certainly, 10 minutes of that and I want to leave the country (Fieldnotes, May 2012).

Even in Campsfield House, with only two housing units, staff assured me, detainees aspired to live on 'yellow block' rather than on 'blue'.

Such institutional demarcation helped staff and detainees make sense of the population and of the centre. Conceiving of the building in this way was also productive, fostering a means and mode of governance in an environment in where staff frequently complained that they had few tools to enforce behaviour. In its intersection with racial and ethnic categories, room allocation offered a familiar localized form of governmentality through which staff controlled the population (Foucault, 1991).

Once distributed to the housing units most detainees made little attempt to personalize their rooms. Walls were usually left unadorned, and few used bed linen other than that which was distributed to them by the officers. At the same time, however, their rooms were meaningful to them and many did rely on them as places of (relative) sanctuary. Adah, for instance, when she was not praying, spent a lot of time in her room. She had borrowed a copy of the musical *Grease* from the library, which she watched everyday alone. 'It cheers me up', she told me brightly, 'the music is so good. I try to dance' (Nigeria, YW).

Permitted a limited number of personal items, women and men stored tea, coffee, and food from the centre shop (and occasionally from the dining hall) in their rooms, a habit which staff tried to discourage by searching rooms and discarding items they deemed contraband. Although such objects should only have included fresh food illicitly brought in from the dining area, detainees complained staff overstepped their role and threw away unopened foodstuffs they had legally purchased. 'Last week they took food from us', Ola lamented. 'How can I commit suicide with milk, butter? Some people get hungry at night. I bought that food from the shop. These rules, they just make life uncomfortable' (Brazil, YW).

For those who were on the main housing units, each day in detention was marked by monotonous similarity. 'Every day is the same', Amya complained. 'You wake up and it is the same boring days. I am fed up' (Gambia, YW). Punctuated only by the certainty of meals, official counts, and room checks, time passed slowly. The lack of options was boring and painful.

During the week, 'legal visits', an institutional term of art that includes meetings with onsite immigration officers as well as lawyers, consular representatives, or anyone with an appointment in an official capacity, usually occur in the morning, with social and domestic visits happening later in the day. All IRCs must offer a minimum level of activity, access to arts and crafts, fresh air, sporting equipment, English as a second language courses, the internet, religion, healthcare, visitors, and lawyers (UKBA, 2008). In addition to these contractual obligations, many centre staff innovate, bringing in individuals and community groups to extend the establishment's limited regime. IRCs also organize one-off events around religious calendars and the seasons, ranging from football matches and barbeques or a summer fete, to Ramadan, Diwali, and Christmas. In those equipped with 'cultural kitchens' detainees may cook meals for a small group of friends.

For most, a typical day starts late. Detainees, generally, slept in. If there was no legal visit in the morning, there was little reason to get out of bed before lunch. When asked how he passed his day at Colnbrook, Viku reported: 'I just lie down. I just lay in the bed and watch TV' (Moldova, CB). In Brook House, Daaud a 19-year-old boy who had recently completed a prison term griped, 'All I do is eat and sleep. That's all I know what to do. I'm lost in here. And there's nobody here to help. I can't ask them [other men], and I can't ask the officers. All they want to know is whether I want to go off the unit. I just want to go home' (Somalia, BH).[15]

---

15. As it turned out, Daaud did not spend long in Brook House. Rapidly returned to a young offenders institution, his means of passing the time—distributing drugs—was deemed unsatisfactory.

In each centre, core groups of detainees clustered in certain parts of the centre, taking advantage of the limited resources. While the IT room was heavily used everywhere, as detainees sought to communicate with family and friends or go online, in Yarl's Wood, the arts and craft room was particularly popular as was the hairdresser and the cultural kitchen (see Figures 22 and 23). In these parts of the centre, the pastor optimistically claimed, the women could 'forget where they are . . . because of the atmosphere in those places' (Chaplain, YW).

Reflecting the constitution of the population, the mosque at Campsfield House was heavily used and, since the fieldwork ended, has been significantly expanded under new management. So, too, men took up the option of gym classes enthusiastically. The pool tables were never unattended.

In a lengthy description of activities at Yarl's Wood, Lela first depicted an impressive set of options:

> Activities offers physical exercise of course, [and we have] English and IT lessons in the IT room. The library has all the forms and all the get out of jail

Figure 22. Art and Craft Room, IRC Colnbrook (Photo credit: MF Bosworth).

Figure 23. Art and Craft Room, IRC Campsfield House (Photo credit: S Turnbull).

free books that BID[16] very kindly provide for us. Everywhere you look . . . you'll normally find the vases made out of paper and that kind of stuff so there's a lot of that goes on [in art and craft] . . . The hair . . . salon's usually packed with people all doing each other's hair and nails and things. Discos are put on quite regularly. Every Friday there's a big game of bingo and you can get up to a hundred and twenty women turn up for that, it's very popular. We offer shop vouchers as prizes. The library has literature but it doesn't tend to be widely used cos obviously literacy is, is not as common, you know . . . IT room itself of course has the internet, so people use that . . . we try to observe as many religious festivals as we can but there are hundreds of them so, you know, you can only do what you can do (DCM, YW).

Ena, however, rejected this rosy view, bemoaning that, 'there is nothing to do here' (Gambia, YW). A long-term resident, she found herself increasingly stuck in her room. 'I used to read but now I can't concentrate. I never watched TV before, but now I do. Sometimes I borrow a TV guide from the library and just watch TV' (Gambia, YW). Others were frustrated by the lack of utility of the available activities, preferring training in employable

16. Bail for Immigration Detainees <http://www.biduk.org>.

skills. The art and craft activities, Nimali protested, were infantilizing: 'It's not useful to our life you know. What is going like children things you know. Is not important to our lives, you know. Without that things we can, more things we can learn. But here nothing' (Sri Lanka, YW). Their lives felt frozen as though time had stopped.

Even Lela, despite her initial enthusiasm, appreciated that, 'there's an awful lot of sitting round in groups'. The activities, she acknowledged, were 'just distractions' (DCM, YW), occupying the women while they awaited the outcome of their immigration case or the trip to the airport. 'We can't open the door and let them out', she concluded, 'so let's do what we can. It's just ease the trauma of this because unlike a prison sentence they don't know how long they're here, that's the biggest area of frustration, is that not knowing' (DCM, YW).

Notwithstanding the efforts put in by officers like Lela, wherever they were housed, men and women often reported that it was difficult to join in. They felt uninterested or unable to participate. There were not always enough spaces available for those who wished to take a class. Many found concentrating on activities too great an effort. 'I know that they try to make you do things, and you can do things if you want, like there is a gym, library, TV, but I don't want to do any of these', Anastasiya acknowledged. 'I don't want to do anything; I only want to go out. I would not enjoy anything; I am just focusing my mind about going out of here' (Russia, YW). Likewise, when asked how he passed the time in Tinsley House, Fariborz replied with a laugh, 'Wake up, measure the corridor, measure this place [the courtyard]' (Afghanistan, TH). It was not that he had nothing to do, but that he felt too distracted. 'Mentally I do not enjoy the gym, [or playing] pool. I just don't feel like it', he explained sadly. He could not stomach the education offerings either. 'I have no nerves for classes. I am too anxious. I can't sit in the class for even 5 minutes' (Afghanistan, TH).

Some staff recognized the vulnerability of detainees. Leah, an activities officer at Yarl's Wood, spoke compassionately about the women in her care, describing her job as 'an understanding, patient, caring role. You're teaching many different nationalities, some don't even speak English so you're having to work round a lot of different obstacles but yeah, it's important, it's important to be caring and calm and understanding' (DCO, YW). Others, however, felt that detainees were offered an unfair advantage, and should not be allowed access to gym equipment, games consoles, or other perceived luxuries. Some failed to appreciate why detainees found it difficult to enjoy the opportunities available to them.

For the most part, classes and activities were offered only during weekdays. In the evenings and on the weekends, detainees explained, the centres felt quite different. For those who took advantage of the limited offerings, these periods of time were often challenging. 'There is nothing to do on the weekend', Pam and Ena sighed (Nigeria and Gambia, YW). 'There are no classes, nothing to do', Laili confirmed. 'All we do is stare at each other. It is horrible' (Malaysia, YW). 'Weekends seem much longer', Ishmael agreed (Sierra Leone, TH).

Many also found evenings and nights gruelling, unable to fall and stay asleep or bothered by frightening dreams. 'The worst time is the middle of the night', Amine confided, 'it's all quiet, but I can't sleep' (Algeria, CH). Mia came to the same conclusion. 'During the day is fine', she observed, 'because you come to the library, you talk to people. But when it gets to 9 pm there is nothing to do, no one to talk to. Everybody is in their rooms then' (Gambia, YW). From Campsfield House to Morton Hall, Tina's view was common: 'Everyone cries at night. It's the worst time' (Taiwan, YW).

People dealt with the evening in different ways. Some wiled away the hours watching television or movies. Others, like Ray, talked on the phone or with each other: 'We all stay up until 4 in the morning . . . in [my friend's] room' (Jamaica, TH). Tina made good luck origami paper stars and diamonds, for other women, commenting: 'I can't cry because I have to concentrate' (Taiwan, YW). Many passed the nocturnal hours in religious worship. 'We barely sleep at night', Adah told me. 'We meet in groups to pray at 12 o'clock. We read the bible, and then sing from midnight to 1.30. Then sometimes we sit down and chat' (Nigeria, YW). Finally, there were those who reversed the order of the day. Aadan in Brook House, for instance, who had been unable to sleep without the aid of sleeping pills, had decided to stop taking them. 'They were too strong. They just knocked me out. I couldn't even wake up to piss. So now I sleep in the day and stay awake all night. After midnight I just watch the news until 6 am. Then at 8 am when they unlock us I get breakfast and go to sleep until 10am or so. I get up, shower, have my lunch and then go back to sleep' (Somalia, BH).

Certain issues made particular nights more upsetting. Many were matters well beyond the centre: Worries about children, marital breakups, memories of rape and brutality. Ena, who had endured extensive sexual abuse at the hands of her husband and the men who smuggled her into Britain gave a sense of her desperation.

> The nights are the worst. I can't sleep. I'm up until 4 am. I just cry and cry. Sometimes when I'm really upset, I call my mother [in the Gambia]. But after I tried to overdose and slash my wrists last time, one of my friends called my mother and told her. Now I just try to get her to think I'm ok. My mother passed out when my friend told her what I did. I can never repay my mother. Never. Never. She has done so much for me (Gambia, YW).

Other concerns were closer to home. Removal directions, or monthly reports on the state of their immigration case were often distressing.[17] 'Why don't they just put the report under my door?' Rega angrily demanded. 'I told them to do that. When they call me up instead I spend the whole night worrying. I can't sleep. I don't know what it will be about. They do that on purpose to mess with your mind' (Jamaica, BH).

As Rega's testimony makes clear, in contrast to prisons, where most prisoners look forward to their release date,[18] most of those interviewed were afraid of the endpoint of their detention. Although they recoiled against their confinement, some, particularly those in Yarl's Wood, declared it was preferable to removal or deportation. According to Aatifa, who had been beaten by father and her husband, 'my life is finished in Pakistan. . . I would rather stay here in Yarl's Wood my whole life than go back to Pakistan' (Pakistan, YW). Sunnathurai was of the same view: 'I've only one, two choice me. Either stay in this place or I will get released from this place. I don't go back to my country' (Sri Lanka, CB). Nonetheless, and notwithstanding a tendency for the UK government to hold some people for very long times, for most, detention is brief. Given the rapid turnover of most centres, departure is part of everyday life in detention as well as one of its most distinctive characteristics.

---

17. Each month the Home Office has to issue detainees with a report on the status of their immigration case. Such reports are frequently described by staff and detainees as erroneous. I was shown some examples where the nationality of the person was incorrect, their name, their date of birth and so on. Such small errors can have an enormous impact on their immigration claim, as incorrect names are later recast as 'aliases' and falsification. They also undermine everyone's faith in the immigration caseworkers' abilities to consider claims fairly and accurately.

18. Even in prison some fear release, particularly those who have been incarcerated for a long time, or who will be returning to poverty and homelessness. As criminologists have recently recognized, release from prison, particularly for women, is often a dangerous time (Carlton and Segrave, 2011; 2013).

Release was, usually, a happy occasion, as this field note records. 'Immediately after lunch I saw Mia [Gambia, YW]. She has been released on bail. She asked me to go with her in her room. Many women congratulated her, as did a few officers. The women seemed genuinely happy for her and were hugging her . . . Mia seemed confused, happy and worried' (Fieldnotes, December 2010). However, it was not unusual for men and women to fear departure, even when it signalled a temporary respite from removal. For those, like Mia, heading for the first time to temporary accommodation, release could involve a lengthy trip in an unfamiliar city, armed only with an address and a one-way train ticket. The challenges could feel overwhelming. 'We had one woman the other day', West recalled,

> that was released on bail and we took her to the reception so that she could get on the bus but she didn't. So we were thinking of calling the police to have her removed. She did not want to leave because she had no-one on the outside. We don't release them without an address but here she had friends, and people she knew, and the outside she had no-one (DCO, YW).

If release into the community was taxing, receiving 'removal directions', the paperwork with the date of departure, detainees reported, was even more frightening. 'I tell you what', David proposed, 'getting removal directions is like arranging your own funeral. You say goodbye to everyone and'—Mohammed interjected—'and you never see them again' (Uganda, CB and Somalia, CB). Many resist, filing for judicial review or asylum until the final moments. Such strategies aimed at preventing or delaying departure, ironically embed it further within the daily life of detention.

At Yarl's Wood, Bryn described in some detail her failed removal, revealing both how this event affected others around her and the involvement in it of a variety of institutional staff.

> The plane was at 1.30 on the 21st. They came to me at midnight of the 20th and said 'you need to go'. They did not give me time to take all my stuff I have had here [in the UK] for 11 years now. The only thing I will go back to is the clothes I am wearing. When they come at midnight they would not tell me where I was going. They just said 'come downstairs we need to talk to you'. I said 'I won't go!' They need to tell me why they need to talk to me. One of the women asked and they said that they were going to remove me. I fainted on the floor and they called the doctor. The doctor didn't even touch me but told them I am making problems for no reason. I have very high blood pressure and I am an old woman, and the doctor didn't even come down to touch

my hand and see if I was ok, if was really ill considering I have high blood pressure (Jamaica, YW).

Bryn was not alone in enduring a failed removal. Whereas some never left the IRC, others made it all the way to the airport. David learned his judicial review blocking his deportation had been granted only once he was at Heathrow. 'I saw that big plane Virgin airlines and I was like ooooh . . .' (Uganda, CB). Tina had actually boarded the flight to Taiwan when her judicial review came through (Taiwan, YW). At the most extreme end, Lina described overseeing a failed deportation to Guyana via Barbados while working as an 'overseas escort' for a security company to supplement her income (DCM, YW). The man had been erroneously deported when a judicial review was in place, meaning he had to be returned to detention in the UK. Abassi in Colnbrook, attested that the same thing had happened to him. Mistakenly sent back to Lagos, he was promptly returned to Campsfield House (Nigeria, CH).

To be sure, not everyone was afraid of going home. 'I was never going to stay in England', Khalil assured me. 'I have to go home to my country. I love my country' (Algeria, BH). Yet, everyone wanted to be able to return at a time, and in a manner, of their choosing. Consequently, even those who were happy to leave complained about the amount of luggage they could take and the loss of face they would experience as a result of returning without sufficient gifts. 'I want to go back on my own', Khalil urged. 'I want to get all my stuff, my money, and to buy people things. Maybe go home at the same time with my sister. If I go home alone, just in this [gesturing to his outfit] after having been away for eight years, what will people think?' (Algeria, MH).

Those brought straight from prison might have only the clothes issued to them there. Unable to recuperate their personal possessions before their departure, such people faced an embarrassing return to their home countries, especially if they had been away for some time, Edem pointed out. 'That's the reason why my suitcase in reception' (see Figure 24), he claimed.

I've no more clothes because I can't take seeing them going. So I only have three trousers left there, because I couldn't handle it. Say bring some people just prison clothes, and they want to take him home. We think you know in civilised society they're going to think 'Okay, let at least provide him with a jean or you know, nice hair for him to go at least his country with dignity.' But they don't do that. And then when you see the person and talking, you

Figure 24. Suitcases in storage in reception, IRC Colnbrook (Photo credit: S Turnbull).

can't just ignore them. You have to think 'I have to do something, I'm going to give him one of my trousers, one of my top for him to go. . .' (Togo, CB).

Whether they are returned to their country of birth, bailed, or temporarily admitted to the British community, or sent to another establishment, whenever they leave, detainees exit IRCs in a reverse order of their arrival. As their departure date nears, most of those who are being removed will be plucked from their mainstream housing unit and placed back in the induction unit before being processed, on the day of their departure, out through reception. At Campsfield House, Christopher explained, 'we've got a policy: we put them into short stay unit [SSU] for when they leave as well because it's a controlled unit. And, and it stops disturbing. . . Because if he has to go early in the morning, instead of going to get him out of the blocks, disturbing the blocks, it's in short stay then we just pick them out, skip them off' (DCO, CH). Once on the SSU, he continued, 'all we've got to do is take him from the short stay unit to the reception unit and then hand him over to the escorts, once he's processed' (DCO, CH).

While the SSU in Campsfield House is separated by a metal door from the rest of the centre, within it the men can move around and talk to one another. By contrast, detainees in Brook House and Colnbrook are confined in a cell with one other man. In Tinsley House, where there is no separate induction unit, the men are placed in a separate waiting area on the day of their departure. They may be held there for some hours.

The pains of detention

According to prison sociology, prisons are made and remade through the everyday actions and events made manifest in this chapter (see, inter alia: Sykes, 1958; Carlen, 1983; Bosworth, 1999; Phillips, 2012; Kaufman, 2014). Seemingly banal matters, like the state of people's room, their access to culturally specific hair products or food, as well as more serious issues like security and autonomy, not only define daily life but also hold the key to understanding the purpose of incarceration. Habitually referred to as the 'pains of imprisonment' such matters unveil the effect and nature of punishment. They are, in the words of Gresham Sykes (1958: 64), 'punishment deliberately inflicted by free society', deprivations that 'pose profound threats to the inmate's personality or sense of personal worth' (Sykes, 1958: 64). These are also the factors underpinning the institution's validity and justice (Sparks and Bottoms, 1995; Sparks, Bottoms, and Hay, 1996; Liebling, 2004; Crewe, 2009; 2011).

Detainees reported many pains that related specifically to how the institutions were run. In addition to those already discussed, as in prisons (Ugelvik, 2011), food was a common source of complaint, in terms of portion size, quality, and variety;[19] 'The food is quite bad', Allah complained, 'because it has no salt' (Uganda, YW). 'The way they cook the rice here is very bad', Akash asserted. 'The rice is of very bad quality and I know because that is what we eat a lot. Back home even the beggars would not eat that quality rice. If you go and have a look at the kitchen you will see that no one finishes the food. They have to eat to survive, but most of it is throw away' (Bangladesh, TH). Detainees feared that the vegan and vegetarian options included meat, or the Halal had pork. Many complained that certain cuisines were favoured over others, with a number asserting that 'Asian' spices predominated.

---

19. The menu is on a rota, meaning that long-term detainees face the same options over time and, like institutions all over Britain, on Fridays each centre offers fish, chips, and peas.

While staff members, often employed by sub-contracted companies, prepared the food in IRCs, detainees usually served it. This arrangement generated numerous disputes. Some kitchen workers, favoured their co-nationals, giving them bigger portions, or special treats. Others did the same for their friends. For Arah, there was a 'health and safety issue', in the work conditions. 'There is a fire hazard in the kitchen', she asserted. 'They lock the women who work in there so if there were a fire they cannot get out' (Jamaica, YW).

Healthcare too was widely criticized (Bull et al, 2013). Sometimes the problems were simply practical ones. 'On the enhanced unit, our time for healthcare is 2 pm', Koosha explained, 'but there are no nurses there so they can't give us our medication; if we come back at 3.30 pm they ask why we can't come earlier' (Iran, CB). Often, however, they were more serious. In all centres, for example, detainees complained that, no matter what their ailment, they were just given 'paracetamol'. There was also a widely held belief that the medical team did not believe what they were told. 'They possibly think that because they are in detention they fake their complaints', Arah suggested, before stating categorically that 'there need to be a doctor for 24 hours; the nurse can't do what a doctor can' (Jamaica, YW).

Although staff in healthcare have access to and are meant to use interpreting services, it was not clear that they always did. In any case, even when they spoke English, detainees often appeared to be confused about what medication they had been prescribed. Such uncertainty could have devastating effects. In one tragic example, Abbo from Uganda miscarried the day after taking anti-malaria medication. 'The pain was too bad to leave my room', she recalled, 'but no nurse came. At 3 am the officers got the nurse who gave me only paracetamol. Eventually it came out in the toilet' (Uganda, YW). Convinced that the medication had terminated her pregnancy, she blamed herself and the doctor. 'The next day nobody checked on me', she said. 'I was really, really angry. You've got no hope, no help when you really need it most. I was tortured psychologically and physically because I was really in pain. What have I done to be treated like this?'

For some, matters become unbearable, leading to self-harm and suicide attempts. Amine, who found it hard to sleep, spoke about how he tried to avoid cutting himself. A former heroin addict, who professed also to be a torture survivor, he told me 'in Islam suicide is Haram—forbidden—so when I feel like killing myself, I have a cold shower, I go play football. I try to take my mind off it cutting myself is bad. God gave me a perfect body and when I return to him, the bits I hurt will speak' (Algeria, CH). Nearly everyone reported anxiety or depression, with over 80 per cent of those who completed the MQLD in Yarl's Wood, Tinsley House, and Brook House diagnosed as clinically depressed according to the Hopkins Trauma Scale (Bosworth and Kellezi, 2012; 2013).[20] 'This place is killing me', Naimah moaned, 'I cannot eat. You see my skin [acne]. When I arrived I was very fresh. I am not fresh anymore' (Pakistan, YW).

Detainees also differentiated between centres (Bosworth and Kellezi, 2013). 'The officers treat me better here [Tinsley House] then elsewhere', Fariborz said. 'In Colnbrook you can't fax and they don't listen to what you are saying. Dover had toilet in the room. Colnbrook the same but then there was very strong smells of the toilet and shower. Here it is a good place compare to the other centres' (Afghanistan, TH).

Staff members too had expectations and opinions about each centre. Not only did they distinguish between them like detainees, but they were usually particularly attached to the one in which they worked. At Tinsley House, for instance, many officers disapproved of the harsh regime and techniques of governance in Brook House, despite the fact that it operated with the same Senior Management Team. 'I don't feel like a prison officer', Arvil stated. 'Not so much here. I don't think so much here. Next door, definitely . . . Here, it's more, you're just more of a, a, a security guard, if you like' (DCO, TH).

Opinions about their workplace often overrode their view of their employer.[21] 'When Serco came here . . . they, they wanted to know the, the feeling of staff etcetera, one of the questions in their questionnaire was, Serco this, Serco that', Sean remembered,

and I actually wrote that when I came to Yarl's Wood to work I didn't come to work for group Four Falc of the day or Group Four or GSL and today's Serco. I've always come to work for Yarl's Wood and I will continue to work for Yarl's Wood and I actually said to the centre manager only recently that, 'You can choose where to work but you can't choose your master.' Her reply

20. On the impact of immigration detention on mental health more broadly, see Steel et al, 2006 and Fazel et al, 2011.
21. As the previous chapter made clear in this one area, Morton Hall was subtly different. Older members of staff, who had made their career at the institution when it was a prison, remain emotionally attached to it as a place, but, they argued, the place had been utterly altered by its transformation into an IRC. For them, the prison service made sense, and, if they became too disenchanted with their post at Morton Hall, would be where they would seek remedy (see also Bosworth and Slade, 2014).

to me was, 'Well this is the real world', and I said, 'I understand that but I don't have to like it.' You know so I always come to Yarl's Wood to work but today my master is Serco, tomorrow who knows? (DCO, YW).

For those in Morton Hall, considerable confusion and discomfort surrounded the relationship between HM Prison Service and the Home Office. Staff not only missed working with a custodial population whom they felt they had understood and could help, but they were not happy about their new immigration managers. 'Since we re-roled [job satisfaction is] far less than it used to be. Dealing with women was great, because you got the outcomes. You could help', Jonathan complained. 'But now there's nothing there at all . . . To be fair, because there's not a lot I can do for them . . . And they [the Home Office] are a black art to me. I know nothing about them' (DCO, MH). Faced with a different population, and new masters, this man spoke wistfully of the past, when Morton Hall was a prison, and his job had made sense.

In contrast to such nuanced and, often passionate, staff views about the places in which they worked, and far removed from detainee experiences and complaints, the official Home Office perspective, Paul proclaimed, was that IRCs 'are not meant to be destinations' (Home Office). Detention centres, he implied, are not sites at all. They are just a passageway, a point of departure, a temporary site of identification.[22]

This official interpretation had multiple effects. As non-destinations, IRCs need not (and do not) develop detailed regimes of the kind present in prison. Why create extensive counselling or treatment services, when the population is just passing through? Likewise personal officer schemes, or an estate-wide peer support scheme like the Listeners' programme as in prison, are easily rejected.

Such words manifestly overlook the complex nature of these institutions. They also deny the degree to which IRCs have become a fixed part of the architecture of border control. The numbers within them may yet be small, but such places are entrenched within the legal and rhetorical approach to migration.

Above all, refusing to consider IRCs as destinations discredits the pains of detention, staff ambition, and the experiences of all those working or housed within. In so doing, the Home Office perspective suggests that,

22. In Vanessa Barker's terms (2013b) a 'No-Man's land'.

unlike prisons, the '*interior* quality' of IRCs, is not just unrelated to 'questions of *exterior* legitimacy' (Liebling, 2004: xix), it is irrelevant. These are not meant to be destinations. Their purpose is elsewhere. Detention itself becomes disconnected from that goal.

Conclusion

Paul's testimony offers a glimpse of the scale of the state of denial underpinning the project of border control (Cohen, 2001). In its dissonance with daily life in detention, where women and men sometimes linger for quite some time, and where staff labour long hours for many years, it raises profound questions about how we might judge and understand them. If, in detention, the connection between the form an institution takes and its purpose is broken, how might we hold it to account? What, in such places, restrains power?

Insisting detention is nothing more than a brief interlude does not just limit the regime within these institutions, but also interpolates their relationship to other places of confinement and to the broader, global context in which they are situated. The reliance on a criminal justice imaginary in the institution's design, staffing, and policy is glossed over. The population, drawn predominantly from particular regions around the world, are recast as travellers, their fears, hopes, and relationships within and beyond the institution's walls ignored. Such repudiation is one of the key challenges facing those within such places, and one that they must negotiate everyday. It shapes the relationships people forge within and structures their experience of detention. For these are indeed places with histories, cultures, and enduring qualities which connect to existing patterns of global and local articulations of power and inequality. They are also places where, notwithstanding considerable differences and tensions among them, people form relationships with one another. As the following chapter will argue, the interplay between such internal and external factors is crucial to understanding IRCs.

5

The detention community

Some staff are really nice and some are awful. [The nice ones] cares and treats you right (Alla, Uganda, YW).

There is a fantastic community spirit here. You can see it in how the ladies sit around doing clothes, hair and nails. They are always smiling (Home Office, YW).

Life in detention unfolds in a local context shaped by humdrum matters such as room allocation, the daily timetable, architectural design, access to internet, and food. Institutions, however, are formed by more than their timetable. It is not just the specific 'deprivations' of confinement which define the nature of incarceration, but the beliefs and expectations the confined bring with them (see, inter alia, Sykes, 1958; Irwin, 1970; Earle and Phillips, 2012; Phillips, 2008; 2012; Sparks, Bottoms, and Hay, 1996; Crewe 2009). Detention centres are also shaped by human interactions as well as relationships between and among staff and detainees.

Having sketched out the institutional context in the preceding pages, this chapter concentrates on the relationships detainees and officers build (and sometimes fail to build) in detention and the connections they maintain (and fail to maintain) with friends, family, and lawyers beyond the walls of confinement. Relationships may offer support and relief. They might also be the source of conflict or coercion. In their interactions staff and detainees can reach an understanding, or, conversely, refuse to try. Even when negative, interactions require some acknowledgement. They express hope and desire for recognition, as well as generating or upholding considerable barriers between people. In short, they help us to understand the emotional texture of incarceration under conditions of deportation and removal.

Custodial relationships in a global institution

For the most part, detainees passed their time informally, chatting, playing cards, braiding hair, shaving, drinking tea or coffee, playing pool, watching DVDs, videos, or television together. While officers may be present and participate in some of these activities, detainees spend most of their time with one another. Some of the centres are set up to facilitate such informal interactions. Reflecting gendered expectations about women's behaviour, Yarl's Wood is designed with numerous small 'association' rooms along the activities corridor and on the housing units. Specific national groups of women often congregated in these, chatting to each other and on their mobile phone. When British weather allows, they can also sit in the garden.

Space is less intimately arranged in the men's institutions. Socializing outside the bedrooms primarily occurred around the pool table, the big screen television, the gym, or in the courtyards. As in Yarl's Wood each of the men's IRCs included outdoor space, although in the two high-security facilities—Colnbrook and Brook House—some of the external courtyards doubled up as potential sites for sport and were covered in concrete rather than grass. In them men could enjoy basketball or football when equipment was available; occasionally the centre staff organized tournaments. In Tinsley House and Brook House there were also seating areas outside the institution's shop which, in Brook House, was frequently, and deafeningly, used by men to play dominoes. Tinsley House has recently constructed a quiet lounge room with computers (see Figure 25).

Due to the unstructured nature of the day, men and women often roamed around the centres, walking the corridors either in pairs or alone, sometimes conversing on their mobile phones, at other times silent, trying to pass the time. Many clutched shabby yellow envelopes filled with documents related to their immigration case. Back on the housing units, some lay in bed all day alone, while others assembled in their rooms with friends to pass the time. 'I just stay by myself, yeah, just here by myself', Arah said sadly. 'And, you know, just go through paperworks as you see now, just make, you know, work, I will go through my clothes so many times. Go through paperworks, yeah, so watching the telly' (Jamaica, YW).

Interactions with each other were not always peaceful or happy. Inevitably, in institutions of confinement, where people are stressed, anxious, confused,

Figure 25. Detainee lounge in IRC Tinsley House (Photo credit: G4S).

and frustrated, detainees fought or alienated one another. They sometimes harmed themselves. Disputes could be triggered by minor irritants: taking too long to use the microwave, talking too loudly on the phone. Conflict also reflected pre-existing prejudices. In Yarl's Wood, for instance, the Chinese and Jamaican women taunted each other and on a few occasions threw punches too. Hostilities between these groups reflected enduring racial prejudices as Jamaican and Nigerian women mocked Chinese speech patterns, chanting 'Ching Chow Min', while Chinese nationals accused them of being overly sexual, promiscuous, and aggressive (Bosworth and Kellezi, 2014).

Although, for the most part, IRCs are not associated with the kinds of interpersonal violence among the confined population that mark some prisons, during the fieldwork in Colnbrook, a group of men tied up another in his room in order to beat him. The attack lasted some time before staff realized anything was amiss.[1] Although this fight concerned only those specifically involved in it, its effect on the detainee community was wider,

---

1. The assailants, at least one of whom I had previously interviewed, were immediately transferred to prison. Staff (and other detainees) reported that the assault was drug-related.

Sinnathurai spelled out: 'One guy some—several people beat him up, they want to kill him but they don't have a knife, they don't have nothing. Beat him badly. I don't think we feel safe here' (Sri Lanka, CB). Long after the event, when the perpetrators had been moved to prison or other establishments, fear of violence lingered.

Sometimes, in Yarl's Wood, Amya reported, her frustrations simply boiled over. Although she tried to keep a lid on her emotions, she did not always succeed, lashing out at staff and detainees alike. 'I am so angry in here', she cried,

> I don't go out of my room because I will punch one of the officers. I went out to microwave yesterday and almost killed one girl who took out my food to put hers in, in front of me. I told her 'Do you think I am stupid?' I told her 'I am madder than you! I am so frustrated in here I could kill someone!' So I took her by the throat. The officers came and I denied it all. The other girls in there said nothing. They said they did not see anything. That is why I better stay in my room otherwise I will do something really bad. I am in prison for 7 months for doing nothing. At least if I commit a crime I would deserve being in here. I don't care about anything anymore. I curse at the officers. I just don't care. My friends say I should not fight but I can't control it when they make me angry I can't even see (Gambia, YW).

Hui-Ying, in contrast, turned her frustrations onto herself, cutting her wrists with the lid of a tin of tuna she had bought from the centre shop. 'She is angry', Tina explained on Hui-Ying's behalf. 'She wants to kill herself so everyone knows what Immigration has done to her' (Taiwan, YW). Hui-Ying was not alone in her frustration. Nor did her exasperation flow solely from the inefficient handling of immigration case.[2] Rather, Tina claimed, it reflected the mood of many of the Chinese women in Yarl's Wood where they struggled to follow what was happening and to make themselves understood. 'The Chinese are so angry here', Tina announced. 'They can't communicate, that's why' (Taiwan, YW).

In the men's institutions, moods were similarly dark. 'There's a lot of anger', Joao warned. 'There's a lot of anger and people want to release this anger, and [they] don't know how' (Angola, CB). Some, like Hui-Ying,

2. Having resisted her removal for over a year by refusing to provide information necessary to obtain a travel document, Hui-Ying had recently changed her mind and agreed to return. As the months continued to pass and she was not provided with a ticket, she became increasingly upset at the delay in her return.

harmed or threatened to kill themselves. Others promised future violence. 'I used to see reports from Iraq about suicide bombers and think how can them guys do that, but now I know', one elderly man at Morton Hall threatened (Unknown nationality, MH). Waldo agreed, his vexation evident. 'I'm feeling pain', he stated. 'I'm sat now, I'm thinking, I don't know, my mind is that if I was to go back to my country, I see any British man I shall retaliate. That's what my mind is telling me. Because your people are so wicked . . . they are very wicked. They don't listen to anyone' (Ghana, BH). For Malik the danger lay in his deportation. Going back to Pakistan, he predicted, would make him 'worser. There's drugs there, it's easy to get weapons, if I go back I'll just get worser. I know I will' (Pakistan, BH).

Not all men were so belligerent. In Brook House, a group of Kurdish men had formed a tight peer group, while in all IRCs the Chinese population seemed to coalesce. At Morton Hall, Richard took a mixed approach: 'I spend most of the time with other Zimbabweans, just talking. Maybe my language. I am English as well. Then I've got a few Jamaican friends. English. That's it. Then sometimes I'll just be in my room, watching movie, DVD. That's it' (Zimbabwe, MH).

Whereas nationality could be a source of unity, as Richard suggested—an easy means of recognition—it intersected with class, gender, and also with people's life histories. In Yarl's Wood, the Brazilian community split into those who had worked as nannies and cleaners, others who were generally more educated, and still others who fit neither group. Emilia set herself apart and was ostracized. Young, blonde, and glamorous, heavily made up and habitually clothed in short tight-fitting dresses, she was the ex-girlfriend of a Brazilian gang member who was serving a prison sentence for assaulting her. She met with disapproval from the rest of the Brazilian community and did not interact with them.

In the men's institutions, aspects of masculinity shaped relationships and the extent and quality of interactions. Men often refused to discuss their fears and concerns with one other, either because they did not trust anyone else or because they did not want to burden others who were depressed with their problems. 'It's not going nowhere', Kasun proclaimed, 'you know, my inside feelings, I don't tell no one. I don't tell no one. Not even my mum' (Sri Lanka, TH). Although some assisted with interpreting or helping others to complete bail applications, men commonly described enduring their confinement unaided. 'I don't have no friends in here', Odaawa (Somalia, CB) acknowledged with resignation. 'Each man is alone', Fikru agreed (Eritrea, CH).

Certain activities brought women and men together. In each centre, for instance, the art and craft room was frequented by a particular group of people who would spend their day as a collective talking in small groups with each other and with the staff member on duty while sewing, gluing, and painting. The hair salon in Yarl's Wood was another important location where women talked informally and braided each other's hair. In the men's institutions the pool tables were an important site of informal interactions.

In all the centres, Evangelical Christians bonded over daily prayer. 'I use the chapel everyday', Richard described. 'Every morning and every, every, every evening. We go there, we pray in the morning, pray in the evening. Me and a few more guys, we just go there, we pray. We talk about our stories, about our families' (Zimbabwe, MH). In this environment, he suggested, barriers fell away, enabling men to reach out to one another.

As Adah described in the previous chapter, friendships could be precious. Some forged permanent bonds. 'You make friends you keep for life in here', Ora declared enthusiastically. 'When friends leave and you stay behind it is very hard. Someone women cry for days when their roommates leave' (Nigeria, YW). For most, however, meaningful connections were hard to establish. Language, fear, and the varied length of detention were all significant barriers to intimacy. When asked about whether his friends in detention were helping him cope with his anxiety about removal, Behnam revealed his solitary pain, 'Apart my roommate, I have not made any friends. But he was released. Another man I knew was released too. I have not made friend with anyone else' (Afghan, TH). While some stayed in touch with those who were bailed or temporarily admitted into the British community, on occasion even being visited by their former roommates, most, like Behnam, did not foresee much of a future in their relationships, a factor that dampened their enthusiasm for making friends.

Low levels of trust influenced people's capacity and desire for forging friendships. 'There are people in here I can talk to,' Ariz noted, 'but I can't say they are my friends. It takes a long time to trust people. And I don't know people in here' (Pakistan, TH). Nguyen kept his interactions even with his roommate to a minimum. 'I learn about him, but I don't ask personal questions about him', he stated warily (Vietnam, CB). Detainees struggled to have faith in others not just when they did not share a language, culture or religion, but also because they did not always find them credible. 'I don't trust people', Ariz explained. 'They say that things go back to your caseworker, so I am really worried who I talk to' (Pakistan,

TH). Some, who had previously been tortured or abused found it hard to have faith in anyone.

Laili offered some insight on what it was like to dissimulate. 'When I first came [to Yarl's Wood]', she reminisced, 'I lived in fear because I told them I was from China and I couldn't speak English. I was so scared. And then because the solicitor told me do not speak to anyone because they might be a spy, or that UKBA will put a spy here, so they will try to be friendly to you, and then know everything of you, and then they will disclose . . .' (Malaysia, YW). Her pretence prevented Laili from interacting with staff or detainees: 'I dared not speak to anyone, even the officer' (Malaysia, YW). Attempting to maintain her story affected her mood as well as her interactions, warping her sense of the institution and those around her. '[I felt] like I'm living in a world of fear, can't sleep. Yeah. It's like so scary. Though the place is, the facilities, everything is okay . . . it's so difficult for me to lie' (Malaysia, YW).

Detainees hid other matters from each other, sabotaging their attempts to be themselves around others. Despite their widespread experience of sexual violence, for instance, the women rarely spoke about their experiences of victimization. Few detainees in any centre were openly gay or lesbian. Those with a history of drug or alcohol abuse rarely confessed their addiction, while many who had been in prison were cagey about their criminal record, even when it was immigration-related.

Part of the problem, the women and men appreciated, was their pathways to detention were not all the same due to the arbitrary nature of immigration control. Whereas much of the literature on the criminalization of migration or 'crimmigration', paints a picture of stark control (Stumpf, 2006), in the UK detainees and case law tell a different story (Aliverti, 2012a; 2012b; 2013).[3] Pam made it plain:

> You know the other African women they look at me and say: 'You are criminal.' They say that other person was working with fake documents, why did they bring me in here? They did not bring other people in here. They said that they were taken from work too and with fake documents but don't understand why they took you to prison and not me. All my African sisters look at me as a criminal. Why did they choose me for this? Why did they

3. In her analysis of case files from one British Crown Court and one magistrates' court, Ana Aliverti (2012a; 2012b; 2013) found very few examples where criminal law was invoked. Instead, the state preferred to use administrative powers which are less cumbersome and more efficient.

bring me in here? When the time in prison finished I thought they were going to let me out or send me back home, but they did not. Why did they choose me? Why don't they take me home? What have I done to deserve this? I will be labelled for life (Nigeria, YW).

Pam resisted the label of criminal, particularly given that others who had worked without documents had not been put through the court system. She could not understand why she was singled out, and found her treatment to be painful and confusing. Her identification as a former offender was an emotional burden and a stigma.

Those who were silent about their criminal record may have had good reason, since detainees often expressed concern about the presence of ex-prisoners. 'We are here, [with] strange people', Viku grumbled. 'Like somebody from prison . . . It's different, some drug addicts and . . . it's no good' (Moldova, CB). The problem, Viku went on, lay in the diverse backgrounds of the detained community. '[We are] no supposed to be together', he said. 'If some people who stay long prison sentences supposed to be in another place. Not here. Or, we're supposed to be in another place. But we are together, and we are not safe' (Moldova, CB). Richard, despite being a former prisoner himself, agreed with this view. 'You, you don't know some of the people I'm dealing with', he asserted. 'Like I told you, being locked up with murderers, people that are psychopath, rapist. Others are just a normal person that's just come out of the airport. They took him out of the airport. They took him out of Dover or somewhere, under a truck or something. Everyone's here' (Zimbabwe, MH).

Whereas Viku appeared to be afraid of his peers, declaring himself 'unsafe' in his confinement, the problem for Richard lay in the diversity of those around him. 'In jail it's different', he claimed. 'You communicate with everyone. Everyone speaks English. "Hi, how are you?" You respect each other. Some of the people here don't even speak no English. Nothing' (Zimbabwe, MH). Under these circumstances, not only was detainee solidarity much reduced, but, Richard made clear, the capacity for recognizing the humanity of others was as well. 'You're just in a jungle', he concluded. 'You've got all the animals just on you' (Zimbabwe, MH).

Unlike prisoners, detainees, in principle at least, have greater access to means of communicating with their family members and friends outside. Not only are mobile phones permitted in all British detention centres to facilitate contact with families and lawyers, but also detainees can email using the centre computers. They are entitled to more visits than prisoners and detention centres are relatively porous, welcoming a range of non-custodial figures every day to run programmes and offer legal advice or social visits.

For some, these kinds of interactions eased the pains of detention. Able to communicate widely, women and men did not just reach out to spouses and children, but also to parents, particularly to their mothers, for support. 'My mum makes me happy every time I talk to her', Obiye confided (Somalia, CB). At the same time, however, family contact could exacerbate the strain many felt. Women and men hid their detention from their loved ones, telling their children they were away on work or holiday, pretending to their parents that they were still in gainful employment. 'My father is coming here [to Britain] to visit in two weeks and we have not told him that I am in detention', Dan said anxiously. 'I feel like a criminal being here. My head is down. My pride is gone. I am in a prison' (Mauritius, TH). 'My mother thinks I'm at home', Azra similarly reported (Pakistan, YW). Some argued with their partners who became frustrated at the length of their absence. Others had nobody to call.

In any case, maintaining relationships over the phone was not easy. 'I don't want to talk to my family on the phone', Mansour asserted. 'I have lost any desire to talk to people. It makes me feel sad to talk to them. I don't want them to see me for what I have become' (BOC, TH). Having disguised his absence from his daughter, he was unable to cope with her disappointment at his failure to spend time with her. 'My child said on the phone "Dad you don't love me anymore? Because you have not come to see me." It is like a knife went through my heart. I love her more than myself. I keep telling her that I am way for work. I will never be the same person again when I leave here' (BOC, TH).

Detainees with friends and family in the UK can be visited everyday. Yet, due to people's work schedules, finances, geography, and immigration status, not everyone called on their family and friends in detention. Parents found it emotionally wrenching to be visited by their children and complicated to arrange, often preferring to limit their interaction to the phone. Adan explained, 'My partner comes to visit me with my child. I told her to not come every week because it is expensive. She lives in Birmingham. I told her to come once a month so I get to see my son. I find it very hard when I see him. I talk to him on the phone every day. It makes me very sad when he asks, "Dad when are you coming home?"' (Iraq, TH).

In addition to their friends and family, many detainees were in regular contact with lawyers, volunteers, and other advocates. Following the tenets of the 2001 Detention Centre Rules and the Detention Services Operating Standards (UKBA, 2008), each centre must have a visitor's group. These groups offer social visits to detainees as well some financial assistance and referral services.[4] Other organizations assist detainees in completing bail applications, and can also refer to legal services. Religious representatives, knitting teachers, yoga instructors, university lecturers, artists, and musicians similarly visit their local immigration removal centres.

For some, such visitors offer a lifeline, a kind conversation, a welcome reminder that they had not been forgotten. In the case of a lawyer, they raised the possibility of a way out. Often, however, they were another source of disappointment or confusion, unable to help with the issue that concerned detainees most: their immigration case. Staff and detainees complained bitterly about inadequate lawyers. Allegations were frequently made of corruption, with families outside paying significant sums to individuals who then failed either to show up in court or file the relevant paperwork. Some, it turned out, were not immigration lawyers at all. 'My lawyer did not have a licence', May recounted. 'He kept my case for 6 months, wasting my time and got a lot of money, and they let him in here. They take fingerprints on visitors but they let in unlicensed lawyers? He would come in all the time and they did not check. When I changed lawyer he tried to find out all the information from this one without licence and could not even find his registration' (Jamaica, YW). For those fortunate enough to be granted legal aid, confusion abounded. Many misunderstood the existing legal aid system, believing that their lawyers, 'worked for the government', and, therefore, were 'on the side of' the Home Office (Various, all centres).

Despite the best efforts of visitor groups, some, like Sunnathurai in Colnbrook, remained unimpressed. 'They [local visitor group] try to help me. I think they put me website about my story. End of the day they can't do more than that' (Sri Lanka, CB). More commonly, detainees who were unable to read the signs around the centre, or who had been inattentive or stressed during their induction process, had simply not heard of such organizations.

---

4. A full list of the befriender organizations can be found on the AVID website at: <http://www.aviddetention.org.uk/>.

Like others in custody, detainees found it difficult to maintain ties with the outside world. Many spent considerable time chasing up their lawyers on the phone, complaining that messages were rarely returned. Family relationships often ebbed over time. Under these circumstances, relationships with custodial staff became increasingly important, since they were often the only figures available to offer assistance, sympathy, or advice.

Relationships with staff

Although the literature on penal institutions has concentrated on the perspective of prisoners, a growing body of work argues that the relationship between staff and detainees is a crucial part of prison life, the 'heart of the whole prison system' (Home Office, 1984: paragraph 16; Liebling, Price, and Shefer, 2010: 53; see also Crewe, 2009; Liebling, 2004; Bennett, Crewe, and Wahidin, 2007; Liebling, Price, and Elliott, 1999). Considerable evidence can be found about the importance of staff discretion (Liebling, Price, and Shefer, 2010: 121–80) and effective management (Crawley, 2006; Bennett, 2012) in maintaining good order as well as in shoring up legitimacy in general terms. Studies demonstrate also the effect of positive staff relationships with detainees on specific matters like improving educational attainment (Ministry of Justice, 2006), reducing suicide risk (Liebling, Durie, Stiles, and Tait, 2005) and encouraging family contact (Prison Reform Trust, 2005). In short, a prison with good staff-prisoner relationships generally is a happier, safer establishment than one without. In Alison Liebling's words (2011: 484), 'the moral quality of prison life is *enacted* and *embodied* by the attitudes and conduct of prison officers'.

As usual, we have little evidence about what staff in detention centres do or think. In IRCs the one available academic study of custodial staff paints a bleak picture of alienated and uncomprehending officers obsessed with security above and beyond care or compassion (Hall, 2012). In the institutions I visited, however, matters varied, complicated not only by diverse management styles but also by the range of employees present at any one time and their distinct powers over and responsibilities towards those in custody.

The staff members with whom detainees have the most contact are uniformed custody officers. These are the women and men who lock and unlock doors, count detainees during roll call, search their rooms, supervise meals, and run activities and education. While they play no official role in determining their immigration case, detention custody officers prepare detainees to leave, and hold the responsibility for handing them over to the escort staff on forced returns as well as uncontested ones. DCOs must make available information on a variety of matters pertaining to people's immigration case, including a list of immigration lawyers. Welfare officers may help women and men complete bail application, file out applications, and track down their possessions.

Each centre deployed their staff slightly differently. Whereas most allowed for a certain amount of specialism—enabling officers to concentrate their time and hone their skills in particular sections of the centre or on specific tasks—all requested them to fulfil other functions as well. At Campsfield House two men went into detail: 'I'm operational staff so I'm based within visits, gatehouse, detainee reception', Ben told me. 'Basically anywhere that somebody comes first, I'm one of the people that work in those areas. And that's what I do' (DCO, CH). 'Me, I'm from regimes', Chris chipped in. 'I mainly do activities and those speak for itself really, mainly sports, football, cricket, in the fitness week doing competitions. All the fun stuff really' (DCO, CH).[5]

Sometimes, staff roles changed. 'When I first started', Alexander recalled, 'I was in the short stay unit, you know. But then when they, they changed things around I got put on the blocks, but I still go in there when they're short of people, you know' (DCO, CH). Those working on the housing units (the 'blocks' or the 'wings'), had the most contact with detainees. 'We're basically the people they come to first, you know', Alexander went on. 'If they need property, if they need receipts or to see immigration, any of that stuff—we'll be doing that for them. We'll do all their faxing, mostly all their copying, we'll be sending out their lettering, their letters' (DCO, CH). Wing officers may also need to sort out their institutional needs. 'We'll get additional clothing for them', Alexander commented, 'there's certain days for their bedding [to be replaced]'. Trying to come up with an analogous job he painted an incongruously cosy picture of community, 'It's

---

5. At some centres, like Yarl's Wood, 'activities staff' members are differentiated from the rest by their uniform. Everywhere those who staff the gymnasium dress in tracksuits, rather than collared shirts. They also all undergo specific health and safety training for physical activity.

like you move to a neighbourhood and, and, this is the office you go to, you know, that handles everything else for you' (DCO, CH).

Many DCOs, particularly those employed in Campsfield House, Yarl's Wood and Tinsley House presented themselves as helpful and caring professionals. 'I like to look at this work as more caring than security-wise', Alisa reported, 'because you're in a secure environment anyway and I think you've gotta have empathy for the people that are here, you know. Sometimes, no fault of their own, through poverty and things they could be here so, you know, I think that you've got, you've gotta understand why they're here, yeah' (DCO, TH). The detainees, her words suggest, were defined by more than their incarceration.

Detainees varied in their opinion about the custodial staff. While for the most part they were guardedly positive about them,[6] women and men in all centres were often confused about and suspicious of the precise role of the DCOs and their source of authority. 'They [the custodial staff] say they are here to help, but really they are all working together', Sanjeewa argued. 'It is a business. The judges are also working for immigration. They are not impartial, if they were impartial they would listen to both sides of the story, but they only believe UKBA' (Sri Lanka, CH). Such suspicions affected how detainees interacted with staff. In a focus group interview in Tinsley House, for instance, where staff-detainee relationships seemed to be particularly good, it became clear that the population of young Afghan men referred to immigration and custody staff alike as 'police'. 'They are all the same for us', the young men attested. 'They all wear uniforms'.

Accusations of incompetence were, likewise, common. Ex-prisoners, in particular, tended to perceive DCOs as less professional and capable, often comparing them unfavourably to prison officers. 'It's like as long as you got clean record and you got security clearance pass, you will get job in G4S', Malik asserted contemptuously. 'Maybe few of them have training but I think most of them got no training how to deal with other person, emotions. . . I don't think so they are like professional like prison officers' (Pakistan, BH). Whereas some, like Koosha criticized officers for their lack of professionalism, stating angrily that, 'some officers make you stressed,

---

6. According to the terms of the MQLD survey, for instance, most detainees in Brook House, Yarl's Wood, and Tinsley House perceived custodial staff members to be honest and kind, they could understand what staff told them and could communicate with them easily (Bosworth and Kellezi, 2013).

because some officers can't do their job properly' (Iran, CB), others like Ania, preferred them, finding more informal relationships easier to manage than the rigid ones she had experienced in prison (Poland, YW).

In reflecting on their role and their relationships with detainees, staff often emphasized the importance of respect and fairness. They were also mindful of the particular legal status of those in their care. 'You've got to try and respect them while they're there', Alver proposed, 'because they're not there for punishment. They've done . . . If they've been to prison, they've done their punishment. They're there to sort their immigration case out . . .' (DCO, TH). At the same time, officers were often confused by the implications of holding detainees in secure environments, unsure about whether or not they might be dangerous. Why were they detained if they were not a threat?

Not everyone was bothered. For Allen, their lack of British citizenship was sufficient. 'Personally I don't agree with immigration . . .', he announced defiantly. 'I mean, I'm one of the world's worst, you know, "kick 'em out, keep 'em out"'. Nonetheless, he appreciated, 'it's my job, I've gotta be professional. I can't let . . . We've all got prejudices, we've all got our . . . prejudices. We've all got our own mindset. You know, the older you get, the more stuck that becomes. But yeah, you've just gotta leave it all outside the door. Do your job, get on with your job.' His 'philosophy', under these circumstances, he went on, 'is treat everybody how you'd like to be treated yourself. I wouldn't like to be treated like a bag of shit so I don't treat somebody like a bag of shit. It's, it's why I've always, you know, it's the way I've been brought up, it's the way I've always carried on' (DCO, TH).

Staff felt it was important to exercise their authority. 'They need to be strong enough to know when they have to say no', Alvis put it, 'and also strong enough to know that when they should say yes' (DCO, TH). Officers also generally advocated consistency. The women 'need to know that you're gonna say no to some things', Leah proclaimed, 'so they know where they stand as well and they like that . . . if they get an officer that's not standing by the rules they get confused' (DCO, YW).

Detainees also valued consistency, and were very critical when they felt that staff failed to administer rules or offer assistance fairly. 'Who they like, they favour', Sunnathurai grumbled. 'Who they don't like, they give them hard time . . . Man over there, [gesturing to an officer reading the paper] him, he's all right. And some of the officers are like him. Fine. They will do, like care for detainees. Some of them, they don't give a shit about detainees'

(Sri Lanka, CB). Warming to his theme, Sunnathurai went on, gradually becoming more agitated, 'even they don't do nothing to detainees, that doesn't matter, but they always give hard time. They provoke them, they wind them up. And when they do something against them, they take into rule 40, writing a file, everything. Make them worst' (Sri Lanka, CB).

Custodial staff were only occasionally explicitly antagonistic or derogatory towards detainees in front of the research team.[7] One such exception occurred in Morton Hall, within earshot not only of the researcher but also of the other detainees. Two staff members, speaking loudly in the welfare office referred to a man from the DRC who had been given removal directions that morning and was visibly upset.

DICK (DCO): You see Didier today?
JOHN (DCO): Yeah, he knows he's going back to the Congo. He can't do
             anything about it now.
DICK (DCO): Yeah he's just crying all the time. He cried all the way through
             visits.
JOHN (DCO): Yeah—he cries like this [gestures].
[Both laugh out loud]
DICK (DCO): It's like—carry on crying mate but if you are on your bed, make
             sure I can see you're still breathing and let me get on with earning
             my money (Fieldnotes, April 2012).

While Dick and John's callousness was shocking and does not sit well with their 'duty of care' towards Didier, they were not the only ones evidently uncomfortable with detainees' emotions. Nor were they alone in their contempt and desire to distance themselves from what they were witnessing. Officers detached themselves from the emotional pain of those they confined in a number of ways (see also Hall, 2010; 2012). Some couched the matter in gendered terms. For a long-term employee of the prison service, whose previous experience had all been with women, 'it was strange for us when I saw them [men] cry in front of us. I didn't know what to do', Arabella admitted. 'Because, you know, we weren't trained for that. We trained more like, you know, "boys don't cry"' (DCO, MH).

Others, like Dick and John, racialized the emotions they witnessed. For them, expressions of happiness, fury, or sorrow were attributed to cultural stereotypes. 'The Jamaican way of life', Todd claimed, 'is totally, you know,

---

7. Although negative cultural stereotypes and sweeping statements about national groups were not uncommon in the relative privacy of interviews.

raising their arms and raising their voice. But it's their, it's their culture. Get used to it' (Todd, DCO, YW).

Most simply learnt how to compartmentalize their feelings. 'I've learnt to detach myself ninety-five percent of the time', Mishal attested, 'because if I didn't then I wouldn't be here anymore . . . Very early on I learnt to sort of keep myself separate from their issues because there's just so many of them. And not to resent UKBA', she added (DCM, CB).[8] Although they often recognized detainees' emotions, staff like Mishal were able to stand apart, denying not just the pains they witnessed, but, more importantly, any personal responsibility they had in creating such suffering. In so doing, not only could they continue to work in the establishment, but maintain a sense of normalcy in their life outside. 'You leave this job behind as much as you can when you walk out the main gate because of certain things that you, you can't sit down and discuss with your kids and your wife', Alvis revealed. 'I mean, fortunately my drive's about half an hour home which is long enough to get over it before I walk in the front door' (DCO, TH).

While all staff acknowledged the pressures of their job, most (also) drew pleasure from their interactions with detainees. 'I find it very easy to talk to them', one officer commented in Tinsley House. 'There are a lot of intelligent guys in here' (DCO, TH). His colleague, Barry, agreed. 'You become friendly with some of them, like friends and you have very interesting conversations. But', he paused, acknowledging the men's anxieties, 'you feel helpless. What can you do?' (DCO, TH).

Indeed, staff in all the centres found their jobs rewarding, despite significant misgivings about pay, conditions, and relations with senior management. 'I just enjoy the whole job as a whole', Alver enthused,

> Just getting everyone fed, ensuring that they've all had a meal. I get a certain buzz out of working, well, certainly down Brook House. Getting through the day knowing that I've done everything I can to assist all the detainees I can do with the two other officers on the wing. Which is a lot to ask: three to

8. The case which 'taught' her the necessity of emotional distance, she went on, involved 'a very young looking resident who probably looked about fourteen but he was eighteen, over eighteen and he stopped eating and drinking for two weeks and I felt a lump in my throat trying to convince this guy that you need to eat and sort yourself out and he was just lying there in a paper suit and I just couldn't get him, listening to his story I couldn't get it out of my mind when I went home . . . cos I thought like he was just a kid and he's having to deal with things that we take for granted, like we were born with, born British so we've not had to worry about "I need to stay here. I need to sort out", you know, all these basic things that we take for granted' (DCM, CB).

one hundred, maybe one hundred and twenty-odd male detainees on there. Which is a lot to go through. Especially when you've got a door to open and close, because it's all controlled there. And then you've got the office, where they come in with issues that they've got. And issuing out just simple things like toilet roll, and all, all the daily things that you need. And then just walking around the wing making sure everyone's safe, and there's nothing that's going to hurt them. Just ensuring the safety of them while they're there in our care. I get quite a buzz out of doing that really (DCO, TH).

While Alvis depicts the satisfactions of fulfilling the process of his job, others emphasized their contact with the detainees. 'You grow as a person', Alana claimed, 'when you find out, you know, all these, you know, people from different countries and, you know, their backgrounds' (DCO, TH). In Yarl's Wood, Leah felt the same. 'Working here has developed me as a person confidence-wise', she said. 'I've come a long way since I started' (DCO, YW).

Partly job satisfaction flowed from a sense of competence. Staff were particularly enthusiastic when they felt their work was valued and appreciated. In Leah's case, detainees regularly made her gifts in art and craft, praising her and in other ways expressing their gratitude for her help. This kind of recognition, she made clear, was both very welcome and in stark contrast to how she felt treated by her superior officers. 'I feel recognised', she said,

through the ladies a hell of a lot. I get Christmas presents, I get birthday presents, I'm not allowed to accept them but I do, I put them in the office, I'm not gonna say no. I'm not taking them anywhere, I'm putting them in the office. I've got, I've got baskets of like paper flowers, I've got other baskets, I've got baskets with my name on it . . . it, it, that itself is rewarding and just to know that they really appreciate me and I've got the comments book now as well which some of the comments in there are amazing, you know.

However, staff satisfaction was not simply a result of mutual recognition. Often it flowed from quite the opposite—from their differences. Alana, who above described the detainee's backgrounds as reinforcing her sense of self, went on to explain her emotional response to the men in her care. 'It's interesting', she reflected, 'people's lives, the way they've unravelled. I mean, this guy that I was talking about, he told me that he used to be like into drugs and things like that and how he got himself out of drugs. And you're sort of like you know, "his life's like a film"' (DCO, TH). In this account, Alana's interactions with otherness and difference rather than alienating, stimulated and energized her. In words that were echoed throughout the staff interviews, she stated, 'It's very interesting. People are interesting, you know, and you know, every day is different. There's not one day that's the same' (DCO, TH).

Such a response to alterity appears at first glance to be quite distinct from the contempt expressed earlier by Dick and John. In both cases, however, the officers objectify the detainees, effectively denying their shared humanity. As such, this view often went hand in hand with a staged indifference. At Morton Hall, for instance, fieldnotes record,

> Fry and Windsor units have an office in the entrance hall for the officers. When the doors are closed detainees have to knock and wait. This keeps the distance between the officers and detainees. The officers don't seem to be too patient about detainees not knocking. They also don't allow detainees to linger at the windows. I was in one of the unit offices this morning. One male officer told a detainee hanging out at one of the windows 'what are you, an officer? No. Sod off then!' (Fieldnotes, May 2012).

At other times, conflict between staff and detainees was more spontaneous. In Yarl's Wood, Alla described conflict in the dining hall, when a DCO intervened in a dispute between two detainees:

> One of the women was given two spoons of rice and that was not enough for her. Some people just need more food. So she complained and did raise a voice a little bit. The staff lady told her not to raise her voice, and that her tax money pays for her food. That annoyed all the other women who started making a big fuss and throwing the food on the floor. Everyone reacted together (Uganda, YW).

Indeed, many staff believed that they had to endure far more aggressive behaviour than their counterparts in prison, behaviour that shaped their interactions with those under their care. Dickson was direct: 'Some of these guys are very abusive, very aggressive, very violent.' As a result, he thought staff ought to be careful and try to minimize the possibility of discord. 'I think it's best to think of ourselves as professional friends', he said. 'We need to ask and engage them. When you do that, the men can open up and tell you lots of stories.' Yet, such interactions could not be genuine, he hastened to add, 'since most of them lie' (DCO, CB). Professional friends, in other words, are not really friends at all.

There was some variation among the centres in the survey responses, which were also apparent in the fieldwork. Overall, men confined in IRC Brook House felt they were treated less humanely than the women in Yarl's

Wood or men in Tinsley House. They also reported higher levels of dissatisfaction with the custodial staff, whom they perceived to be less honest and fair than staff elsewhere. Brook House detainees struggled to comprehend staff, and found it harder to make themselves understood than those in Yarl's Wood and Tinsley House (Bosworth and Kellezi, 2012).

Since completing the fieldwork, Brook House has undergone significant changes in its staffing and approach. However, at the time of the research, it was still recovering from its first two years of operation that had been marred by a series of violent disturbances. Detainees lit fires on units, attacked staff, and refused to return to their rooms for the evening. Arvil, who had worked at Brook House during its most tumultuous period, before transferring to Tinsley House, described its effect on his sense of self. 'At Brook House I got . . . I didn't realise, but I probably got myself into a state, because involved in a lot of bad things, witnessed a lot of bad things. It come to a point, I wasn't even aware I was hitting my wife in bed' (DCO, TH).

Notwithstanding an official view that matters had been resolved, many staff in Brook House appeared to be nervous and inexperienced (HMIP, 2010). The institutional anxiety was further evident in the design of the wing unit offices, where the desks had been built up so high that they were awkward to see over. In my fieldnotes I describe them as 'five feet high'. At five foot two inches that meant I had to stand on my tiptoes and crane my neck to talk to staff sitting below. Officers had effectively barricaded themselves in; a decision they blamed on the detainees, who, they said, otherwise grabbed office stationery or crowded their space. On many of my visits to the living unit, staff remained cloistered in the office, leaving only one individual in the common area to answer questions, assist the men on the block, or join them in a game of table tennis. Thus, although most of the detainees were taller than me, and could have seen over the ledge, the message communicated remained the same: do not bother us.

While most day-to-day interactions between staff and detainees were informal, IRCs had also created a range of official mechanisms for communicating with and eliciting detainee views. Whereas the centre managers at Campsfield House and Morton Hall chaired weekly detainee consultation sessions, which any man could attend along with the designated detainee representatives and various members of the SMT and the IMB, Yarl's Wood ran a range of groups. At the first two, the topic of the agenda shifted, enabling a regular consideration of issues such as food, equipment, religious provision and, other services. In contrast, Yarl's Wood attempted to hive off matters into specific committees. They also ran nationality-specific events. As my fieldnotes record, however, none had a very good turn out. 'Chinese women welfare focus meeting. Nobody comes, only Tina who was (a) personally requested and (b) has something she wants to deal with' (Fieldnotes, July 2010). The following month: 'The centre organised a focus group for Pakistani women to cover impact of flooding in Pakistan, plans for charity. Nobody came, so the Welfare Officer rounded some women up: two came, four staff' (Fieldnotes, August 2010).

A much smaller group of custodial officers oversee the uniformed members of staff. Known collectively as the 'Senior Management Team' or SMT, they include the Centre Manager, the Deputy Centre Manager and then, usually, Heads of security, operations, activities, healthcare. These men and women do not wear uniforms and spend much of their day physically apart from the detainees, sequestered on the senior management corridor, attending meetings and liaising with the Home Office (whom they refer to as their 'client' or 'customer'). They do spend some of their day talking to DCOs and DCMs as well as walking around the centres, although their visibility in the centres varied considerably.

Some of the Senior Management Team rise through the ranks from the uniformed staff within IRCs, others have moved from private prisons, or, on occasion, from other sectors of the private custody business. All but one of the centre managers I interviewed were former prison governors, with experience in public sector and private prisons.[9]

In a number of the centres, DCOs expressed considerable resentment towards their superior officers. Typically, their complaints centred on mundane issues like rostering, pay, and holiday scheduling. Such practical matters were exacerbated by a widespread view that their efforts were not appreciated. At Colnbrook, Mahmoud moaned about having to work three out of four weekends. Promotions were scarce, he said, and staff felt pressured by being constantly evaluated. Some DCOs were frustrated by a perceived lack of institutional support. 'Management and UKBA tell us to make sure that detainees are doing things', Dickson reported, 'but then

---

9. The exception was the centre manager at the time at Campsfield House who had moved into his role from one in human resources in GEO. When he left his post (and GEO), to put together an alternative bid for Campsfield's contract on behalf of another company, (MITIE) he was replaced by his deputy, who had previously been Head of Residence at HMP Grendon.

they don't give us the power to make them do it. For example, the men sometimes refuse to produce an ID card. But what can we do?' (DCO, CB).

Few admitted to aspiring to a place in the Senior Management Team. As Alana put it, 'I've done the control room, I've done detainee reception, I was a fire officer for four years, I've, you know, I've seen, I've done everything that I wanted to do, to gain the experience and the knowledge, but I don't want to be somebody's boss, I don't want to lead somebody. I'm quite happy being part of the team' (DCO, TH). Allen, her colleague at Tinsley House agreed. 'I've been offered manager's side of things', he claimed, 'but I can't (whispers), I can't do that. No it's, just float along, do the job' (DCO, TH).

Even those who aspired to more were not always aiming at a career in custody. Ammon, for example, saw a range of options in his future:

> Someone was saying to me that they wanted to go into the enforcement team at UKBA. You can use it as a stepping-stone to get into the police force, prison service. You know, it's quite, for some people it's quite, looks quite good on people's CV. Because obviously with us, we get the Home Office stamp, and, you know, that counts for a lot, especially like fire brigade, police force. That looks quite good on the CV. So, you know, some people do use it for that. And we have been told, you know, great stepping-stone if that's, you know, that's what you want to get into. So there are options, a lot of options out there, you know. If it doesn't work it out the way you want it to work out, you've got other options to fall back onto. Which is quite good (DCO, TH).

Others were more cynical. Arvil, who had been employed for two years as a custody officer, originally at Brook House before being transferred to Tinsley House, took a dim view of his job and its security. 'I just see it at the moment, it's a job, pays my bills', he declared scornfully.

> In today's climate nobody knows whether they've got a job from one minute to another. You've only got to have a couple of comment, racist comments made against you, and it could be quite tricky. Because, you know, right or wrong, it's, it's a job you do have to be careful with in who you talk to. You know, because there's always gonna be somebody who's gonna be, make allegations somewhere along the line. So I've really got no, no plans. I just take it, the job day by day (DCO, TH).

While reflecting the upshot of a particular incident—where an officer at Tinsley House had recently been sacked for responding to a detainee 'with too much force'—Arvil's mistrust and sense of the precarious nature of his job ran deep. Although protected by their citizenship and undeniably more powerful than those they guarded, these low skilled, poorly paid, private sector custody workers were also subject to the vagaries of the post-Fordist marketplace (De Giorgi, 2010; Lerman and Page, 2012). Enforcing border control in the name of the state, they worked long hours without much job security for companies whose priorities rest with their shareholders and the bottom line.

In addition to the custodial staff, each removal centre houses a complement of Home Office employees who interview detainees, passing information between them and their off-site caseworkers. The IRC-based immigration staff members are overseen by the centre's Immigration Manager, who must also monitor and enforce the contract with the private company. Balancing these two sets of responsibilities can be arduous. 'One minute', an Immigration Manager explained, 'you're arguing [with the private company] about fried eggs[10]. . . then you're heavily involved in someone's [a detainee's immigration] case'. Under these circumstances, she admitted, contract monitoring was often placed on the 'back burner. The detainees happen in real time', she pointed out. 'They're right up here in your faces so you have to deal with them. I can sort out the fried eggs tomorrow' (Home Office).

Over 20 months of fieldwork I did not see many Home Office staff walking around the IRCs. Their offices were usually located on a separate corridor, or, as at Morton Hall, outside the walls of the institution itself. Even though the Immigration Manager must regularly inspect the physical conditions of the centre to ensure that information posted on the walls is up to date and the areas clean, I rarely noticed them doing so. In Colnbrook, immigration staff acknowledged that they were nervous about going onto the landings. Although 'the feeling here now is easier and better', than a year ago, when she admitted to being 'fearful about going onto units', Rosie (Home Office, CB) acknowledged that neither she nor her staff were at ease. 'Don't go at lunch time because someone will throw a bun at you!'

---

10. IRCs are contractually obligated to provide certain kinds as well as amounts of food. In this case, the Immigration Manager was referring to an IRC that was failing to offer a sufficient range of cooked eggs for breakfast. It was her job to establish why this was happening and how to resolve it. While she could fine the centre for failing to meet its contract, she preferred to try to fix the problem less formally. In this case, she told me, the lack of fried eggs reflected problems in the staffing in the kitchen and training of detainee-employees. It was soon sorted out.

Elle laughed (Home Office, CB). 'There are certain times of day when men are tense, like lock up', Rosie admitted (Home Office, CB).

The problem, Rosie stated, was simple: 'The type of people we've got here don't want to be here' (Home Office, CB). As a result, the men were often hostile. 'If I'm not called a fucking bitch once a day, it's a surprise', she commented bitterly. 'You have to be thick-skinned to do this job' (Home Office, CB). Elle agreed. 'They are threats to us and our staff', she said. The problem, she went on, was not limited to verbal abuse: 'We are exposed to risk on a daily basis—infections, diseases, fleas' (Home Office, CB).

Under these conditions, it was not surprising to find that detainees in all centres reported poor relations with most immigration staff (Bosworth and Kellezi, 2012). The problem, Haroun professed was that detainees rarely saw them. 'Immigration officer never talked to me here', he said. 'They only call you to tell me what they hear from you. But they never come to associate with people so . . . You hardly know who is an immigration officer because they only call you to say your progress report, or they give you information you should be deported. They're not concerned with anybody' (Gambia, CH). Ava took a different view. From her perspective, the problem with the Home Office staff related to their limited sphere of influence. 'I'd say they were polite', she proposed,

> Not really nice, but they were courteous, go through it, 'any questions? Okay, such and such. If you go back and you think you have some questions, contact us here or do this here, do that here'. Told me what to do, and that was it—two, three minutes on all the occasions I've been there, that's the way it's been. They're just the messengers really . . . they have no control over what happens. They're just the messengers, they just do papers . . . if you have any questions relating to your particular case, I think they forward it to your case worker or something, . . . as I said, they're just the messengers (Cameroon, YW).

On either count, and notwithstanding some exceptions, immigration officers appear to be separate from the detained community.

It was not just the detainees who often found their interactions with onsite immigration staff unsatisfactory, but custody officers did, too. In Morton Hall, where the officers were still adjusting to the new reality of working in an IRC rather than a prison, custody staff were vocal about their troubles with the Home Office. Near the end of the fieldwork, officers became particularly frustrated with the delay in facilitating the removal of a man whose father was dying. The detainee wanted to leave and had provided all the necessary documents. However, immigration staff had failed to obtain a ticket for him. The custody officers were furious. 'You know that bloke whose dad's dying? I'm still trying to get UKBA to sort a travelling document for him. I told UKBA two days ago they haven't sorted it out. They've got his passport and he's still waiting. They're crap, absolute crap', one officer said. Another staff member, sought to resolve the problem over the phone, calling the immigration officers working next door. 'Sorry to be a pest', she murmured diffidently, 'but you remember the man whose father is dying? We asked you about it yesterday . . .' She finished the call. 'I think I'll go over there and put some pressure on them. I'll put on my best sad face' (NGO, MH).

It was not just the bureaucratic inefficiency that frustrated custodial staff, but also the immigration officers' inexperience of working in a custodial environment. Immigration officers, they complained, were too rigid, too often fearful of ex-offenders, naïve and in their emphasis on compliance with immigration matters, unhelpful in securing day-to-day management and good order. In their narrow focus on immigration matters, they argued, such figures compromised the capacity of custody officers to govern and control, impinging on their realm with matters located elsewhere.

In their interactions with immigration officers, staff and detainees reveal the complex power relations enveloping the IRC and shaping relations within them. Unlike prisons, where those who work directly with the prisoners—officers and psychologists—have the most influence over their experience, in detention, power rests with the Home Office. Indeed, although the staff member above sought to speed up the immigration process through a personal intervention, putting on 'my best sad face', she was unlikely to succeed for the reasons identified earlier by Ava; the onsite Home Office employees have little influence over the time it takes for cases to be resolved, nor, they assured me, its outcome. 'We are inbetweeners', Elle admitted with some regret in Colnbrook. 'It is not my fault that someone didn't get bail' (Home Office, CB).[11]

The final figure in detention works offsite. Immigration caseworkers rarely if ever meet the women and men whose fate they determine, and usually communicate through the onsite immigration staff.[12] This system, in

---

11. Bail is determined by an immigration judge, just as the decision to temporarily admit can only be made offsite by the caseworker. Or, more accurately, by their caseworker's supervisor. Whereas the decision to deport or remove can be made by a fairly low-level immigration officer, decisions to release can only be authorized by senior staff within the Home Office. (For a critical account of this system as it pertains to ex-prisoners, see HMIP and ICIBI, 2012.)

12. On emerging research into the decision-making of caseworkers see Bosworth and Bradford, forthcoming. See also HMIP and ICIBI, 2012.

which the most important decisions occur elsewhere, gives detention centres a peculiar cast and one that bears some similarity to that in other sites of liminal confinement including death row and prison remand wings where uncertainty is legion and the pains of confinement are profound (Abu-Jamal, 1996; HMIP, 2012b). Like prisoners awaiting trial or anticipating execution, detainees live temporally split lives, enduring their confinement in the present, while constantly looking ahead, fearful of what is yet to come.

Conclusion

There are many layers to the detention 'community'. Notwithstanding the immigration officer's snug view of female companionship in Yarl's Wood with which this chapter opened, detainees are often divided from one another by language, culture, and geography. Unlike prisons, IRCs are not easily interpreted, or governed, through the lens of conviviality (Earle and Phillips, 2012; Phillips, 2012). Levels of trust are low and emotions run high. Custodial staff also report tensions among their own cohort, particularly with officers of higher grades. Everyone's working relationship with the Home Office can be combative. Nonetheless, for the most part, people rub along together, however uneasily. The diversity of the population is both a barrier to congenial relations and, sometimes, a factor in them. Staff and detainees found variety stimulating as well as alienating.

Yet, IRCs are volatile. Detainees regularly refuse food, raise their voices, and self-harm. Over the past decade there have been many escapes and large-scale disturbances. Staff have limited options. 'The officers . . . can't do anything', Allen complained. 'They can't give them extra time. They can't do anything. They can't take away their privileges. Nothing. Because they're not . . . They're only detained, they're not incarcerated' (DCO, TH). In the next two chapters, I will direct my attention to these paradoxes, seeking to explain the nature and effect of the uncertainty within such places. If prison sociologists are right, the everyday interactions between staff and detainees reveal institutions structured by ambivalence, where people come together, not always understanding or recognizing one another. Such uncertainty is both the form and effect of power in detention, always and everywhere an uncomfortable and uneasy mode of governance.

6

Uncertainty, identity, and power in detention

Today I overheard a Namibian woman on the phone calling the Immigration Advisory Service: 'Hello? I'm calling from Yarl's Wood. I need your help.' Straight to the point. A call into the dark (Fieldnotes, August 2010).

You know, you can't live a life, not knowing what's gonna happen tomorrow. You can't. The door is locked. You don't know what's gonna happen tomorrow (Richard, Zimbabwe, MH).

IRCs are uncertain and inconsistent places. Designated sites for foreigners awaiting removal, deportation or the determination of their asylum case, they are justified by and legitimate a politics of identity, in which 'foreigners' are dangerous and unwelcome,[1] no matter what their connection to Britain and in which they are nationalized as Pakistani or Chinese etc, broad categories that elide regional, class, gender, and ethnic variance. Nonetheless, and notwithstanding the considerable resources of the state in identifying and expelling detainees, it is not always easy to force people to leave. Identity, it turns out, is not only a slippery concept, but also hard to prove.

As we have seen, detainees challenge their identification through legal and informal means. They may espouse an equivalent form of citizenship based on a moral hierarchy (as workers, mothers, Christians), duration of

---

1. See, for instance, Home Secretary Theresa May's speech at the 2013 Conservative party conference in which she not only manages to connect terrorism to immigration control, but makes it clear that in her view ex-prisoners are not entitled to the protections of the Human Rights Act <http://www.ein.org.uk/news/home-secretary-announce-massive-shake-immigration-law>.

British residence, or through rhetorical appeals to human rights ideals. However circumscribed in legal terms, such bids for recognition can unsettle staff, draw detainees together, and act as a powerful coping mechanism. On the other hand, counter-claims and challenges can also make matters worse. Failure to 'comply' with the process of identification may alienate custodial and immigration staff, while insistence on an alternative identity can be brushed aside. Narratives of identity sometimes divide detainees from one another, and, when they fail to prevent removal, may lead to greater disappointment and frustration.

In this chapter I concentrate on such discrepancies within IRCs and their unsettling and uncertain effects. Drawing once again on the words of staff and detainees, I explore how both groups cope with the fickle nature of life in detention, and how insecurity shapes their identity and sense of self. In so doing, I suggest that, while such inconsistencies justify detention and flow from it, the confusion within such places reveals disquiet and dissonance about border control and the exercise of power that it entails. Uncertainty, in other words, is both a means of governance and a potential site of resistance.

Unlike the 'responsibilized' subjects of criminal justice, who, however attenuated, remain part of the community and retain some agency, detainees, with their status as 'strangers', by definition cannot belong. Stripped of their past, with their future denied, they are always already destined for elsewhere. Their uncertain status is the source (and price) of our security. Ambiguous figures, as strangers they are one of the means by which we know ourselves, a symbolic mechanism for carving out a wider British identity (Ahmed, 2000; Bosworth and Guild, 2008). In the detention centres, however, identity is not experienced metaphorically. It is painful and confusing to be labelled a stranger and unwelcome. Many contest it. Some succeed. Bringing criminological literature and feminist theory to bear on first-hand accounts I begin to assemble a critique of IRCs grounded in the words, experiences, and identities of those within the centres, a task to which the remainder of this book is devoted.

Uncertainty, risk, and identity: sovereign power in a global age

Scholars across a number of fields have been asserting for decades that we live in uncertain times. Our historical period, they say, is shaped by economic, social, and environmental insecurity (Douglas and Wildavsky, 1982; Beck, 1992; 1999; Garland, 2001; Hannah-Moffat and O'Malley, 2005). Many of the risks we face are global: they include nuclear weapons, terrorism, the unequal availability of food and water, peak oil, the upsurge in drug resistant illnesses, and a host of potentially lethal new viruses. Globalization and mass mobility are the outcome and the cause of insecurity (Young, 1999; Melossi, 2003; Aas, 2012; Huysmans, 2006; Sassen, 1999; Bauman, 1998), as factors simultaneously enhancing and eroding the power of the sovereign (nation) state (Garland, 1996; Bosworth and Guild, 2008).

Governments and the private sector have responded to uncertainty in many ways, evident in the proliferation of forms of expert knowledge, actuarial tools, and insurance (O'Malley, 2004; Hacking, 1990; Feeley and Simon, 1992; 1994; Baker and Simon, 2002; Ericson, 2008), new practices of policing (Ericson and Haggerty, 1997), criminalization and punishment (Zedner, 2007a; Ramsay, 2010; Garland, 2001; Hannah-Moffat, 2005), the rise of punitive sentiment (Bottoms, 1983; Ericson, 2007; Pratt, 2007), 'data mining', and the endless collection, collation, and retention of information on us all (Schinkel, 2011). Through such methods, states and private enterprise seek not only to tighten their control over present dangers, but also to target the future, minimizing potential threats (Zedner, 2007; Ramsay, 2012).

Such practices and their accompanying discourses of dangerousness, risk, and security, are now so embedded in our social institutions they appear largely self-evident and uncontested. Yet, an obsession with risk and security has had a profoundly deleterious effect, altering our bonds with one another by shifting our relationship with the state (Zedner, 2003; 2007b; 2010; 2013; see also Cole, 2003; 2007; Loader and Walker, 2007). As we trade away our legal protections in the name of security, the basis of citizenship, and therefore, who we are, is irrevocably damaged.

Through risk assessment tools and other technologies, as well as in the legal bargains they strike, governments seek to create governable, or 'responsibilized' subjects (Garland, 1996; Rose, 2000; 2001; Bosworth, 2007b; 2009). Such subjects must regulate themselves in order to avoid sanctions. These attempts to 'inscribe the norms of self-control more deeply into the soul of each citizen' (Rose, 2000: 1409), entail a psychic cost as intimacy and self-identity, previously considered outside the gaze of the state, are opened to its sphere of influence, thereby hollowing out notions of privacy and authenticity (Giddens, 1991; see also Foucault, 1978). Those who refuse the deal, or who are excluded from its logic, as well as those who are unable to acquiesce with its requirements, are inexorably cast as the appropriate target of increasingly punitive interventions and social exclusion (Rose, 2000).

In terms of border control, a concern with risk has recast migration as a 'security problem' (Bigo, 2002; Huysmans and Squire, 2009). The effects of this discursive and legal shift have been manifold, as states have made it increasingly more difficult to enter or to remain (Huysmans, 2006; Zedner, 2005). Such concerns explain how it is that people get to detention. Detainees, marked by their skin colour, nationality, irregular immigration status, criminal record, or poverty as risky, are easy targets of state intervention and exclusion. So, too, discourses of risk and dangerousness easily attach to detention centres due to their physical resemblance to prison (see, inter alia, Stumpf, 2006; 2013; Aliverti, 2012a; 2012b; 2013; Zedner, 2010; Bosworth and Guild, 2008; Bigo, 2002; Huysmans, 2006).

Once inside, however, the logic of risk begins to dissipate. Unlike prisoners, who, having failed to police themselves, must be exhorted to do so while incarcerated through work, education, drug treatment, and the pains of imprisonment (Bosworth, 2007b), detainees are not asked to change. While some work and education are available, they are only offered to pass the time. Similarly, despite being held in secure institutions, detainees undergo no formal security classification. The centres themselves, notwithstanding considerable material differences among them, are likewise not allocated security levels. There is no official pathway through the immigration estate, even as people circulate around it regularly.

Always already deportable, forever marked as strangers (Ahmed, 2000), detainees have no destination other than 'home'. Detention centres, in this view, are part of the 'Ban-opticon' (Bigo, 2008). Their task is simply 'return to sender' (Broeders, 2010).

These characteristics of detention have been the subject of previous chapters in which I have demonstrated their paradoxical and contested nature. Notwithstanding the fierce rhetoric about them, removal centres, I have shown, have no straightforward outcome or effect. Sites of identification, they struggle to reduce a multitude of identities to the single axis of citizenship. Designed to facilitate deportation or removal, they witness the return of around half their population each year to the wider British community. Under these circumstances, their organizing principle as well as their mode of governance, is not risk, but uncertainty (see also Griffiths, 2013). The question that remains, is what is its effect?

From uncertainty to estrangement

One of the defining aspects of a period of detention is that nobody knows for sure how long it will last. Notwithstanding case law, and immigration rules that call for confinement to be limited to those whose deportation is 'imminent', some people are kept in custody even when it is quite clear that their deportation or removal cannot proceed due to a lack of documents or the political conditions in their country of origin.[2] Those who are issued removal directions may delay their departure by filing fresh asylum claims or a judicial review. Others refuse to get on the plane, earning a short respite. Still others resist on board, a mortifying and dangerous practice that, on commercial flights may prevent departure, but on charter ones, where deportees are outnumbered by as many as three to one by escort staff, is unlikely to have much effect.

Until intervention from the Home Affairs Select Committee, following complaints from HMIP (2012d), the Home Office routinely over-booked flights, leaving detainees unsure whether they would actually leave the country or not. While this practice should have been suspended, so that no-one should be sent to the airport without a seat on a plane, HMIP (2014a) continues to find evidence of it. In any case, in the week leading up to a charter flight more women and men maybe issued with removal directions than end up leaving, since case workers assume that a certain proportion will avoid expulsion.[3]

The lack of clarity over the duration of confinement has a number of effects, from the design of the buildings and their daily regime to how officers and detainees value themselves. It also influences how people get along with one another and how they perceive the outcome of other people's cases. While detainees often described the deportation of others as unnerving and sad, its regular occurrence an unwelcome reminder of their likely future, some felt their odds of being allowed to remain improved if others were expelled. 'It feels like a lottery here sometimes', Ania admitted. 'So I think that if ten people get deported that that will improve *my* chances of staying' (Poland, YW).

2. On 23 October, 2013, for instance in *R (on the application of Giwa) v Secretary of State for the Home Department* [2013] EWHC 3189 (Admin), the High Court ruled that 53 months of detention pending removal was lawful but 'pushed to the limit of what is capable of being considered reasonable', in a decision that seemed far removed from Woolf's opinion in the 1984 *Hardial Singh* case.
3. For an official account of a removals process, see HMIP, 2014b.

Without knowing for sure how long anyone would be with them, staff assured me, it was too difficult to devise detailed programmes of work or education. Open university, widely available in prison, was impossible they claimed; certified training courses, very difficult. Even a structured art class would be challenging when you did not know who would attend each day, while psychological counselling for sexual violence or other trauma would be pointless. You simply would not want to 'open a can of worms' like that, Reginald, a counsellor at Yarl's Wood proclaimed, unless you knew how long you had to work with the women. To do otherwise would be dangerous, he thought, leaving them more vulnerable than ever.

Although usually couched in terms of the present, the real barrier to the regime, a senior member of staff suggested, lay in the future. The detainees were not coming back, so why bother doing anything with them? In this line of reasoning, as in so many others in detention, the institution was often compared to the prison. 'There is a logic to prisons that make total sense', Henry argued. 'You do education because prisons rehabilitate and they will be going into the community. But here they are just going to be removed' (SMT, YW). For those allegedly without a future in Britain, day-to-day activities were not only hard to justify, Henry made clear, they were difficult to imagine. Why would you bother?

Centres are also hampered by their design. It is not just their securitization, which made internal circulation awkward, but also that many centres had been deliberately built to hold people briefly. Their layout was not conducive to work, education, or leisure activities.[4] 'Brook House', Nicholas observed, 'is lacking in outside space, quality outside space and activity rooms inside'. The reason, he said, was that 'it was designed to be a very short term centre and in reality it isn't a short term centre at all' (SMT, BH). Although keenly aware of the problem, the centre was finding it difficult to solve. 'We've only got so many rooms that are gyms and one library and where would these things take place?' Nicholas went on, anxiously. 'We can't take over the courtyards to run volleyball or football all the time because that's the only outside spaces that most of the guys can go to. So at a football match we'll maybe get twenty or thirty people out there, but what do the other three hundred and seventy five do?' (SMT, BH).

---

4. Needless to say, Category B prisons such as HMP Peterborough, built to a similar design, manage to run regimes. However, they operate with more staff and, as is the point, within a different custodial framework in which work, education, and treatment is expected and in which the residence of the population is more stable.

Notwithstanding their considerable limitations, all centres do offer some work and education. Increasingly, they seek to assist with counselling as well. In so doing, IRCs and those within them weave an awkward and contradictory path, between the Home Office's insistence that they are not destinations in their own right, and their day-to-day reality as a place of residence, no matter how long, for hundreds of unhappy women and men.

'You need to do something with them while you've got them', Scot argued, 'especially if they're going to be here for a long time. Just for their own sanity, you know? Anybody would get bored, shut up in any-where with nothing to do after probably a week, never mind a month or two months or three months. There's only so much you can do to amuse yourself before you get too bored, isn't it?' (SMT, YW). Ania agreed. Life in Yarl's Wood, without the structured regime of a prison was boring. Time slowed. 'In prison', she said, 'you know what to do every day. You know what will happen so you just get on with it and the days pass by' (Poland, YW).

Henry, a member of the Senior Management Team, offered a different interpretation. 'All those extra things we do', he asserted, 'like knitting club, and activities we do basically because they keep the women occupied and busy, and busy women are easier to control' (SMT, YW). Tapping into a familiar custodial narrative, Henry saw danger in idleness. The regime, in his view, had to be a carefully calibrated means of managing the popula-tion. Activities also needed to fit into the budget.

Like Scot's interpretation, Henry's view of detention was grounded in the day-to-day life of the institution. Primarily concerned with governing the present, these two officers seemed wilfully unaware of the detainees' preoccupation with their future, or their sorrow about the rupture with their past. Boredom, though very real, paled into insignificance relative to the uncertainty detainees felt about where they were going and what they were leaving behind. Such emotions took their toll. 'I'm so tired', Ziggy declared when talking of his time in Brook House. 'I'm so tired' (Jamaica, BH). Unwilling to relinquish his children, and thus refusing to comply with Home Office demands that he do so, he lost weight, fought with his girlfriend over the phone, and sank further into depression. The days stretched on.

Not knowing when they might be given their travel date made rou-tine interactions with onsite immigration officers upsetting. 'When you're here, when you're detained', Arah described, 'you don't know how long you're going to be here for. Yeah, you don't know . . . so each time they call you [to] legals . . . people start crying . . . Because nothing good comes from legal, nothing good' (Jamaica, YW). Such anxiety and lack of certainty made it exhausting for many to plan or even to imagine life outside the centre. Although some people, like Ava, in a view echoing the official Home Office perspective on such places, rejected the confines of the centres, pronouncing, 'this is just the beginning, this is just a passage. This is nothing to me. There's plenty out there for me, I just can't wait' (Cameroon, YW), more often those I spoke to were troubled and anxious. For them, the uncertainty of detention blocked their ability to imagine prospects beyond it. 'Right now, when I plan for the future', Richard confessed, 'I don't know. I'm scared' (Zimbabwe, MH). 'My mother is dead, my father is dead', Ishmail wailed. 'I was an only child. Who will look after me?' (Pakistan, CB).

Many officers were sympathetic. At the most basic level, they appreciated, doubt affected how detainees used their time in the centre. 'They can't plan their day', Mary pointed out, 'because they don't know how long they're here for' (DCO, CH). Why bother interacting with others, or taking advantage of the limited regime if you are unsure from one day to the next how long your stay will be? Uncertainty, in this view, explained why many women and men spent most of their time in their rooms.

Ambiguity over the duration of detention, staff acknowledged, was more than just logistical, however. It was also emotionally taxing. 'The biggest problem the ladies have', Ryan noted, 'is the uncertainty of not knowing when they're getting out. Be it onto a plane or into the community. If they knew, then they would, they would be able to deal with it better . . . they need to know what's happening to them . . . that is the biggest issue for them' (SMT, YW).

The lack of resolution about the outcome or duration of detention, this officer contended, was not just a problem for the detainees. It had a wider effect, defining the institution itself. Referring to it as 'the biggest difference between this environment and a prison environment', Ryan articulated a view common at all levels of the institution: 'you go to prison, you've been sentenced, you know before you even walk through the door into the prison when you're coming out again. Here, the ladies come into here and they haven't got a clue when they're getting out of here. And that is the hardest thing.' Lela, a colleague from Yarl's Wood, was in accord: 'The most difficult thing they deal with is the not knowing how long they are going to be here . . . when you go to prison you know how long your sentence is but here they don't know' (DCM, YW). Such uncertainty, moreover, she contended, was profoundly unfair. 'I know of a woman who spent her time in prison and they released her early. Then they brought her here and she spent as long in here as she spent in prison. That is not fair. Why release her early and then make her serve a longer sentence in here?' (DCM, YW).

Indeed, while staff at all levels and in the Home Office were quick to point out that lengthy periods of confinement could sometimes be caused by detainees refusing to cooperate, I did not find anyone who supported open ended detention. Instead, most believed that it should be capped at six months, and, where possible, that people should be held for much shorter periods.[5] 'It should be 6 months, no more', Leah attested. 'Then they should tag them and release them. They can call them back in when they get their travel documents' (DCO, YW). Ryan, her superior officer, who had worked for many years in prisons, concurred: 'They just need to change the law to get rid of indefinite detention', he said. 'We don't hold any prisoners like that. It doesn't make sense' (SMT, YW).

In our conversations about return, detainees often worried about logistical matters. Uncertainty about a departure date made it difficult to arrange plans with relatives, work, or housing at the other end. Resident in the UK since childhood, David was unsure how or where to find accommodation in Kampala and planned like a 'tourist' to commence his return abroad at a hotel. 'I told them just to drop me at a 5-star hotel', he joked. 'I'm a tourist, innit? That's secure' (Uganda, CB).

As David appreciated, leaving the UK was rarely the end of a person's voyage. Not only may asylum seekers be sent back to third countries under the Dublin III Regulation,[6] but even when detainees are returned to their country of origin, they are unlikely to be transported directly to their hometown or village. Flights set them down in major airports, leaving

---

5. Indeed, it is worth recalling that Britain is the sole member of the EU with no upper time limit to detention. It has not signed up to an 18-month maximum under the 2008 European Returns Directive (Directive 2008/115/EC). Denmark, which also did not sign the Directive, has nonetheless implemented its guidance into national law.

6. This agreement, between European member states establishes the procedures of a European-wide asylum process, in which asylum seekers can be returned (subject to Human Rights protections) to their original point of entry to the EU. It superseded an earlier agreement, known as Dublin II which had itself replaced the Dublin Convention <http://eur-lex.europa.eu/LexUriServ/LexUriServ.do?uri=OJ:L:2003:050:0001:0010: EN:PDF>.

internal transportation up to them. Plans they may have made do not always work out.[7] 'One of the women who left the other days was told she would get £2000–3000 for going back but she only got £100. And when she arrived in Nigeria they would not let her in without money', Fawn reported.[8] 'So she had to give them the equivalent of £70 to be let in the country. And it costs £50 to go from airport to the village where she lives. She had to call on old friends that she had not heard for many years to get the money to go back home. And she ended up in a village and had to learn how to work the land again. That is the worst place to get back to. The worst kind of poverty. It is slavery' (Nigeria, YW).

As we have already seen, men and women were often concerned about the manner of their return. Those who had been unexpectedly arrested at work, after a traffic stop, or while signing on as asylum claimants, had usually been unable to recuperate their possessions. For them, Gena explained, 'is not that being deported is a problem. It's like going with respect is, you know, is a thing for them—very important . . . Three people have told me the same thing. Say: "I'm going to Ghana, but only if you know, I get a chance to just go home, get my things. That's all I need, nothing else more than that. That's why I need bail." But even bail is not given to people' (India, YW). Fawn was adamant: returning without any gifts would look bad. 'When you go back from here people expect you would have a lot of money', she maintained, 'It is so shameful that I have no money to show for these 3 years. They will say that if I have no money I must have been a prostitute or broken the law' (Nigeria, YW). Bassam agreed. 'If I go home alone, just in this [gestures to his outfit] after having been away for eight years', he asked, 'what will people think?' (Algeria, BH). Returning without gifts would prolong and exacerbate the stigma of detention. It would

---

7. In this project although I remain in contact with a few former detainees, I did not follow people home. However, claims like this one, that money which had been promised by the British state to those who agreed to return, did not materialize were commonplace among detainees and staff. Elsewhere, academic accounts of the deportation experience show similar practical difficulties of return and readjustment (Brotherton and Barrios, 2009; 2011; Drotbohm, 2011).

8. Fawn is referring here to AVR, assisted voluntary return, a scheme administered by an international organization (IOM at the time of the research, Refugee Action at the time of writing), by which certain detainees who agree to return are offered a financial incentive to go. This scheme exists throughout Europe and beyond. More information about it can be found at the Home Office website <http://www.ukba.homeoffice.gov.uk/aboutus/workingwithus/workingwithasylum/assistedvoluntaryreturn/avrim/>.

change how others perceived them, and in so doing, would affect how they saw themselves.

Some, like Richard, were scared of the process itself. 'I don't know what's gonna happen to me', he murmured. 'I've heard people been cuffed up, put on a plane by force' (Zimbabwe, MH). Such fears were exacerbated in October 2010, when G4S escort officers suffocated long-term British resident, Jimmy Mubenga, whom they alleged, was resisting his removal on board a British Airways flight destined for Angola. Although G4S was not prosecuted under the Corporate Manslaughter Act, Mubenga's death was subsequently ruled to be an unlawful killing. The following year, the coroner, Karon Monaghan published a damning report that included evidence of 'pervasive racism' within the company (Monaghan, 2013). In March 2014, the Crown Prosecution Service (CPS) announced they were charging three G4S guards with manslaughter (M. Taylor, 2014).

At Yarl's Wood, the management issued a letter in an attempt to alleviate women's fears.

> As some of you may have heard from TV and news reports Mr Jimmy Mubenga sadly passed away on the twelfth of October whilst on an escort removal. This, like any loss of life, is a tragedy and we have the deepest sympathy for his family and friends. We understand that this news may have caused you additional distress during a difficult time in your lives. As usual, please speak to our staff if there is anything we can do to help and support you. We would like to invite you to make use of our counselling services through the additional drop-in clinics running next week, venue, central counsellor office, day, Monday, Wednesday and Friday, time, ten AM to four PM (Serco, YW).

Such official reassurance had little impact, however, the women reported. Not only did they mistrust the authorities but, in any case, in each centre before and after Mubenga was killed, other stories circulated of ill treatment during attempted removals.

At Yarl's Wood, Arah had recently been returned from Heathrow covered in bruises when she refused to leave without her property. Whereas officials maintained she had been disruptive and violent, hurting herself in the process, she declared the wounds to be a result of a beating she sustained inside the escort van. She was not the only one to make such claims. Emilia, the young woman who had been victimized by her Brazilian boyfriend in the UK before securing his criminal conviction, dreaded return to Brazil, where she feared his friends and family would retaliate. Having been given removal directions, she was told she would be able to talk one last time to immigration at the airport to plead her case. 'They ask you if you want to go. I know that, we all know that', Emilia stated indignantly.

> But when I got there see nobody. I stay in van from 9 to 3 pm. Nobody talk to me. Then two men and a woman [escorts from G4S] take me to plane. They grab my neck. They twist my arm with those things [handcuffs]. Yeah, I scream and cry 'I no go back!' So the pilot, he says 'I do not take her'. And they bring me back here. Then a mans comes to my room to take photo of my arm. I say 'I feel bad, my head hurts'. He say, 'ok you go to doctor tomorrow'. But that doctor, he no good. He racist. He don't ask how I feel. He just ask me why I came to England. He no help. I don't know why (Brazil, YW).

The implication of such treatment, Arah, concluded was obvious: 'They are trained harshly to treat us they way they do' (Jamaica, YW).

Less controversially, yet painful nonetheless, were accounts of individuals who wished to leave, but were unable to depart due to administrative error or delay. Already, we have seen the story of Pam, an elderly woman from Nigeria, who was held in Yarl's Wood for over six months, despite agreeing to leave as soon as she arrived from prison. 'I am tired', she complained, 'I just want to go home. I don't care about applying for anything. I don't want anything. I just want to go home' (Nigeria, YW). Pam was not resisting deportation, instead, her travel documents had been mislaid by the authorities when she applied for voluntary return. The setback was excruciating. 'What have I done to deserve this?' she cried out one day. 'They caught me with false documents and they took me to prison and I did my time. Why are they still keeping me here? I want to go home. What have I done to deserve this and being punished? There are people who don't want to go and they send them back, but I want to go and they keep me here. I have been in here five months' (Nigeria, YW).[9]

While the cause of Pam's protracted stay was known, in other cases, the reasons for delay were unclear, creating yet another source of institutional uncertainty. 'You just get stuck in this place', Richard asserted. 'You get people that are wanting to go back to their country, and they're stuck here. So you just don't understand where he's going and where he's coming from' (Zimbabwe, MH). In both circumstances, detainees (and some staff) often attributed their treatment to malice. 'Once you annoy immigration', Asa

9. Eventually, in December 2011, Pam was finally returned to Nigeria. We have since lost touch.

grimly proclaimed, 'by refusing to go on a flight, or transfer to another centre, they will do anything they can to pay you back, like cancelling flights for those who want to go, and sending back those that what to stay without giving them chance to appeal their decision' (Kenya, TH).

These examples capture the affective dimension of the particular configuration of power, identity, and uncertainty inherent in IRCs. A lack of agency hurts. It is frightening and frustrating, confusing and alienating.

In order to manage their pain, fear, and confusion, women and men look for an explanation. Some, like Pam, seek it within: 'what have I done to deserve this?' she demanded (Nigeria, YW). Others (also) look for someone else to blame, differentiating themselves from other less deserving individuals, whom, they claim, have been unfairly treated better.

In their search for explanation, detainees often focus their attention on their immigration caseworker. Such people, whom they rarely meet, can assume monstrous dimensions in their imagination. 'The most horrible person in my case is the case worker', Odaawa averred. 'Even though she had all my documents, my passport, for six months. And she was denying that she had any knowledge. And later she admitted and then sent it to my lawyer in Scotland' (Somalia, CB). Complaints are also racialized. 'My caseworker now is from Jamaica', Agim protested. 'They don't like us. All Africa does not like us. They don't want us Europeans in Britain' (Albania, TH).

In these interpretations, inconsistencies and delays in decision-making appear vindictive rather than disorganized, those confined as innocent victims of the unfair decision-making of bureaucrats.[10] In other ways as well, detainees searched around for 'techniques of neutralisation', a means to 'reject their rejecters' and cope with their confinement (Sykes and Matza, 1957). Some excoriated the British public. 'The British are wicked and selfish, and lazy as well', Waldo angrily proclaimed (Ghana, BH). Others, planned to cut ties altogether. 'Even if I become the president, prime minister of Kenya and they invite me to come here I will never come back', Asa burst out (Kenya, TH). Commonly, women and men appealed to the higher loyalties of human rights norms. 'Okay, keep me in detention or whatever, but treating me like that, you don't have the right really', Giv

---

10. For more on vindictiveness and state power in immigration control (in the US) see Brotherton and Barrios, 2013; on vindictiveness and penal power in the UK, see Young 1999; 2003a.

challenged. 'If you do, if you're saying you do have the right to treat me like that, then the third world countries, you are the worser than them. Because they are dictator. If you are thinking like that, you are dictator as well. But this country, thank God, they claiming they respect the human right law. So what is this all about?' (Iran, CB). Most denied any responsibility for their pathway to detention. 'I didn't come as a criminal from my country', Ridoy pointed out. 'I came as a child. If anything, your, your country and this country have made me the criminal, if that's how they want to label me' (Bangladesh, MH).

Beyond releasing pent up anger, however, such rhetoric had little effect. Border control targets those whose identity has been already fixed as foreign, rather than criminal law, where the identity of offenders is linked to behaviour and can, therefore, change. The mere fact they are in detention is evidence enough of detainees' deportability. Consequently, attempts to deny the power of the state are much less likely to succeed. Under these circumstances, the malice accorded to the Home Office and the wider British public, rather than neutralizing their stigma (Sykes and Matza, 1957; Goffman, 1968), often exacerbated their ontological insecurity and increased the pains of detention.

For many, immigration control felt like betrayal. 'They don't care about the fact that I have been here 15 years and that my family is in exile', Asa cried out indignantly. The state, in his view, was vindictive and deliberately hurtful. 'Why did my caseworker tell the Kenyan High commission that I am an asylum seeker here, when they know that the minimum prison sentence for someone who claims asylum is 2 years of imprisonment?' he wanted to know. 'My mother had health problems and she put money together to go and buy a house for me at the Kenyan border. She died soon after because of worry that I was in here. So UKBA is responsible for the death of my mother' (Kenya, TH). The denial of agency was painful Asa made clear, not just because he was unable to make his own decisions, but because the state had intervened in his intimate relationships, separating him from his family before abandoning him altogether. 'They don't care that I have a son here and will never see him again if I leave! . . . Where I am to go when I arrive there and I have no one, no phone to call anyone and no money?' (Kenya, TH), he demanded pitifully, pleading for help that never came.

As with so many in detention, Asa struggled to reconcile himself to his fate. His options were limited. Detention not only engendered a sense of personal insecurity and sorrow by cutting his intimate ties, but, due to its uncertain duration, was difficult to manage, let alone resist. His asylum case denied, all that Asa could do to register his anger was to refuse to produce the requisite information to obtain travel documents for his flight. In blocking such requests, he merely condemned himself to a longer period of confinement, compounding his vulnerabilities and exacerbating the pains of detention.

In this instance, the utility of the open-ended nature of detention is manifest. Uncertainty can evidently be an effective means of control. Yet Asa's words move us not just because he is unable to act, overpowered by the state. His story is troubling because of its emotional cast. The excision of family ties and his sense of abandonment are hard to ignore. In a liberal democracy the family and our intimate lives are meant to be outside the state's purview, private matters, for us alone. Whereas some populations, prisoners, the poor, children and the mentally ill, exist outside these expectations due to questions over their desert and/or mental capacity, it is not self-evident why the lack of citizenship should justify similar treatment.

It is here that much of the labour of detention occurs and its effects become clear, as those who are foreign are recast as strangers. Gradually, yet intractably, Asa was stripped of those intimate ties which rendered him recognizable and human. His mother was already dead; his 15 years residence discounted, trumped by a criminal conviction. His son, too, was to be denied to him. Finally, after a year in detention, he was deported in the Spring 2011. We have since lost touch.

Conceiving of testimonies in terms of estrangement enables us to revisit the isolation of detention. It illuminates the relational and affective nature of power and offers another explanation of why women and men find it hard to forge bonds with one another in custody, fearful of long-term stigmatization whether or not they are deported. The uncertainty of detention does not just enable the state to rend detainees from their loved ones and from Britain, but it can also change their view of themselves. 'Always being told you are a liar', Amanda pointed out, 'it can push too much down' (Brazil, YW). Her friend Ola agreed, insisting furiously, 'I'm a subject now [of the Home Office], not a person. As a subject we can't say anything' (Brazil, YW). Divided from themselves, it is no surprise that they are often unable to join together with others. Their alienation is humiliating. 'I feel like stranger in this country, feel like shit', Ola exclaimed (Brazil, YW). Such rupture all too often leads to bitterness and rage. 'To some extent, you actually start to feel hatred against the British', Frank observed. 'Because when I came here at first I asked that okay, I accepted me, I'm part of the community, okay everything's working okay. Until now when it comes like this' (Zimbabwe, MH).

Like uncertainty, estrangement has spatial dimensions. We may feel out of place in particular locales or everywhere. Even in detention, certain areas are less alienating than others. The mood in the art and craft rooms, and in the gym and church was often lighter, and staff less formal. In the education corridor, detainees' pictures often adorned the walls. In the mosque at Colnbrook, a man, who had learned calligraphy in Iran, crafted intricate decorations. Outside, columns and a dome have been painted on the walls surrounding its entrance.

Gyms resembled sports areas in other places, sweaty activity accompanied by a loud soundtrack emanating from a radio or CD-player. 'I go to the gym all day' Ania reported,

> Usually I go from ten till twelve in the morning, then from two till five in the afternoon . . . And then I go from half past seven till nine . . . Literally every day. I mean I don't obviously just run non stop for all that time. Sometimes I run or exercise, sometimes I just play sports. But I make sure . . . I'm basically there all the time. Helps me cope, takes the stress out of . . . By the time I get in bed at night I'm so tired I sleep. They say it's good for depression (Poland, YW).

Staff likewise differentiated between certain spaces. 'When I'm in that art room', Leah proudly announced, 'it doesn't even feel like I'm in Yarl's Wood' (DCO, YW). Activities staff described their work in the gym in similar terms, perceiving it as distinct from the rest of detention, a 'normal', positive and happy space. 'Take yesterday at work', Ben remarked happily, 'well I got to play football in the evening, badminton in the morning, I had a bit of cricket and volleyball in the afternoon, I had a workout in a gym, you know what I mean? It's like "You've got any easy life ain't ya?"' (DCO, CH).

Such nonchalance was, in many respects, disingenuous. Just as much as Elle and Rosie, the Home Office employees who would rather be sequestered in their offices than confront the outcome of immigration policy or their role in it and risk having a 'bun thrown at' them, Leah and Ben expended considerable effort in denying their part in the logic of border control. While the art and crafts room was indeed a more informal space than elsewhere, to imagine it did not 'feel like Yarl's Wood', Leah had to ignore the keys around her belt, the locked cabinets in which all equipment was held, available only on request, and the barred window. Ben would have had to do the same. Both, most pertinently, had to overlook the women and men themselves. Their own peace of mind, in other words, rested on overlapping forms of estrangement (Ahmed, 2000), alienation from themselves, and denial of those in their care (Cohen, 2001).

Estrangement varies over time. Sometimes, relationships break down only to be repaired. Often, however, feelings worsen. In detention, women and men usually grew more upset and agitated the longer they were confined, reporting higher levels of depression and complaining far more about their immigration case and living conditions (Bosworth and Kellezi, 2012; 2013). As time in detention dragged on, most people found it harder not only to pass the time, but also to look ahead. They began to lose hope, and in so doing, lost confidence and their sense of self.

Such issues reveal the importance of detail in understanding detention. The decision to remove is experienced in the past, present, and future, as women and men seek to resist it, fear it, and try to make sense of it or reconcile themselves to it. While an institutional ethnography might expect to concentrate primarily on the spatial aspect of uncertainty, in detention, the temporal nature of it was acutely felt. These institutions which seem familiar, in their similarities with other sites of custody operate with specific metrics and logic. Characterized by matters of identity and uncertainty, rather than regime and conditions, they are places where time trumps space and where identity is constantly under review. They are sites where their inhabitants are meant to disappear, even though many remain.

In refusing detainees the right to reside in Britain and to determine the hour or means of their departure, the Home Office not only seized their future but negated (denied) their past. In so doing, the threat of deportation destabilized people's sense of self. Tahir expressed matters neatly: 'My whole life is going to be erased. Just imagine that! You know, when you erase old numbers from your mobile phone? Just imagine your whole life was erased just like that' (Sudan, CH). Living in England since he was a young child, Tahir felt little connection with his country of birth. The Sudan, he mused, was unrecognizable and unreal; a locale he only knew through television. A place, he said, where only bad things happened. 'I have lived here [the UK] since I was 5 . . . I can't go to the Sudan', he exclaimed. 'It's 3rd world, mosquitoes, people dying everyday on TV' (Sudan, CH). Unmoored from his past and unable to imagine his future, Tahir struggled to cope in the present, angry and confused about his treatment and its justification.

Whereas Tahir stressed the cultural effects of his estrangement, Bryn, who was arrested at her workplace for immigration offences, emphasized the material nature of her predicament. 'I have nothing, apart this clothes I am wearing', she professed. 'I have been in the country for 11 years now and I am leaving with nothing, no clothes, no belonging. As if my life while I was here does not exist' (Jamaica, YW). Leaving without her belongings would not just be mortifying, as Fawn had complained, but it would imply that she had had no life at all. Banished without her possessions, Bryn began to doubt her own existence.

For Edon the problems were intertwined. 'Going home is not easy', he pointed out. 'Things have changed so much. You don't have any more connections; you don't know any more people so how can you get a job. Plus, you have learned a new way of life, so how can you get used to that?' (Albania, TH). Having made the decision to leave, he had detached himself from his past and embraced new practices and ideas in the UK. This rupture had material and cultural effects, changing his 'way of life', his habits, desires, and expectations and eroding his prior connections, making it tough to get a job or to fit in. Doubly sundered, first from Albania and now from the UK, he worried he would be a stranger everywhere.

Not everyone felt alienated. Many had always intended on returning, usually once their remittances were no longer necessary. Such people, whose pay in the UK covered the education, medical treatment, and housing bills of family members back home, tended to worry far more about the material consequences of their detention than others, concerned at having 'let down' their dependants in their country of origin. Although many had not seen their family members for many years, their sense of self-identity remained tied to them. 'I am 32 now', Pal said. 'I want to spend my life with my family. I don't want to waste time'. Over a nine-year period in the UK, during which he had worked in construction, made British friends and lived with a British girlfriend, he had maintained a family back in Albania. 'What is the point of me being here and my family being back home?' he asked. 'I don't want to be here alone. The work has gone down now. There is not much money . . . Life is very expensive even here. But at least I have bought a shop for my wife to become hairdresser in my village' (Albania, TH).

Like migrants anywhere, detainees could be nostalgic, waxing lyrical about food, landscape, and community in their home paradise. Even those who did not want to leave the UK perceived superior qualities in their home culture and lifestyle. The food (and weather!) were invariably better. People were friendlier, more trustworthy and generous. 'In my country', Agrin asserted, 'people will give you anything you ask for, no questions asked, not like here in England. In my country if you went there and called out on a street "I need help", all the people they would rush down and see what you needed. Not like here' (Kurd, Iran, BH).

Men were particularly nostalgic about the women back home. 'Girls in UK', Farid, who had lived in the UK for ten years, grumbled, 'are only after the money. If you have money then they like you' (Morocco, TH). British women were so different, others attested, that they were dangerous. Not only were they promiscuous and unreliable, but they could corrupt other, better, women, from home. 'My cousin married an Albanian girl and brought her here', Visar alleged, 'and after a few years, she did it to him like the English girls. She said she wanted to go out on her own, and she wanted him to take her on holidays like the friends of hers husbands did. So then she left him. I told him not to bring his wife here. I knew he would be in trouble' (Albania, TH).

For many, religion was a comfort, a mechanism not just for coping with uncertainty, but also for explaining it. 'I don't know what will happen. Nobody does', Malik murmured, 'but whatever happens it was written before. Only God knows. God knows everything' (Pakistan, BH). Echoing Malik's fatalism, but with a more positive interpretation of her circumstances, Gena professed that, 'it looks I've come here for a reason. Because I have touched so many people's heart. And spiritually I've come out from my bad behaviour' (India, YW). 'You have put my body in prison but my mind is free', Tina avowed. 'My mind is gone to God and gone up there and you cannot imprison it' (Taiwan, YW). Still others, like Ava, found sustenance in comparison. 'Sometimes when you listen to some of the things some of the women have been through, look at yourself say "Why are you complaining?" you know?' she remarked. 'So you know, some of your things sound so small as compared to what some of them have been through. So instead of being distressed, you kind of feel a bit grateful or that sort of thing. I should feel ashamed for feeling bad' (Cameroon, YW).

Often, however, uncertainty about the future prevented detainees from doing anything or connecting with anyone. A lack of trust and clarity drove a wedge between people and was often hard to bear. 'I heard that there's some detainees here, because they want to get out they bring, they take information from other detainees and, you know, be a problem', Arah reported nervously. 'So they pass information on, yeah. Yeah, so we're even getting scared of each other in this way' (Jamaica, YW). With little capacity for self-determination, living under conditions of profound uncertainty, detainees easily felt alienated from one another. This unease consolidated their estrangement, fracturing their sense of self and their relationships with others.

Officers were not inured from such matters. Not only were they sometimes troubled by the fairness of open-ended detention, but the lack of certainty about its duration also exposed their limited sphere of influence, raising unsettling questions about their own role and identity. 'The ladies get frustrated', Ryan observed, 'and then they'll start talking to us saying, "I've been here this long. Why am I still here? What can we do?" And the staff can't answer their questions, or can't do anything to help them with that because it's purely a UKBA issue . . . That's the hardest thing for the staff to deal with' (SMT, YW).

While the differentiation from immigration staff was often a deliberate ploy of DCOs, a means of avoiding blame and a way of initiating rapport with detainees, officers resented their lack of influence. Often their confusion arose from unmet expectations about custodial work. 'I thought I was gonna be more like a prison officer, like I've seen on TV', Allen admitted, 'but because of the nature of the business, it's got to be more softly, softly approach' (DCO, TH). At other times it sprang from compassion, as they worried about particular women and men. Frequently it connected to pragmatic problems of management, as the Home Office decided to move women and men without warning, or prevented them from participating in centre activities when they refused to comply with immigration requests for information.

As the frontline personnel, DCOs have the most contact with detainees. Without an organized regime and with no official influence over immigration matters, staff may be unsure of the purpose of their interactions with detainees or of the form they should take. In each centre I witnessed staff members going well beyond their official role, procuring items for detainees, posting their mail, designing specifically tailored activities to help them pass the weekend, monitoring their wellbeing.

Many officers enjoyed their job. As we have already seen, a number of them explicitly emphasized the diversity of the population as an unlikely source of stimulation. 'I've always liked geography', Mary declared earnestly, 'and learning about other people's cultures' (DCO, CH). Alana agreed. 'I enjoy coming into work everyday', she commented enthusiastically. 'It's a different, different challenge, every single day. Different people. I love meeting new people' (DCO, TH). Most of all, she enjoyed her interactions with them. 'I like, I like playing pool with the detainees, I like chatting with them. We're, you know, we don't just talk about their [immigration] cases' (DCO, TH).

In this interpretation of their work, Mary and Alana, like Leah and Ben earlier, neatly sidestepped more difficult ethical questions about their job. Unlike Leah and Ben they acknowledged the detainees, but primarily as exemplars of 'culture'. Interpreting difference as 'culture' rather than power, they were not alienated, but rather felt sustained by diversity, finding within it a *raison d'être* ludicrously at odds with the aim of the institution. In this view of ethnicity, they reflected a general approach adopted throughout the IRCs, where, under the banner of 'diversity', cultural events, including British national holidays, like the Queen's Jubilee and St George's Day were celebrated alongside Chinese New Year, Eid, and Diwali. Such festive multiculturalism, no doubt helped everyone pass the time. It rested, however, on one important condition, as Alana noted: silence over detainees' immigration cases.

In their reluctance to acknowledge the wider context of removal and deportation, officers are greatly assisted by the split governance of immigration detention. Even the onside immigration officers play no official role in the decision-making process, shuffling papers to and from the caseworkers. Nonetheless, on both counts, staff members are only partly successful. As the testimony from Fawn revealed, onsite immigration staff loom large in the imagination of the detainees. In the survey, too, they were clearly considered separate to DCOs and given short shrift by the respondents (Bosworth and Kellezi, 2012; 2013). The DCOs were also frequently accused of working for the Home Office.

Like the DCOs, onsite immigration officers often distinguished themselves from the caseworkers, decrying the decision-making process and calling for face-to-face contact. At the same time, however, the immigration staff I spoke to valued their role and identity as agents of the Home Office, proud to uphold border control and accepting its basic premise. Aware of their low institutional status, however, many felt embattled and bitter, insufficiently supported by the Home Office and unfairly criticized by custodial staff and detainees for doing their job. Under those circumstances, they often relied on the language of security to reinforce their sense of self, offering a palatable explanation for their job that was, otherwise, difficult to understand or justify.

Whichever perspective we take, it is clear that it is not just the identity of the detainees that is uncertain in IRCs. Each subject position is contested and, to some degree, uncomfortable. Custody officers, in particular, are often torn in many directions. Unless the state is prepared to use force, custodial work requires some engagement from those confined. Staff accounts reveal not just the affective nature of power and confinement, but also how the identity of the officers intertwined with that of the women and men they secure. In their claims and their interactions, the possibility of recognition, however contingent, emerges, pointing to the potential for an alternative set of arrangements.

Yet, countervailing forces keep such human instincts in check. Staff were constantly enjoined not to get too close. There was to be no emailing or phone contact during detention; and no contact, of any sort, after deportation or removal. 'Empathy not sympathy', they obediently parroted, a catchphrase widely used that, in defiance of dictionary definition, sought to restrict engagement with the people in their care.

With limited training, poor job security and low pay, staff encountered additional disincentives to commit emotionally to their career or to those in their care. Many worked at more than one trade, ranging from local supermarkets to other security work as bouncers. Financially stretched, such people were unlikely to challenge the rulebook.

Some took on occasional jobs in 'overseas escorting', accompanying women and men on the airplane, a task that they were careful not to admit to detainees, but one which had an inevitable effect on how they interacted with them. One day in Yarl's Wood, while I was in the cultural kitchen, a young female DCO who had been seconded from elsewhere in Serco was introduced as someone who lived near me. As it turned out, my fieldnotes record, 'She actually works for Serco's overseas escort unit and is about to be seconded to Christmas Island [off the coast of Australia] for six months. Whenever she mentioned her overseas escorting she lowered her voice so that the women couldn't hear: "I don't talk about what I do here. I don't tell them. It would be difficult if they knew that I'm the person who might take them back"' (Fieldnotes, July 2010). Another member of staff in the same institution who supplemented her income in this way only 'escorted' women and children from the family unit, neatly, in her mind, keeping the two parts of her job separate, demonstrating the capacity and necessity of denial in this uncertain institution.[11]

Although both women were able to reconcile themselves to the painful effects and implications of their escorting trade, at some level they remained alive to the ethically contested nature of this additional labour, and its intersection with their mundane tasks within the centre. Each of the private companies operate well beyond the walls of the detention centres, offering a range of career paths to their employees in which the particularity of detention work erodes, absorbed into a wide-ranging set of security practices. Under these circumstances staff simultaneously are provided an expansive language and justification for their job, while its specific purpose becomes increasingly fuzzy.

Conclusion

Uncertainty characterized all aspects of the detention experience not just the period of detention. It existed on many registers, affecting how people interacted with one another as well as how they perceived themselves. It stretched across time and space, unfixing and denying people's past while dictating their present and colonizing their future. It is the constant backdrop to detention and its outcome.

Under these circumstances, staff and detainees' capacity for trust is diminished. Their agency and self-realization are restrained. Everyone is alienated, albeit to varying degrees, separate from one another and from themselves. Unable to predict or shape their future, detainees struggled to maintain a clear narrative of identity. With the relevance of their time in Britain denied, they lost their bearings. Who would they be upon return, they wondered?

In a visit to an IRC at the early stages of this project, when I was securing research access, a centre manager complained that senior civil servants

---

11. When asked about overseas work, most staff were quick to point out how exhausting it is, since they rarely disembark at the destination, but rather immediately fly home, having delivered the former detainee. This woman was an exception, claiming to have benefited from a free three-day 'holiday' in Jamaica, when her plane was unable to return due to the Volcanic ash cloud of 2010 which prevented air traffic over Britain for three days. This one experience still brought her considerable pleasure as she reminisced about staying in a beach front property courtesy of the Home Office.

in the Home Office referred to detainees as 'stock and flow' rather than as people. Riley, a senior caseworker in the Home Office, echoed his concerns: 'I can't get over, sometimes, how badly we as an organization deal with individuals. We don't consider them as individuals. I mean case workers, they don't even call them by their name!' Elsewhere, a young detention custody officer at Campsfield House, wondered why the Home Office could not allocate detainees to IRCs more efficiently, 'like Sainsburys', aware of the location of all their items for sale and any gaps on the shelves that needed to be filled. In such accounts, vitiated by management-speak, detainees were dehumanized, objectified, and commercialized.

Such objectification is a key outcome and justification of immigration detention, closely linked to the politics of uncertainty and denial (Cohen, 2001). Whereas risk management seeks to create governable subjects, the management of uncertainty objectifies. Those in detention do not need to 'responsibilize', since they are not coming back. Their identities are fixed as always, already gone. They are strangers; 'those who are in their very proximity, already recognised as not belonging, as being out of place' (Ahmed, 2000: 21).

For those governing these institutions, such uncertainty is, quite literally, hard to manage. A member of the Senior Management Team at Campsfield tried to explain. 'Most days go past very, very quietly with nothing happening at all . . . ' Lindsay began,

> very little happens. But it takes one person to walk through the door in the wrong set of circumstances and then that can lead to . . . a really difficult incident be that they might have the propensity to self-harm or they might incite others into, you know, radicalising. Or they might, you know, set fire to the place or something like that. And that's the element of the unknown that's both a challenge and the thing that sort of gets the heart racing and also what keeps you awake at night (laughter). Because you worry that at any given time one of the 216 chaps, mostly we don't know very much about, could do something which would put themselves or others, including, you know, fellow residents as well as staff, at risk, you know? I think it's a very, it's a fragile thing in Campsfield, you know? And at the moment, the equilibrium's okay. But I think historically it's always been a sort of flash in the pan type environment. We're, we're calm most of the time but when something goes wrong, it goes badly wrong, you know, seven people climb over the fence or, you know, they set fire to the place. Then you've got, you know, two hundred guys pushing their way through a gate in, in, in, you know, out of the centre essentially . . . most days are normal, they're settled and but then

there's always that thing at the back of your mind that, like, you know, it's got the potential to go like that (SMT, CH).

Such insecurity, that permeates all aspects of the centres flows in many directions, not all of which operate in the interest of the state. In a diverse and multicultural society like Britain, the 'stranger' often has claims upon us after all. As Haroun from Campsfield House pointed out, Britain relies on immigrants:

> If you notice who work at post office? Is mostly Asian and all these people. Check it for yourself. Who work in the hospital? Check all of these place, yeah. All of these place is outside foreigners coming in. And you don't see British people doing those . . . If all these people strike, Britain went down and they all know that, you understand (Unknown nationality, CH).

Culturally, too, the border is perpetually traversed, as food, religion, music, and other forms of expression that originated elsewhere have become central to the British way of life. Casting out strangers, under these circumstances, takes considerable effort. It is painful not just for those being excluded but also for the ones forcing them out.

Uncertainty, in other words, is by definition, an unsettling and unsettled mode of governance. A focus on it does more than illuminate power from above, it also challenges a singular view of control, underlining the pertinence of individual struggles and relationships alongside coercion. The inconsistencies of detention creates profound ontological insecurity, primarily among the detainees, but also among the staff. Denied recognition, placed in a low-trust environment in which they are prevented from exercising agency on all but a few matters, it is no wonder that detainees exhibit high levels of depression and distress (Bosworth and Kellezi, 2012). And yet, such a pessimistic view does not tell the whole story. Uncertainty sometimes brings people together. It can disrupt the flow of power and control at the same time as it is their medium. It raises the possibility of things being otherwise (Hemmings, 2012; Pedwell and Whitehead, 2012). In spite of itself, as we shall see in the following chapter, it may offer some grounds for challenge and resistance.

7

Ambivalence and estrangement in detention

> I really don't know why I'm working here any more. I used to know, criminals were criminals and we were detaining them. But now I don't know. I just don't understand why the government wants to keep families apart. Any man who has a child doesn't pose a flight risk . . . it took me a few months to realise that what we are doing doesn't make much sense, and it's expensive for everyone (Colin, DCO, MH).

> If we're not criminals, why you put officers with uniform? And if you look at us as criminals, then you put professional officers who knows his job! (Giv, Iran, CB).

In this final chapter, I revisit the questions with which this study opened. What are IRCs for? How can we understand them? On what basis might we appraise their success? How can we determine their failings? Given their financial and human costs, not to mention their apparent inefficiencies, evident in the growing number of long-term detainees, as well as in the significant proportion of people returned to the community without expulsion, such questions demand a response. Yet the theoretical framework in which to pose them remains hazy.

On what basis might we judge an institution like an immigration removal centre that transcends the sovereign state in which it is located? Where is power located in such a place? How is it experienced? Who should have a say in any debate over detention, when the community inside (not to mention those who are affected by their custody) are not fellows of a single political community (Fraser, 2007)? How would they register their views and by what means would we recognize them? Such questions are part of a broader discussion of whether the liberal political project extends to foreigners

(Fraser, 2007; 2008; Honig, 2001; Benhabib, 2004, 2006; Bosniak, 2008; see also Barker, 2013; Bosworth, 2013; Gibney, 2013). As such, they remind us of the role of IRCs in shoring up liberal political power.

Concentrating on staff accounts, this chapter explores what happens to assumptions about state power if we place ambivalence, estrangement, and uncertainty at the heart of our analysis. How can we understand it, and how might we challenge it? Returning to the questions posed in the introduction, what are detention centres for? How are they justified?

The purpose of detention

Notwithstanding the apparent political enthusiasm in Britain and other countries for tightening the border and for detaining irregular migrants, the purpose and effect of detention and other methods of border control remain deeply contested. Staff members were not immune to such questions. 'When I first started here', Alana recollected,

> I thought it was just everybody's gonna be deported and that's it. But over the years and learning how the system works and whatever, I would say it's a stop point. It's a stop point to actually find out whether they're gonna come, go, stay. [To find out] what they're doing . . . It's not a final 'Goodbye you're out of the country', because we've released far more people than seem to go on flights (DCO, TH).

Officers were similarly unsure about their day-to-day responsibilities. Like detainees, they often struggled to understand the nature of the institution where they worked. Although their most common point of comparison, like the detainees, was with the prison, staff often preferred alternative views of IRCs as community centres, hospitals, or schools. In a conversation about methods of managing those at risk of suicide or self harm, Lela described the mechanisms used at Yarl's Wood[1] as being

> like a, a stricter boarding school if you like, for some of the people here and there are those who will always be needier than others and, you know, we

---

1. In common with their colleagues at all IRCs, staff at Yarl's Wood were meant to monitor detainees for indications of suicide and self-harm. Those considered at risk would be dealt with according to the tenets of the 'Assessment Care in Detention and Teamwork' (ACDT) programme, adopted from the Prison service's ACCT equivalent. Details about the overall scheme can be found on the Home Office website, although local practice varied slightly <http://www.ukba.homeoffice.gov.uk/sitecontent/documents/policyandlaw/detention-services-orders/assessment-care-in-detention.pdf?view=Binary>.

do have them who quite like the attention of, of being monitored. It's only when it gets really intrusive (laughter) that they start saying, 'I think I'm better now' (DCM, YW).

Many found the incoherence of their role and responsibilities uncomfortable. While such reaction could lead to sympathy for the women and men in their care, it also generated hostility and mistrust. Officers were particularly aware of, and uneasy about, the politicized nature of their job, concerned about how their profession was perceived by people outside detention.[2] Troy, who had come to custody work after a long career in manufacturing that had been derailed by the economic crisis of 2008, claimed never to speak of his work outside detention. Although he enjoyed his job, he did not want others to know what he did. 'If you meet somebody for the first time', he observed,

> it's a normal part of conversations, 'Oh what do you do for a living?' 'Oh what do you do?' You go to a party, you go to the pub, you bump into somebody or whatever, it's a common thing people ask isn't it? If it's strangers, I normally say 'Oh I work for the Home Office.' 'Oh what do you do at the Home Office?' 'Oh I'm involved in the back room stuff.' I don't want to discuss Yarl's Wood . . . So I never tell anybody I work for Yarl's Wood. I work for the Home Office. Back room stuff you know, looking at numbers, and things like that (DCO, YW).

Not everyone was embarrassed by their career. Many were proud of their work and keen to dispel negative perceptions. Such attitudes could take many forms. In their comparisons with prison officers, whom they believed were dependent on the prison adjudication system to maintain order, DCOs commonly espoused particular expertise in 'de-escalating' problems without recourse to a punishment system. 'When I visit a prison', Mishal reflected, 'it feels very different. The staff there have loads of sanctions. All we have are our interpersonal skills' (DCM, CB). While staff often complained about their inability to punish detainees, officers were also proud of their skills in managing them without such blunt compulsion. Particularly in Yarl's Wood and Tinsley House, staff stressed the 'caring' aspect of their role, minimizing its coercive element.

---

2. In at least one IRC, staff training included sessions on discussing media representations of immigration and its impact on staff perceptions of detainees (personal communication, former centre manager).

Others simply denied that problems occurred. One day at Yarl's Wood, for example, when I was quietly eating lunch in the family unit dining hall, I was approached by a young female officer who wanted to know what I thought of the centre in general, and of the family unit, in particular.[3] Irritated by my evasive answer, Lida was scornful: 'You know the ex-residents lie don't you? They just sugar coat [sic] it for the newspaper. There's no problem in here' (DCO, YW).

The vehemence of her response and her refusal to acknowledge readily available evidence to the contrary were striking. It was also common. Even the most sympathetic of staff—who could be compassionate, warm, and concerned about particular individuals—found it difficult to accept that there was a general 'problem' in detention.

It is possible that Lida was unaware of the pain the women and children in her care endured. Yet, their desperation felt close, as we stood together in the lunch room that was decorated with children's paintings and contained a small number of family groups huddled together. She may also have been referring to a particular event that she believed had misrepresented life in Yarl's Wood. The institution at the time was often in the news. Both responses, however, miss the implications of her denial. Lida was pained by these accusations. Acknowledging the damage of detention was too threatening to her sense of self, so she simply refuted their allegations (Cohen, 2001).

In their accounts, Troy and Lida expressed considerable discomfort in the role of the detention custody officer. Whereas Troy could not bring himself to admit publically to his profession, Lida would not accept the effect of her work. Each reacted to discussion of their work negatively. Instead of pride they felt shame and anger, sentiments that led to deceit and repudiation. In these unpleasant feelings, they are revealed to be doubly alienated, from themselves as well as from those in their care.

Not everyone was afraid of confronting the impact of their work, and not all were unaware of its effects. Many had found a way of acknowledging the pains of at least some of those they confined, expressing concern about certain events and regret over the detention of particular individuals. In this vein, officers were open about the challenges they faced in managing

---

3. This interaction occurred as Yarl's Wood was in the transitional phase, still accepting young children in family groups, but in fewer numbers as the Home Office looked for alternative measures.

violence, coming to terms with children in detention, and accepting the deportation of long-term British residents. Officers were, likewise, anxious about the wider immigration system, unclear about its parameters and justification, critical of daily practices. Yet, eventually, even the most sympathetic among the staff shied away from the implications of their accounts. In this movement, from recognition to alienation and estrangement, the power (and the pain) of detention is made manifest. It is here, in other words, that alternatives must be sought.

Violence as a source of ambivalence

For the most part, the violence which concerned staff was that perpetrated by the detainees against themselves: suicide and self-harm. Each of the centres ran a 'violence reduction' programme. Adapted from the prison service, most of these systems emphasized prevention. At Colnbrook, as in prison, the violence reduction programme was also linked to room allocation decisions.

Each centre maintained an Excel file on suicide and self-harm attempts. Some, like Yarl's Wood, recorded a third category of 'raised awareness'. This label, Lina explained 'expresses a staff member's concern for residents that is more subjective; I can't cope, I am finding it difficult, history of depression and self-harm. The individual is not verbalising an intention but we are a bit worried' (DCM, YW). Most IRCs also monitored and recorded instances of bullying as a distinct type of violence. Detainees considered at risk of suicide and self-harm were put on a register and placed under varying levels of surveillance from a 'constant watch' to informal conversations every few days. Those who were bullied were monitored less formally. Alleged aggressors were also kept under scrutiny.

Concern about such matters was widespread. In Yarl's Wood, Sean recalled, 'When I first took this job . . . I was thinking to myself, "Crikey, I wonder how many years I have to go before I see suicides and self harm?" Well, (laughter) the first week going live into the job, wooh . . . it, it was, yes I, I've, I've had to deal with many, many, many, many cases of suicide and self harm . . . '. Over his ten-year career, he said, 'I've seen many, many things, you know, from someone ironing themselves to pouring boiling water over themselves, to cutting themselves, all kinds of things, swallowing washing tablets, all kinds of things, yeah' (DCO, YW). Such actions, he believed, were a method of 'coping', however harmful. His job was to assist the women in finding an alternative outlet for their emotions.

Officers were not always sympathetic. Sometimes self-harm was considered to be a step too far, generating ridicule. When Hui-Ying slashed herself, one staff member's response was harsh. 'Silly girl!' Lesa snapped. 'You know they [the women] complain that we don't give them everything they ask for, but when we do they do stupid things like that!' (DCO, YW). Another woman, who was the subject of special intervention from the local NHS mental health team, had scars all over her body from self-inflicted wounds. A photograph of her hung in the staff corridor alongside other so-called 'development nominal', terminology adopted from policing, to refer to known suspects, that in detention usually applies to those considered difficult to control. Underneath this particular woman's picture a staff member had written, 'uses her self-harm to manipulate staff'.

Sentiments like these coloured institutional responses to other forms of self-harm enacted in protest. Hunger strikes, in particular, were carefully monitored. Referred to in official parlance as 'food refusal', a phrase that neutralizes their historical and ideological associations with political prisoners, they had to be disrupted as quickly as possible. On one occasion, the media erroneously reported that a hunger strike had broken out in Yarl's Wood. The response from the Serco management team was swift. 'You may have seen the headline', Luna announced at a staff meeting:

> 'Yarl's Wood hunger strike started yesterday at teatime'. . . But it's Campsfield House that has a food refusal, not Yarl's Wood. It has caused a lot of media furore as would be expected. My sympathies to Campsfield House, they are also the centre of attention from activists. My concern is that these things have legs and will grow. As you know we had one before. So everyone pay close attention! Get those SIRs[4] moving! We need to be vigilant and careful (SMT, YW).

Fearful that the media report might inspire women to resist, senior staff sought to prevent disruption through an information gathering exercise. Security Incident Reports are logged and analysed by the centre's security department, who then determine what action to take.

The thankfully rare practice of lip sewing, more common in Australian detention centres, was also viewed with suspicion. At Colnbrook, Jeanine,

---

4. Security Incident Reports.

who was otherwise sympathetic to the men, taking time out from her own life after her shift ended to procure items for their cultural and religious services that were otherwise unavailable, assured me that when men acted that way, they really only 'pretended' to sew their lips together. They just 'loop a few threads' through their lips, she contended, always leaving enough room to smoke a cigarette (DCM, CB).

Even in Tinsley House, where many officers prided themselves on their caring approach towards detainees, staff members were unsure how to handle bodily demonstration. When an Iranian man, whose torture claim was initially rejected by the Home Office sewed his lips together in protest, staff were unnerved. Alana, who oversaw his release, referred to it as 'one of the more difficult moments' in her career. 'The last person that I did who was released was a gentleman that sewed his mouth up', she began, 'so that, that was difficult because I actually had to look at him with his mouth sewn up and ask him all these questions' (DCO, TH). While evidently upset about having to 'look at him with his mouth sewn up', Alana rapidly edged away from his bodily suffering to more familiar territory: his lack of English. 'You know, I, my Arabic like I said, is okay', she observed,

> but it's not good enough for interpreting, so I had his friend who he was quite happy to have in there interpreting as well, so I was getting the gist of it, but there were certain words that I said, 'Now, hold on, can you explain exactly what that means to me?' So, that was, that was a long, three hour assessment. So they can vary from half an hour to sometimes a whole day, so, yeah (DCO, TH).

In this encounter, the embodied nature of the man's suffering and his dissent literally made it too emotionally taxing for Alana to look at him. Perceiving but finding it difficult to see this man's damaged mouth, she turned, as others have before her, to bureaucracy and procedure (Arendt, 1963; Milgram, 1974; Bauman, 1989; Cohen, 2001). In so doing, Alana successfully transformed this man, who initially troubled her peace of mind, into a 'long, three hour assessment'. Yet, traces of her ambivalence remained, exposing the effort required in making sense of what had happened and her role in it.

Although for the most part centres function peacefully enough, the threat of force is always present. Staff must maintain order and discipline, and, when required, facilitate an enforced removal. However much officers may not wish to see it or fail to understand it in that way, detainees often experience their actions and that of the wider immigration system as violence,

VIOLENCE AS A SOURCE OF AMBIVALENCE

forced upon them, techniques designed to hurt. 'At the end of the day', Giv maintained, 'you know, he's got a uniform, he can do whatever he wants' (Iran, CB). Correcting himself, he went on, 'Not whatever he wants. If he does it to someone who knows the rule, how the rule work, so he can make him do step back from what he doing. But some people, the one who specially can't speak English, doesn't know the rule whatever, he take advantage of them. And they really make them very stressed, frustrating' (Iran, CB). This power imbalance, which, as Giv reminds us, needs to be situated in constitutive qualities of the detained population, created all sorts of fears among those who were captive, some of which may have been grounded in their personal experience in the UK, others of which related to their lives elsewhere. Certain fears sprang from the experience of detention itself.

People's concerns were often gendered. Pam was anxious about the trip to the airport. 'I am really scared they will be violent', she confided 'and who knows they can rape you on the way to the airport. There is no one who cares or would do anything to them' (Nigeria, YW). Pam's worries about deportation, she made clear, were amplified by her previous experiences in Nigeria as well as by a broader cultural attitude at Yarl's Wood, where, she alleged, women and staff engaged in inappropriate sexual relations:

> The way they [male staff] look at you. I am too old for these things, and I would never do it for anything. If an immigration officer asked me to have sex with me I would never allow it. Even for getting out of here I would never do it. There are some women here that are very loose, the way they talk to the officers and play with them. You have no idea what happens here. The women officers don't know what happens but a lot of bad things happen here.

Although others, like Iola from Serbia, claimed that, to the contrary, male officers kept their distance from the women and were far less flirtatious with them than prison officers, in 2010 a detention custody officer was sacked for having sex with a detainee who fell pregnant. Three years later a former detainee accused three officers of sexual abuse and, at the time of writing, a legal case remains underway.[5]

Women's anxiety about sexual assault often related to their previous experiences of victimization. As Ena put it, 'They [the male staff] are

5. In 2013, HMIP reported no evidence of institutionalized exploitation, although in January 2014, Women for Refugee Women countered with a report of their own, which included

alright. But still, I don't trust them. They are men after all' (Gambia, YW). Not only had many women like Ena been raped by a family member, but some had been assaulted by a police officer or by other men in positions of power in their country of origin. 'When you go to the police in Pakistan', Aatifa exclaimed bitterly, 'first they rape you and then they ask you what you need when you go to report domestic violence' (Pakistan, YW). Still others, who had reported sexual or domestic assault that had occurred in Britain to the British police, had been swept into detention as a result. They were also being held in an environment where they regularly witnessed physical coercion. During fieldwork in Yarl's Wood, the panic alarm was pulled on a number of occasions, calling staff to subdue a fight between the women. Likewise, the 'stop all movements' siren sounded frequently, potentially signalling the forceful removal of a woman from her room to the segregation unit or to an outside escort service, as well as facilitating a headcount if necessary.

Yet, the British detention system evinces little understanding of the gendered nature of the exercise of coercion. Instead, the pain and worry inherent in strategies of force are neutered by their official appellation as 'C&R' ('control & restraint') as well as by more colloquial terminology, in which force is renamed 'wrapping up' and 'laying on of hands'. Instruction in 'control and restraint' is moderated by official guidelines. It is an important part of the officers' initial training and must be regularly renewed. Talk of 'C&R', or 'wrapping someone up' was common and much was made of the requirement that even the 'civilian' teachers in art and craft and education, who did not wear uniforms, had to possess these skills.[6]

Some staff struggled within this environment. At Tinsley House, a young female member of staff asserted one day, 'horrible things happen here! How can they treat people so inhumanly? When they deported the husband of my assistant they had to hold her down on the floor, three of them, when she was pregnant, and take him away by force. He had a lot of cuts and bruises on his whole arms because they dragged him away.'

---

one allegation of sexual assault and three claims of staff violence within the centre (Girma et al, 2014). This report has led to a national campaign, 'Set Her Free' to 'end the detention of women who seek asylum'.

6. Practices varied. Whereas art craft and education in Yarl's Wood and Colnbrook were both run by DCOs in uniform, in Campsfield House and Tinsley House, they were taught by artists and trained ESOL teachers who did not. At Brook House, the man running art and craft was a former secondary school teacher, while the ESOL teacher had previously worked as a DCO.

Pausing, Caren collected herself, adding nervously, 'but I should probably not tell you these things' (DCO, TH). Also at Tinsley House, Alana was ambivalent. On the one hand, she asserted, physically restraining detainees was 'fantastically empowering because as a, as a female and someone who was quite, I wouldn't have said physical cos I'm not physical . . . it was empowering, it made me feel like, actually, I can control with, with other people we, we can control somebody' (DCO, TH). On the other hand, she admitted, 'I don't like violence, I don't like being, I hate doing contact and restraint [sic], I absolutely hate it, but if it's necessary, I'll do it' (DCO, TH).

Others resisted physical coercion altogether, claiming that such techniques were unnecessary or ineffective. 'One thing I'm very proud of in my job', Sean asserted, 'after being here for nearly ten years, I've never had to lay hands on anyone in, in, in anger as you might put it, I've never had to use control and restraint. I've had to hold ladies' arms to stop them hurting themselves but I've never had to use control and restraint. I've used other skills and I'm very proud of that, yes' (DCO, YW). Stan, also at Yarl's Wood, initially agreed, claiming that, 'a good rapport can de-escalate quite a few situations'. Yet, he warned, 'you've always got that line where a good rapport doesn't go' (DCO, YW).

In Tinsley House, Barry, echoed such views. 'We've always said as a rule we de-escalate. If we put hands on, we've failed. So we don't like to fight. We don't', he began (DCO, TH). Unlike Sean, however, Barry had used force, an unwanted outcome that he struggled to reconcile with his averred dislike of violence. 'Someone who's highly aggressive', he explained, 'we will eventually get them down to sitting down and talking normally. That's how we go. We don't go, "right, let's have it." You know, we're not violent people. We don't like to be violent. Why would I want to inflict harm on people, but sometimes you have to do that'. Ultimately, the fault lay with the detainees, he decided. 'I mean I've been bitten, I've been seriously injured, I've been urinated over. And that's all from their side, not from our side. You know, so then you have to go through life now thinking, "why would someone do that? Is it sheer desperation, or is it the fact that they just want to hurt someone?"' (DCO, TH).

Some refused to be drawn into wider questions about order. For them, matters were easily resolved if you just knew how. According to Allen, the solution was gendered.

Sometimes I think it's better actually to have a woman going in sorting something out than a bloke, you know. Cos they'll, you know, they'll look at a lumpy jumper and they'll be happy: A young lady talking to 'em rather than an old git like me going in. Yeah, sometimes, you know, to de-escalate a situation, your best tool, if they're up for it, send the girls in. It works every time (DCO, TH).

Allen's senior colleague Angus took matters further. For him, day-to-day life was easily managed. Force, in his view, related only to the question of deportation, a matter, which, he argued, had nothing to do with him and his work. 'If you keep them fed well, they're happy; they'll do things', Angus asserted confidently. 'If they're not fed well, then they get bickery, they get maudly and they get angry, and then you have problems. But if you eat well and you sleep well and things like that, then makes for a good place doesn't it?' (DCM, TH).

Yet, the truth was, just as they used C&R to control women and men in detention, the staff also enforced removals. While they do not put detainees on the plane (unless they are working as escorts), they are responsible for preparing them to leave, a job that will, sometimes, entail force. Allen described how he managed this experience. 'I, I had one guy', he recalled,

> he refused to go point blank. He had his wife and kids here, about three or four kids, and he wouldn't leave his room. And myself and two other guys had to go in and forcibly remove him. He had a picture of his little girl, his wife and kiddies and that, and that was . . . it wasn't hard but I found it a bit. At the time I was thinking 'You twat, can't believe what you're doing'. You know 'Fucking twat, what are you doing to this poor man?'

As he recognized the man as a father, Allen, who was otherwise uncompromising in his attitudes to detainees and supported tight immigration controls, was momentarily disconcerted. However, he went on, he soon recovered. 'Then it went "ching!"—the emotional side switched off and rational went in. Yeah. Gotta do it.' According to Allen, 'if you haven't got that switch it's very difficult, it's very difficult to, to get on with the job, you know'. It was not just that the 'switch' stopped him from acknowledging his feelings, but that it enabled him to 'sit down for a moment and pause and think, you know, reflect'. Without the ability to make that emotional break, he asserted, 'you're in the wrong job' (DCO, TH).

Warming to his theme, Allen presented his job as one of striking a balance. 'You're totally in the wrong job', he averred, 'if you're "Oh fuck 'em, they're only detainees. Get 'em out the door." Well sorry, but you're [also] in the wrong job if you think "Poor bastard, what's he going back to?"' Adopting a familiar turn of phrase, he went on, 'you know, it's not sympathy, it's empathy, you know, empathise with the guys. So yeah, you're totally in the wrong job if you, if you've got that bollocks attitude as I call it, you know.' The ideal, he believed, was to find a middle way:

> You can't just be, you can't be rational and emotional all, rational all the time or dictorial [sic] all the time. You've got, there's gotta be a little point where you have that little emotional side and it comes in, yeah fine. It's more of a check for you actually, it's more of a check for you. You know, you're still in touch with reality, you're still in touch with the world. You need that. If you haven't got it for this job, there's the door, away you go (DCO, TH).

In such lengthy reflection, and notwithstanding his own admitted prejudices against immigration, Allen grasped the inherent tension in what was being asked of him: to forcibly remove a fellow human being. Such action can only occur when fellowship is denied. Power, his account makes clear, can only flow through alienation. Yet, this man whom he was wrestling on the ground was not unfamiliar. He was a father. He had a wife. He was someone whom Allen was physically grappling, touching, coercing. A man whose pain and resistance he was witnessing and being asked to deny.

Allen was not alone in citing the importance of empathy over sympathy as a means of reconciling himself to such a task. Guards in all centres used such language. Empathy was highly valued. Sympathy was suspect. While the dictionary distinction between these terms is not great, and in fact empathy would seem to be more closely connected to recognition than sympathy,[7] in removal centres the terms had specific meanings that were understood to differ markedly. Empathy was rational. It sprang from an informed understanding that related to their specialized roles as custody officers in which the diversity of the population was merely cultural, questions of power and inequality set aside. Sympathy, by contrast, was emotional and unreliable. It emphasized feelings. It was unprofessional.

In fact, separating understanding from compassion is a tall order. One usually leads to the other. Both rest on recognition. Under these circumstances, talk about rationality was not sufficient in reconciling staff to enforcing removal. Some of them turned to alternative explanations.

Sean, an experienced officer at Yarl's Wood, who appeared to be an otherwise thoughtful and compassionate man, popular with the women and

---

7. In his work on denial and atrocity, for instance, Stanley Cohen (2001: 72) defines empathy as: 'awareness of the consciousness of others'. Too much empathy, he observes, 'causes the observer distress' (Cohen, 2001: 72).

friendly to the research team, deployed a disturbing and blunt analogy. 'I mentioned to you I worked in the abattoir', he began,

> and whilst it's a strange analogy, how an animal is slaughtered—it has to go with dignity. If you bully it you'll get all kinds of reactions. If, once again, we come back to the calm personality, if things are quiet and calm it can go to the point of slaughter, job over. As I said, this is a strange analogy but equally with people, if you're calm, if you're attentive and reliable and you'll have established all those qualities with this person, this lady, long before her RDs, [removal directions] then maybe you'll get a good result, maybe the result will go the way you, you want to because at the end of the day, we are a removal centre and that's part and parcel of what we do but it's how you achieve the end and there, there should be no, it shouldn't be a hard way. If the lady is having a difficult time, it shouldn't be a hard way of doing it . . . So yeah, lots of empathy and, and patience, and, and but at the end of the day it has to be the way the contract says (DCO, YW).

As with Allen's lengthy reflection, there is a lot to assess in Sean's testimony. Notwithstanding his acknowledgement of the 'strangeness' of the analogy he drew between persuading a woman to accept the terms of her removal directions and go home and transporting an animal to its death at the abattoir, the level of dehumanization in his comparison is startling, as is his unconscious appreciation of the parallels between death and deportation. Simultaneously aware, yet in denial of the impact and implication of his work, Sean revealed empathy and patience as a means of enforcing a social execution, before turning, rapidly, to the safety of the contract.

In these cases, the officers were phlegmatic. 'It's gotta be done', Allen observed (DCO, TH). 'We are a removal centre and that's part and parcel of what we do', Sean acknowledged, 'it has to be the way the contract says' (DCO, YW). Such a view ceded their agency, skilfully avoiding reflection about their personal responsibility. While Allen emphasized 'reason' over 'emotion', a shift, which he characterized as prizing empathy over sympathy, Sean cited 'calmness' and dignity as the prerequisites for empathy. Yet, their ambivalence remained palpable. By the end of each man's testimony, they sounded far less sure of understanding without compassion, with Sean concluding, 'I'm as pleased as punch if, if the flight is called off and, and I can switch round then and be so happy for her and, you know, it all changes again. It, it's, I've always said, It's a very, very strange job this. It, it's so complex in, in many ways' (DCO, YW).

It was not just violence that led staff (and detainees) to question what they were doing and who they were. Both groups were also often ambivalent about specific populations, finding children and long-term British residents particularly challenging. In their reservations and concerns about such groups, we catch further glimpses of the emotional demands inherent in enacting border control.

Detaining children

The detention of children in the UK has long been contentious (Campbell, Baqueriza, and Ingram, 2011; Bhui, 2013a).[8] Unlike adults, the confinement of young people for immigration matters stirs popular sympathies. Evidence about the long-term psychological damage of incarceration apparent in both groups, is more persuasive in the young than similar evidence about the negative effects of detention on those over the age of 18 (Lorek et al, 2009; Dudley et al, 2012).

At the time of the fieldwork in Yarl's Wood, there were still a small number of children present. On 16 December 2010, deputy Prime Minister Nick Clegg pledged to end this 'shameful' practice, acknowledging the hard work of those campaigning against it (Mulholland and Stratten, 2010).[9] In fact, children continue to be detained in family groups, albeit at far lower numbers and for much shorter periods at Cedars as well as in Tinsley House (HMIP, 2013). In any case, Lina testily remarked,

> One thing everyone always forgets is that the majority of these women are mothers. Back when they would talk about the family unit, when it was the jewel in the crown of Yarl's Wood, all singing all dancing, I would remind them that the women here are mothers too. And they don't get to say goodnight to their children, or to take them into bed or even always to speak to them on the phone (DCM, YW).

While Yarl's Wood offers extended visits for children, in a bid to mitigate their separation, few women take up this option, fearful of having their

8. It is contentious elsewhere too. See <http://endchilddetention.org> for more details of campaigns against child detention around the globe.
9. His speech can be watched on YouTube at <https://www.youtube.com/watch?v=uShP1R TqqwQ&feature=player_embedded>. Accessed 14 April 2014.

children taken away or unable to afford the visit.[10] Instead, research conducted by BID published in 2013 uncovered widespread evidence of family separation and a growing reliance on emergency foster care. Fewer children are locked up. But their mothers continue to be confined.

Staff were keenly aware of the criticisms levelled at detaining children and often raised the issue in conversation. Senior staff were clear: 'Personally, and I think I speak for quite a lot of the staff here', Henry told me, 'I don't think there's anybody that enjoyed detaining children within the centre . . . I was proud of the job that we did do', he said, 'and the way that we looked after the families and the children when they were in the centre' (SMT, YW). But he wanted to make sure I understood it was a political decision. Staff did not approve. 'It was a government decision to detain children, in family units, for immigration purposes. So we were here to make sure that we did that job to the best of our ability and provided the best level of care we could to families. Personally I mean, I am pleased that we don't have children within the centre anymore' (SMT, YW).

In contrast to Henry's clear account of what was at stake, a number of staff described the situation as more complicated. Many insisted that they had not 'damaged' anyone, and that the children in Yarl's Wood had been perfectly happy. 'Children bounce back', Dorothy urged confidently. 'They may be sad for the first few days, but then they always bounce back' (DCO, YW). Stacey, her colleague who worked in the nursery, agreed. 'Kids this age don't seem to notice', she said in response to a question about what the children made of the location of the nursery within a detention centre, 'All they think is—toys!' (DCO, YW).

Indeed, a number of staff at Yarl's Wood and Tinsley House enjoyed the presence of children in the institution. 'I know I shouldn't say this because children shouldn't be here', Lexi confessed, 'but I'll miss them. I liked working with children' (DCO, YW). Young people lifted the mood of the centre. With them she had been able to do different things. They did not complain like the adults. She felt as though she could play with them, rather than control them. She could, in short, be someone different with them than just a guard. Even so, she conceded ruefully, 'children shouldn't be in detention. I know that' (DCO, YW).

---

10. Some, like May and Meg perceived in the policy a dubious attempt to gloss over the problems facing women in detention, refusing to take up the offer because it would just 'make the centre look good, like they care' (Jamaica, YW).

As Lexi's words imply, the presence of children affected staff member's sense of themselves as well as their view of the institution. Yet, as was so often the case in these complicated institutions, staff opinions were confused and inconsistent. In Tinsley House, where a new short-term family unit was being renovated, officers were worried about what it would be like once parents and children arrived. They were preparing themselves for trouble, fearful that, given the change in policy about child detention, only 'difficult' families would be detained. Under these circumstances, they feared they would have to use their new powers of control and restraint with children more frequently. 'We're doing a different stage [of training]', Alana reported, 'where we can actually control children and that's the worrying part' (DCO, TH).

In the past, Alana had restrained a child, but had not been trained in any particular technique to do so. The absence of protocol, rather than the means of family unification or their removal, or even the fact that she worked in a job where she had to physically coerce young people, had made her very uncomfortable. 'We had an absolute fractious family, that was a mother and three children' she reminisced.

> The mother was reunited with her children here. She'd been in prison for eight years, so her children didn't even know her and they were reunited and they were gonna be shipped out . . . There was a seventeen year old boy, a twelve year old daughter and an eight year old daughter. And the twelve year old daughter was in this room—not with these curtains I might add— actually tried to hang herself. So, as a restraint, I have to stop that, you know? And I'm physically holding her, and getting her down, and she was just so violent, just punching me, you know? So legally, I didn't really have anything that I could restrain her with because we didn't have those powers but as, you know, it was my, my protectiveness, you know, but I had to do it. I had to stop her because that's my caring part. I couldn't let her kill herself (short laugh) you know?

In the new family centre, Alana added, matters were going to be much better. 'Now we've got tools . . . we can actually manage and control a child without actually hurting them. So it's, it's a great relief. Cos I was always worried that it was gonna be all this physical violence and again I, I hate all that, but it's not, it's, it's very, it's quite relaxed actually because everything just calms down and goes slower' (DCO, TH).

Allen, who had found it difficult to restrain an adult man, had recently moved to the family unit. There, his 'sole responsibility is the care of the children', he said. 'That's it. The parents are secondary—I look after the children' (DCO, TH). When asked what skills he would need to do his job in that particular part of the centre, he responded with a textbook account: 'Decency, integrity, that's what you've got, that's what you've got to have when you're looking after children.' Such values, however, failed to eliminate everyone's anxieties about the effect of this form of border control. Alver, for instance, who had recently moved from Brook House to Tinsley House to work in the family unit spoke of his disquiet, 'I've gone from a Category B prison to a Travel Lodge', he began, 'and then, like, for instance the first family I had were, there were children. And to see children in a detention centre, I'd never seen that. And I'll admit I froze when I saw it. I thought, "this is completely different", I'm used to seeing adult males, and now I've got mum, two-year-old and four-year-old. It's very strange situation to be in' (DCM, TH).

Unlike adults, staff also found it difficult to ignore questions about what would happen to children after removal. 'You know, I mean, we can have girls coming in here, 14 year old girls, 15 year old girls that have never been—say Somalia—they've never been to Somalia, they've lived over here', Allen grimaced. 'They're going back there, they're gonna probably marry a 50 year old uncle, get female circumcision. And they, we've got to send them back. You know, it's tough' (DCO, TH). Weary of the pain of others, Allen could see no solution to the task before him. All that he was left with is his words from before, 'you can't sympathise with them but you've got to empathise with somebody. You can't sympathise, you've got to empathise with them. And while they're here, you've just got to give them the best you can. And at the end of the day they've got to go, and you've got to be detached . . . the emotional side, you've got to switch off altogether' (DCO, TH). The children would be deported, and, by restraining his personal engagement (sympathy) with them, Allen would manage his unease.

Deporting long-term British residents

Just as children challenged staff members' abilities to detach themselves emotionally from the more thorny ethical aspects of their job, so too long-term residents, a number of whom had served prison sentences, constituted another large group of detainees about whom staff were ambivalent. In contrast to much hostile media and political rhetoric against about this group, officers were often sympathetic. In part, their compassion sprang from practical matters. Staff typically found those who had lived in Britain for many years easier to manage, and, with their higher rates of English language proficiency, more familiar. Officers also worried about the fairness of inflicting further punishment, uncomfortable with a system in which offenders effectively received two custodial terms. 'I reckon they should give them special conditions', Leah asserted, 'make them report to the police for a year when their sentence is over. And then, once they're proved that they are law abiding, let them stay' (DCO, YW).

Those who had lived in the UK since childhood could be particularly vexing for staff. As one officer observed in Colnbrook about a man facing deportation due to his criminal record, staff sometimes found the immigration law difficult to reconcile with their own sense of fairness. 'Today, I was speaking to one gentleman', Asma told me,

> he's been detained here for over two years and he's been living in England since he was six and he's a Somali national. Now, the reason why he has been detained for so long is that he has more than 35 offences. But I think he said that 20 of those offences are from when he was under 18. But to me, I feel like he's a product of this society because when he came here when he was six, what did he know? (DCO, CB).

Echoing Ridoy's words from the previous chapter, Asma did not think it was fair to expel this man when his criminal activity occurred after a life in Britain. He was 'a product of this society', not of Somalia. He was, in short, recognizable, not a stranger at all.

To be sure, not all ex-offenders were treated with compassion. Immigration officers in particular tended to perceive them as troublemakers. Some were actively fearful of them. Certain institutions, like Campsfield House, minimized the numbers of former prisoners, linking their presence to the need for greater security. 'Our regime is, you know, incredibly relaxed', Bob pronounced. 'We don't have any MAPPA-1s.[11] We have certain MAPPAs, but we don't have any MAPPA-1s or 2s. Or we shouldn't have, and if we do they get removed very, very quickly, within sort

---

11. Ex-prisoners under 'Multi-Agency Public Protection Arrangements'. 'A set of statutory arrangements to assess and manage the risk posed by certain sexual and violent offenders' (Ministry of Justice, 2012: 1), MAPPAs bring together prison, police, and probation staff in the management of offenders. They are numbered on a scale in which category 1 refers to sex offenders, category 2 to those convicted of certain violent offences, and category 3 are 'Other Dangerous Offenders: offenders who do not qualify under Categories 1 or 2 but have been assessed as currently posing a risk of serious harm' (Ministry of Justice, 2012: 2).

of forty-eight hours, if it gets to that stage' (DCO, CH). The presence or, in this case the absence, of such people, he observed, shaped the nature of the centre's regime: 'we don't have need for any rehab, or to address the needs of an addict or someone like that . . . we accept only those guys who are in for offences like cultivating cannabis, fraudulent [sic] . . . We have a few rapes and bits and bobs', he went on breezily, 'some paedophilia. But we don't really have murderers or anything like that' (DCO, CH).

Even in the more securitized establishments like Colnbrook and Brook House, where the SMT corridor included photographs of detainees on MAPPA, and the proportions of ex-prisoners were high, views about them were inconsistent. Indeed, while stories circulated everywhere of dangerous ex-offenders—whom staff and detainees rumoured were more likely to be released by the Home Office than more deserving men—it was clear that long-term residents, criminal or otherwise, challenged the staff in ways that new arrivals, and even asylum seekers did not.

As with their ambivalence about children, violence and self-harm, staff views on long-term UK residents illuminate the destabilizing impact of recognition in an institution designed to facilitate removal. In contrast to the accepted position expressed by sociologist Zygmunt Bauman (1991), that ambivalence arises from unknowability and the stranger, these examples suggest that, in detention, ambivalence sprang more readily from familiarity. Those who could speak English fluently, children who might resemble your own, people in pain; they were the hard cases.

Writing in the final decade of the twentieth century, just after the fall of the Berlin Wall, sociologist Zygmunt Bauman (1991: 51) asserted categorically that, 'There are friends and enemies. And there are strangers'. For Bauman (1991: 61), the stranger was 'the bane of modernity . . . an entity ineradicably *ambivalent* blurring a boundary line vital to the construction of a particular social order or a particular life-world'. The otherwise curious insistence of modern neo-liberal states on regulating and incarcerating groups whose arrival and existence they cannot prevent, in his view, sprang from a desire for order.

Yet, from within a multicultural society like the UK, with its long tradition of colonial and post-colonial rule and influence and of offering sanctuary to the politically dispossessed, Bauman's pessimistic insistence on the irrevocable mistrust of the stranger seems over-stated and, in its emphasis on the view from nowhere, paternalistic (Ahmed, 2000). Who, after all, decides who is the stranger? How do we recognize this figure among our various and varied friends and enemies?

To be sure, the state can and does wield considerable power over foreigners, particularly those without documents or who have served a criminal sentence. However, for every such individual, restricted and controlled by the state, far more foreigners live among us as part of our community. Indeed, sometimes those whom we assume to be outsiders are, in fact, just like us (Girling et al, 1999). Even those who are subject to stringent controls—perhaps even those who are deported—may experience state power in a variety of ways; the truth is that we simply do not know much about the subjective experience of penal power under conditions of globalization.

Unlike caseworkers, policy makers and politicians, safely removed from daily contact, custodial and onsite Home Office employees must forge relationships with those judged unwelcome in order for the institution to run. In these messy, human encounters, staff sometimes find that those deemed unsuitable for residence, are familiar after all. When that happens, staff members may call into question their job and their sense of self. In order to minimize such negative emotions, they turn away (Cohen, 2001). In this denial and rupture once again we return to the politics of estrangement and alienation, in which IRCs are situated and to which they contribute.

Alienation, estrangement, and border control

Primarily employed by the private sector, DCOs embody the vulnerabilities of neo-liberalism and the alienation of the working class. Poorly paid and insecure, with limited personal influence or capital, officers often struggled to consolidate a coherent sense of self in their own right. They were also warned not to complain.'When we start working here', Caren confided, 'we sign a contract that says we are not allowed to make public what happens in here, and we would get fired and even prosecuted if we do' (DCO, TH).

It was not just that officers were concerned they might lose their jobs. They were also unsure about the broader context in which they worked. The immigration system did not always make sense. 'It's so confusing', Mary complained, 'why some people are deported and not another. Just when you think you've got a handle on it, something happens that changes it all over again' (DCO, CH).

Some found the lack of certainty thrilling. 'You have no idea what you're gonna come in to do today and that's part of its attraction I think for, for many of us', Lela noted. 'On the other hand', she contended, 'it can be extremely frustrating if you've planned to do something that you don't like and then all of a sudden Yarl's Wood kind of derails that plan shall we say and alters things'. Above, all, she said, it was an emotional job. 'I've had some tragic duties, I've, I've sat with a woman while she aborted her baby with medication but then I've had the joy of going to say to somebody, "Pack your stuff you're being released". So you know, it's a job of, I'm not gonna use the word "rollercoaster" because it isn't a reality TV programme, it is real life. But it is, it can swing either way, you know? So it is an amazing job' (DCM, YW).

Dealing with confusion and with a distraught population, is not easy. Many coped by turning away. Yet, too much distance, officers appreciated, was not always a safe or effective response. Notwithstanding his earlier comparison between deportation and the slaughterhouse, Sean did not perceive the women in Yarl's Wood to be animals. They are 'not room numbers or, or anything like that', he stated. 'They're individual people and they have names so I will learn their names and I always address them by name' (DCO, YW). For those who were struggling, feeling suicidal or depressed, he promised, 'I'll take you to one side and we'll talk and talk it over and I'll be with you as long as possible . . . that's my method of, of getting them through it . . . I give them myself, I give them my time and my, my experience and my, my, well whatever's needed really to, to get them through this emotional period. It could be a short time until it subsides but yeah' (DCO, YW).

Indeed, disaffection was seen to underpin many problems in the Home Office. Immigration officers themselves criticized their organization on these grounds. Caseworkers 'only see them on paper', Paul protested. 'They don't come here, so it's easy for them to say, "oh well he committed a crime, we can't let him out"' (Home Office). Grievances such as these reveal the salience of face-to-face contact in fostering understanding. 'Sometimes I think our contractors do a better job of treating them as individuals than we do', Riley concluded (Home Office).

Detainees were particularly critical. For some, it was simple. Immigration officers did not know what they were doing. 'I don't know your country, about your country [Australia]', Sami observed. 'People, immigration officers only twenty years old, five years old, twenty years old, how many, how they know to our countries? Only experience, personal experience, someone can decide. Just he had my passport photocopy' (Pakistan, CB). For this man, the immigration staff's ignorance was compounded by their lack of face-to-face interaction with those whose lives they were determining. In the absence of experience, he apprehended, paperwork was all important.

Such a relational gap, Frank pointed out, made it easy for caseworkers to deny their humanity. 'It's like, it's like a slaughterhouse!' he expostulated, echoing Sean's terminology. 'They don't look at you like okay . . . to them we're all the same. Once you're in here, you just like an animal. No rights whatsoever and all that' (Zimbabwe, MH). Without a personal connection, Frank realized, he had become unrecognizable to those deciding his future.

By keeping caseworkers elsewhere the Home Office, has created a bureaucratically complicated system. Paperwork could be more conveniently administered, if the decision-maker was housed in the same building. Yet, as Frank and Sami appreciated, power without human contact is difficult to restrain. The estrangement, inherent in the bureaucratic organization of the immigration system, in other words, is integral to control. In this separation the purpose of detention is made clear.

Conclusion

Diversity and mobility raises profound challenges not just for how power operates, but for our understanding of it. Many officers were aware, however fleetingly, of the pains they were inflicting in the name of border control. In their moments of doubt and ambiguity, we bear witness not only to the effort expended in expulsion, but also to the possibility of thinking otherwise. Staff and detainee testimonies reveal the pains and the pleasures of alterity, the difficulties in excluding those we recognize, the ways in which our shared attributes are denied (Ahmed, 2000; 2004). In these moments, we have witnessed the importance of gender and class as factors uniting those in detention with their guards. We have also seen how matters of nationality and race can divide. Power flows through these identities, and may also be blocked by them.[12]

12. For a related discussion on identity in prisons, see Bosworth and Carrabine, 2001; Phillips, 2012; Kaufman, 2014.

Despite their doubts, staff proceeded as required. The contract must be followed. As they overcome their qualms, the purpose of IRCs as a site of alienation and estrangement is laid bare, while the facilitating role of the private sector comes into focus.

As in any modern institution, bureaucracy and paperwork offer an important bulwark against feelings. The economic precariousness of the private sector staff render them particularly vulnerable, unable or unlikely to refuse what is being asked of them. In any case, the internal division of labour, where the decision-making occurs off site and is merely administered in these custodial settings does much to assuage guilt. 'The law's the law', Arvil intoned. 'We're just the, we're the messengers that get shot each time we've got to do it' (DCO, TH). Though cognizant of blame, Arvil conveniently disregards his own role in border control, turning it back to the government.

Such denial was not easily done, however. Individuals broke through their barriers occasionally capturing their attention and compassion. In these moments, when individual officers recognized detainees as fellow human beings, they were often troubled by their claims and experiences. Although confusing, relationships with detainees led officers to a more stable and legitimate sense of self. 'A lot of detainees have said to me "Miss, you're like a mum to me." Or, you know? "I respect you. 'Cos . . . you're like, you're just like mum", you know?' Alisa said proudly (DCO, TH). Alver, too, felt he built lasting relationships. 'I had a Christmas card last year from a detainee. He said, "thanks very much for your help. Merry, merry Christmas", basically. It was really nice to know that a detainee . . . I think he'd been out for, like, two months or something, still remembers you' (DCM, TH).

In such interactions, punctuated by recognition and desire, the salience and potential of proximity in challenging estrangement is made clear. Officers struggled most in understanding border control in these kinds of face-to-face encounters. Their own sense of identity also depended on them. Power, such instances bring home, is not an abstract quality circulating from an unknown point. It is, instead, wielded among people. It is embodied and made real in face-to-face encounters as well as spread, shored up and replicated through more anonymous bureaucratic mechanisms.

It is in the interaction between these different forms, that power and control in detention are rendered simultaneously more complete and precarious than in other custodial institutions. Forcing out those who have been living among us all along is not straightforward. In order to cope with their feelings, staff needed to turn away, and keep their distance, not only from detainees, but also from themselves. They not only had to emphasize differences from those whom they recognized, but they had to become alienated from themselves. In their encounters with detainees, officers appreciated the challenge of detention and its costs. Staff were aware of shared humanity despite difference, an awareness which, if left unchecked, led to shame and confusion, unpleasant emotions which made it difficult to do their job. 'At the end of the day', as Ammon put it, 'we're all human beings. We all live, live together, so gotta just treat each other the way you'd like to be treated yourself' (DCO, TH).

Conclusion

Irrevocably foreign?

We are human. We are human, not animals. We have hearts. We have feelings (Sami, Pakistan, CB).

Purpose of Yarl's Wood? Well other than the fact that they detain people that are illegally in this country or obviously overstayed, etcetera. After they've walked through the door, the purpose of Yarl's Wood is to, to care and support these people until they leave and prepare them for their onward journey, basically. That's all we can do and do it to the best of our ability and I don't see that we've failed before, we haven't failed I don't think in anything (Leah, DCO, YW).

Detention centres confound many usual categories of analysis, defying neat explanation. Prison-like yet not penal, they are filled with people recognizable but foreign. They are overseen by uniformed custody officers who possess little power. Those who make the decisions are located elsewhere. As spaces in which foreign nationals may be held for indefinite periods of time, IRCs have no assured outcome or inherent purpose beyond providing secure housing. Neither staff nor detainees know how long a period of confinement will last, nor who will succeed in challenging their expulsion.

While the banalities of daily life, the provision of food and comfort of the living areas are not entirely irrelevant, they are of secondary importance to most of the population, whose past and future are imbricated in their present. Physically located in the UK, IRCs and their detained population exist simultaneously elsewhere. These places are a threshold to another country, the staging zone for another life. Those within, reduced to their nationality are always, already, out of place.

It is not just in their institutional life that IRCs challenge us to rethink penal power, but also in their population. These are, as one former centre manager observed, places of 'hyper diversity'. People inside do not just differ by nationality but, even within the same national group, according to religion, ethnicity, gender, sexuality, age, and class. Detainees find it hard to relate to many of their peers, while staff members labour to keep up with the ever-changing population. Custody officers struggle to articulate a clear sense of purpose in their work, and find themselves troubled by individual cases. Their relationship to the Home Office is often fraught while that with detainees is not always clear. Detention custody officers are frequently alienated from the Senior Management Team, while both groups may mistrust or fear their corporate head. Their jobs are difficult and insecure, subject to the vagaries of a contract that is regularly (and ruthlessly) put out to tender.

In contrast to our usual expectations about risk and dangerousness, in detention it is those who are familiar who are difficult to govern, not those who are different. Staff find it hard to coerce women and men whom they recognize and with whom they connect. People are linked by aspirations, accents, and religion. They may share a history of migration, an ethnic background, a socio-economic class. Simply living in close quarters and interacting daily can bring people together. Detainees often struggle to make sense of their treatment. For them and for those who guard them, 'citizenship' is not always a sufficiently compelling mode of differentiation or justification of custody.

In order to make sense of these paradoxes, we need to place detention centres in a wider context of border control. While women and men tend to experience their confinement as an individual sorrow and a personal frustration, broader patterns are apparent in their accounts and in the state response to them. In these patterns, a vocabulary of understanding and, therefore, a pathway to alternatives may emerge.

Estrangement and mass mobility

Under conditions of mass mobility, paradoxically encouraged by neoliberal globalization but also frequently resented by established citizens, states around the world have tightened border control, making it more difficult for large sections of the global population to enter legally or to remain. Such developments follow predictable, racialized pathways, in which, despite long-standing chains of migration sustained by colonial and post-colonial relations with the economically developed North, citizens from the global South have been particularly disadvantaged (see, inter alia, Aas, 2007a; 2007b; 2013; Balibar, 2004; 2005; Guild, 2009; Sassen, 2007).

The impact of these developments, detainees made clear, is painful. One such man, a singer-songwriter called Sylas, whom I met at Campsfield House in the first days of the project, explained. Originally from Jamaica, Sylas had overstayed a visitor's visa. By the time he came to the attention of the Home Office, he had resided undocumented in the UK for eight years and was living with a British woman and their two children. Sylas' links to Britain did not end there. 'In this country now, I've a family', he said. 'I've got grandad, I've aunts, I've uncle, cousins, all that'. Facing imminent and likely permanent separation from these loved ones, Sylas underlined that his goals were not unusual: 'I want that freedom of speech, our rights, just like any normal family'. His status as a detainee, however, he recognized, rendered such an outcome unlikely. As he commented ruefully, 'we can't get that' (Jamaica, CH). David came to a similar conclusion: 'It's all about taking people away from their family, kicking them out, innit?' (Uganda, CB).

Globalization and mass mobility have also had a profound impact on contemporary criminal justice and criminal law (Aas and Bosworth, 2013). Increasingly pressed into the service of border control, prisons (Kaufman, 2012; Ugelvik, 2012; Kaufman and Bosworth, 2013), police (Weber, 2013; Bowling, 2010; Bowling and Sheptycki, 2011), and the criminal law (Stumpf, 2006; Aliverti, 2012a; 2012b; Dauvergne, 2008) have become global in outlook and effect, even while a rhetoric of national pre-eminence has grown and flourished. At the same time, we have witnessed in many jurisdictions a flurry of new immigration offences and the construction of fresh immigration detention centres (Aliverti, 2013; Bosworth, 2012; Wilsher, 2012; Makaremi, 2009b; Brotherton and Barrios, 2011; Kanstroom, 2012; Grewcock, 2010; Dow, 2004; Pratt, 2005). The implication of these developments, notably in regard to the criminalization of migration control, is not lost on those subject to them. 'Sometimes I feel like I'm in prison', Malika (Pakistan, YW) remarked sadly, while Emmanuel lamented bitterly, 'they treat us worse than their own criminals' (Togo, CB).

In these testimonies we glimpse the personal effect of such border control practices as detention. Treated 'worse than' criminals, separated from their children, 'kicked out', their aspirations thwarted, detainees seek, often fruitlessly, for language and a position from which to make sense of and challenge their treatment. 'I know it's not a prison', Puneet acknowledged, 'I know it's called a detention centre or a removal centre or whatever but it is a prison' (India, MH). 'It's not my choice to be here fighting for my human rights', Masani angrily pronounced. 'We don't have any choice' (Uganda, YW).

Officers also struggle to understand their job and its purpose. Working in a secure environment that often resembles the prison, they are not there to punish. Yet, they must maintain order and enable the state to eject women and men who often do not want to leave. As a putatively non-punitive custodial environment, IRCs operate not just without the same temporal limits of a criminal sentence, but also without the mechanisms of governance available in the prison estate. There are no adjudications and, while detainees can be briefly removed from association, the decision to do so has to be authorized by the onsite immigration staff. 'It's difficult to control people here', Tony remarked, 'because you can't punish them' (DCO, MH). Instead, staff members are advised to draw on other interpersonal skills, interacting with detainees in order to secure their compliance.

Though limited in their goals, in such interactions and in the connections they forge with one another, staff and detainees remind us that institutions rely on human relationships. That such personal relations emerge under conditions of deportation, in sites which are meant to be temporary, when detainees have already been designated unwelcome, illuminates a fundamental tension at the heart of border control: identity is broader than identification. Not all strangers are unfamiliar.

In acknowledging our shared humanity, we free the space to ask a series of questions. Can we justify the costs of detention? Are Britain (the US, Australia, France) prepared to turn away so many whose histories and daily life, in a multicultural, post-colonial society, they might share? What would it take to imagine and enact a different approach to border control? Is there space for more amicability under conditions of mass mobility? What are the main barriers to hospitality?

While I appreciate that there is little political will to ease migration policy, and considerable public demand to tighten it further, often prompted by a self-interested media and cynical politicians, those in detention, workers and detainees, aspire to a different system. If there is any point in ethnographic studies, it must surely be this: to advocate recognition and moderation.

Making sense of detention

There is considerable variation in the nature and justification of immigration detention, internationally and within nation states. From tents and dormitories to high-security cellular accommodation, detention centres take many forms. Whereas Australia prefers to build them offshore, sometimes in other sovereign territories altogether, in the UK they tend to surround the country's main airports. The Maltese government favours tents. The Greeks sometimes use shipping containers.

The population within detention centres is heterogeneous. Nearly all of those detained in Australia are refugees arriving by boat. Those who fly in tend to be housed in the community. There is also a handful (c. 50) of time-served foreign prisoners and some visa overstayers (Grewcock, 2011). As might be expected, in Southern European states like Greece, Malta, Spain, and Italy, very many arrive and are duly detained. Such nations also confine significant sums of people trying to leave. The detention centre at Athens airport, for instance, overflows with non-EU nationals caught as they seek to fly North (Fili, 2013).

In 2006, the European Parliament published a briefing paper by Elspeth Guild on the range of immigration detention practices in EU member states. According to her there are five main types of detention: 'Open camps: detainees can leave and return (subject to some restrictions)'; 'Closed camps: detainees cannot leave'; 'Administrative: publicly operated', 'Administrative: privately operated', and 'Military' (Guild, 2006: Appendix). Guild deliberately excluded the imprisonment of foreign national offenders from this list, although she noted some important similarities in their treatment, specifically in the moves underway at the time in member states to criminalize certain immigration offences (Aliverti, 2013).

The common feature across all places of detention, Guild argued, was 'their coercive nature' (Guild, 2006). In order to mitigate such pressure she advised governments to pay careful attention to the internal conditions and the grounds for detention. Such places, she warned, risked compromising the principle of liberty of the individual when the legal or political justification for detention is not clear (see also Fordham, Stefanelli, and Eser, 2013).

As might be expected, criminologists have sought to understand the purpose of detention in light of other, more familiar, explanations of custody. Is immigration detention a form of punishment or is it designed to deter? Do detention centres reform those they hold, or simply exclude them? The answers are not apparent.

While Arjen Leerkes and Denis Broeders (2010; 2013) paint a system that adopts the goals we usually associate with punishment, Cetta Mainwearing (2012) found in Malta that the government seeks primarily to deter. Kay Hailbronner (2007) and others identify a punitive rationale, largely directed at the most vulnerable. In some countries like Greece, it seems not to matter what the official aspiration might be, immigration detention all too often fails to meet any acceptable guidelines (Fili, 2013; Bosworth, Fili, and Pickering, 2014; Amnesty International, 2010; 2013; PICUM, 2013; HRW, 2013).

It is understandable that scholars seek to place this practice within existing frameworks. However, it is important to reflect also on the enduring lack of clarity over the purpose and effect of detention. Front line staff and detainees, as well as civil servants within and beyond the detention centre, express considerable ambivalence about particular cases. While most accept the legitimacy of some border control, few wholly applaud detention. Women and men, who had been reporting regularly to the Home Office under the terms of their asylum ad immigration case, did not understand why they had been suddenly swept into custody. Ex-prisoners had often been given little warning of their secondary period of incarceration. Many staff wondered why the detainees could not have been deported or removed from prison.

Often the sticking point was the duration. Nobody supported indefinite confinement. Staff and detainees were also confused by the variety in decision-making. Up to half of those detained are released back to the community, at least for a time. It is not always clear why.

In every circumstance, therefore, detention remains opaque. In contrast to the unequivocal message from politicians, staff and detainees flounder in making sense of where they are or what they do. In their bid to understand, most turn to other institutions, typically the prison, but also slavery and torture, to find a vocabulary through which they can articulate their experiences.

Yet, as places without a clear goal and with limited effect, immigration removal centres are not easily explained by the traditional notions of discipline or coercion. The identity of a detainee cannot be changed by the threat of detention or by its regime (Bosworth, 2012). Citizenship or the right to remain cannot be earned or learned in such places, despite detainees' attempts to do so through motherhood, long-term residence, or other identities. So, too, while detainees are undeniably vulnerable, it is possible to overstate the power of the government. Despite the arbitrary decision-making and extensive powers available to the state in the pursuit of border control, these institutions are not outside the law. Rather, they may be better understood as sites of multiple governance. The state governs them at a distance, contracting them out to the private sector and HM Prison service, while maintaining control over the most important factor, the immigration case.

At the same time, however, the British state can do little without the agreement of other sovereign powers. In immigration matters, unlike punishment, it is not the sole determining authority (Bosworth, 2013). Instead, its power is relational, dependent on other nation states, international agencies and the detainees themselves. Given the trouble in identification, even small actions by individuals may disrupt this power for considerable periods.

Rather than conceiving of immigration removal centres as concentration camps, or forms of discipline or governmentality, such places are best understood as sites of estrangement. Institutions where relationships are sundered and individuals forced out, IRCs recast those among us as 'strangers', unrecognizable no matter how familiar. Thinking about estrangement and its cognate terms of alienation and denial reminds us of the personal nature of the application of power, and its individual costs, while being mindful of structural factors like race, gender, and class. In so doing, it reveals the salience of lived experience in understanding and generating a critique of border control.

As we have seen, IRCs are often confusing. Staff and detainees struggle to understand them, or one another. They are also painful. Those within are denied more than just their liberty. Their hopes and aspirations are thwarted, while their past is erased. Many find it difficult to cope, unable to understand why they are treated in this way. 'Listen to me', Waldo pleaded,

> this place not good for me, it's not good for me. I want to be free, like as you are free, you can move in and move out, without anyone monitoring

you. You can do anything for yourself, you can't just be there if somebody, if somebody, they're regulating you, go and sleep, you go and sleep, wake up, you wake up, . . . I can't do that . . . this is not good for me . . . It's meant for people who, who, who crime makers . . . I'm not one. You know, fraud guys, you know, criminals, you know, liars . . . I'm not supposed to be here, I'm not, I'm not supposed to be here, this is not my place, yeah (Ghana, BH).

While Waldo experienced his pain individually, detention centres create and exist for a broader category of people, who, in their origins in the global south, as well as in their socio-economic class, reveal a predictable, racialized form of exclusion. Yet, in a diverse society like Britain, excluding on the basis of identity is not straightforward. On the one hand, Malik made clear, detention was merely the most recent manifestation of his identity in the UK as an ethnic minority. 'I been here thirty-two years yeah?' he said. 'I'll be honest with you, I seen the racialism, yeah? . . . Our mums used to put you know, oil, that's Asian tradition we are like oiled, mum put on. "Pakis with the greasy hairs, yeah." "Oh you smell of curries"' (Pakistan, BH). On the other hand, he pointed out, matters had changed. 'Everybody eat curries now and everybody put gel on their head.' In fact, Malik suggested, there was a paradox underpinning detention. These days, he claimed, 'is not Asian coming to this country, is EU, European coming to this country. They don't talk about, maybe they are white. But . . . they can't stop them, and they try to blame on . . . you understand, Asian sub-continent' (Pakistan, BH).

Notwithstanding Malik's sense that 'Asians' were singled out by the detention process, one of the reasons why it is difficult—in practical and ethical terms—to expel many of those in detention is that, like him, they have ties in the UK. Even when specific individuals do not, as a multicultural society, many others who are just like them can be found in the wider community. Part of the job of the IRC is therefore to render the familiar opaque. In an inversion of our usual expectations about the culture of control and risk, it is the familiar who is risky, rather than the stranger. Those who belong are difficult (emotionally, morally, in practice) to eject. Rather than disciplined subjects, IRCs merely confirm those foreigners in detention in an identity they always had: as strangers.

Thinking about estrangement directs our attention to the temporal and spatial nature of interactions and the relationships people forge, capturing the affective nature of border control. It illuminates the uncertainty and ambivalence percolating through these sites. While detainees bear the brunt of the politics of estrangement, staff also find detention confounding. 'We may spend six months or however long the detainee's with us, looking after them on a daily basis and giving them whatever they need and having a fairly good interaction, maybe even having a laugh and a joke with them', Alvis began, 'but then when an instruction comes down from UKBA that this person's going on a flight, they need to ignore all that lot and maybe use force in order to move them out of the centre.' This disjuncture in his role, he made clear, was taxing. 'So you need to make friends for six months and then ignore the whole thing and then put handcuffs on them and put them in a van.' Alvis was not sure what to make of it all. 'I don't know whether you're supposed to care an awful lot and then stop at the end of it or whether you're not supposed to care at all, all the way through', he wondered (DCO, TH).

Staff and detainees grapple everyday with such matters. In paying attention to their testimonies, we appreciate the difficulties they face in denying one another and themselves. In so doing, we bear witness to the uneasy operation of power, grasping its costs as well as its effects.

Estrangement captures the affective and contested nature of life in detention as well as its impact. It also reveals the limits of confining people based on their citizenship and illuminates a way forward: recognition. Misrecognition and status denial are not only painful, they erase our shared humanity.

Within the confines, amid the anger, fear and frustration, staff and detainees reach for relationships and a common understanding. Recognition can be unexpected, as Pam appreciated. 'Before when I was in my country', she admitted, 'I thought all white people are the same. But now I look at you, and I look at Leah [DCO] and I know that you are very different and come from different places and different cultures'. Its effects, she suggests, reaching far beyond the walls of Yarl's Wood. 'Why did people who travelled before not tell us how different you are?' she wondered. 'Now I go back to my country and I know' (Nigeria, YW). Closer to home, Leah had a similar view. 'You sit next to these people on the bus every day', she pointed out. 'They are part of the community' (DCO, YW).

Recognition does not happen easily. There are many forces operating to prevent it. As Arvis acknowledged, when the order comes to cut ties, officers must obey or lose their job. The wider political point remains pertinent, however. Expulsion is facilitated through estrangement. To challenge it we need to restate our commitment to human fellowship. 'I want to live like a normal person', Amara observed. 'Just be normal' (Gambia, MH). Political rhetoric rarely gives room to human perspectives such as these.

As I was completing the first draft of this book in the autumn of 2013, a boat filled with men, women, and children from a range of African countries attempting to enter Europe sank one kilometre away from Lampedusa, killing over 350 of them (Davies, 2013a). A few weeks later, the remains of nearly 100 women and children were discovered in the desert in Niger, another group of people who died in their attempt to reach Europe (Hirsch, 2013). Far away on the other side of the world, boats continued to sink en route to Australia (Weber and Pickering, 2011) while women and men were still perishing on the US-Mexican border (Binational Immigration Institute, 2013).

For those who make it to their destination, life remains precarious. Nations continue to restrict access to refugee protection and step up their policing of anyone without documents, while making it harder for families to bring out their relatives, universities to recruit students and employers to hire foreign citizens. While it is possible to live for many years without immigration status, individuals can never be sure how long their presence will be tolerated. Such vulnerability was drawn home in France around the same time of the deaths in Niger and off the coast of Sicily, when the police arrested Leonarda Dibrani, an undocumented Roma teenage girl who had been resident for some years in France. Taken into custody while on a school trip, Leonarda was forcibly extracted from the school bus in front of her peers.

Whereas Leonarda was sent directly to the airport with her family and returned to Albania,[1] numerous others around the world languish in detention centres. In 2013, it became evident that such places are, themselves, not always safe. That summer, reports emerged of sexual coercion in Yarl's Wood (Townsend, 2013). A few months later, statistics were published from Australia alleging regular sexual assaults throughout their detention facilities.[2] Such violence has been widely documented in US detention centres since the 1990s. In the UK too, a number of detainees have died in recent

---

1. The previous month, following his arrest in Paris, another high-profile deportee Khatchik Khachatryan spent two days in jail followed by 28 days in detention at the centre in Vincennes. The first attempt to deport him failed. He was expelled two days later (*L'Humanité*, 2013).
2. Media reports were based on data released by 'Detention Logs' available at <http://detentionlogs.com.au>.

years, either in custody or soon thereafter (D. Taylor, 2014; Rawlinson, 2014). On the opposite side of the world, on Manus Island, Papua New Guinea, one of the offshore sites where Australia sends asylum seekers who arrive by boat, Reza Berati, a young Iranian man was beaten to death under circumstances that remain unclear (Australian Associated Press, 2014).

In each of these examples the humanity of foreigners was denied. In the casual brutality and indifference, as well as in their death and trauma, we see that the usual restraints to power do not apply. These detainees are not fully human.

And yet, each example provoked a torrent of criticism and protest, multitudes came together to appeal for common cause. In Paris, for instance, the school friends of Leonarda joined with students who did not know her, to demonstrate in the streets. Their outrage was such, and the media reporting so sympathetic, that President François Hollande offered the opportunity to Leonarda to return, without her family, to complete her studies. The tragedy of Lampedusa likewise generated significant debate and grief among the Italian media, politicians, and people (Davies, 2013b), while, albeit to a lesser extent, the deaths in the UK and in Papua New Guinea did as well.

Pope Francis explicitly criticized current policies, while President Giorgio Napolitano declared a national day of mourning and awarded posthumous Italian citizenship to those who died. As with Hollande's offer to Leonarda, however, the Italian President did not extend his generosity to everyone; those who survived the boat trip were locked in detention, charged with the criminal offence of arriving without a visa and banned from the funeral. In Australia and Britain, the deaths in custody became the subject of official investigations.

NGOs around the world, with some scholarly and journalistic assistance, bear witness to the suffering caused by border control, counting migrant deaths, gathering testimonies about conditions in detention, depicting life without documents. Charities inspire volunteers to extend friendship and offer basic necessities to the most vulnerable. On Christmas Island, the site of one of the remote detention centres for those who travel to Australia by boat, a local resident reports on new arrivals and events on a Twitter feed, providing evidence about a location that is otherwise impenetrable and largely unaccountable.[3] Lawyers offer their services *pro bono*.

---

3. @gordonthomsonci.

Such examples fit uneasily into many current theoretical explanations of border control which perceive detention centre as the extension of some holistic logic rather than as spaces that contest that logic or have a meaning of their own. In so doing, not only does much scholarship overlook the enduring legal restraints on state power,[4] but it also risks reproducing what it seeks to critique, failing to engage with those who live among us or who wish to do so.

Even as the immigration status of detainees and the institution where they are held cast them as unwelcome and strange, many aspire to familiar goals. They value family ties, are in search of meaningful employment, long for safety, and hope for autonomy. So, too, they belong to a class, a gender, an ethnic and religious group, a community. They are not fully defined or constricted by their passport or nationality. Under these circumstances, empathy and sympathy become difficult to disentangle, and staff, however briefly, may be troubled by what they do. In their hesitation and in detainee laments, the ethical costs of exclusion are exposed.

In their words too, staff and detainees demonstrate how power flows through and creates identity, converting a long-term British resident into a 'stranger', a mother into a 'single female' appropriate for placement in Yarl's Wood, an asylum seeker into a liar. Once again these matters do not proceed without debate or contestation. Women and men continue to argue for their 'right to family life' or their membership of a persecuted group, to avoid *refoulement*.

To be sure, detainees who wish to challenge their immigration case, face an uphill battle. The law, with its neat divisions between citizens and foreigners, and its detailed categories of grounds for exclusion, finds it difficult to include messy, personal matters of affect or desire. Institutional backlogs in the Home Office prevent speedy decision-making, while its critics assert a culture of disbelief permeates its offices (see eg Baillot, Cowan, and Munro, 2013).

IRCs reinforce many of these barriers. Detention centres are also a result of them. These are sites of estrangement, isolated physical spaces where the ties between those within and those outside are cut. Much of the symbolic effort of excising unwelcome foreigners from Britain is accomplished by

---

4. Notwithstanding considerable efforts by various Home Secretaries to minimize access to Human Rights protections, or the state's occasional reluctance to honour its responsibilities of *non-refoulement*, these safeguards remain in place.

the material similarities between detention centres and the prison, buildings which identify and differentiate detainees from other foreigners, as
unwelcome, threatening, and undeserving.

Instead, detainees often expend considerable energy (and money) challenging the identity attributed to them. Staff, too, offer alternative interpretations and understandings. It would be wrong to imagine that everyone
or even many people find a means to defy state power. Most detainees are
removed or deported. Many suffer greatly. Nonetheless, in their accounts
we can hear the potential for 'thinking otherwise' (Hemmings, 2012).
Equally important, we bear witness to the costs of denying them, appreci-
ating the affective nature of power and the emotional impact of exclusion
(Ahmed, 2000; 2004).

Conclusion

Despite their liminal status, and official pronouncements about them,
IRCs, in the shadow of deportation, at the edge of the nation state, are
concrete institutions with an internal world of their own. With timetables,
routines, and cultures, sometimes they resemble and at other times they
depart from the prison. Even though detainees find it hard to fill their day,
and their attention is often elsewhere, worrying about immigration matters, trying to avoid deportation, they proceed through these centres in
a regimented fashion, from reception to removal or release. Staff, despite
a lack of clarity over the purpose of their job, often do their best.

IRCs, as presently constituted, are not inevitable. With some creative
thinking and political willpower, they could be otherwise. In order for that
to happen, however, we must acknowledge those within as fully human
and able to call on us. At the same time, considerable barriers remain. It is
difficult, perhaps even counter-intuitive, to argue for recognition within
an institution defining detainees as 'out of place'. Yet, at least in the UK,
already children are treated quite differently, held only for one week, and
in a deliberately less securitized environment; why could adults not be dealt
with in the same fashion? (Bhui, 2013a; 2013b). It is also worth remember-
ing that Britain managed its migration, for many years, with far less reliance on custody than it does now. Our European neighbours continue, for
the most part, to use detention less frequently. They all limit its duration.

Above all, if detention is the solution, we need to ask what is the problem? As one particularly critical officer expressed it,

They put so much money in here, it is a waste. It is not a solution. There are so many people who will come from the North Africa now. How are they going to sort the problem? By building more places like this? This is not a solution. They spend so much money and it does not help any of them in anyway. People need more than detention (Landon, DCO, TH).

Detainees, like anyone else, need recognition, safety, autonomy, and agency. They deserve hope, dignity, and the opportunity for self-realization. Such matters, though integral to the ideal of citizenship, are not bounded by it. They are inscribed in the human condition and should be cherished and protected as such.

Under conditions of mass mobility, we must be wary of letting fears about economic resources or concerns about social cohesion overcome our commitment to humane ideals. There have always been strangers among us, and as the staff and detainee testimonies throughout this book have shown, they are not so strange after all. 'I like it here. Women can be safe here' (Naimah, Pakistan, YW); 'We are human' (Tahir, Uganda, CH); 'I want to be with my boyfriend' (Elsa, Mauritius, YW); 'I want to get married' (Rod, Nigeria, TH); 'I've got kids, I've got brothers and sisters' (Joao, Angola, CB); 'the most person is important my life my mum. I love her, she love me . . . every day she phone the place, same time' (Ali, Pakistan, BH). In creating institutions where our shared qualities and aspirations are denied, we not only denigrate those within, but risk our own alienation. As we have seen in other historical periods and in respect to other forms of social control, once we strip these aspects from others, it may be only a matter of time before we will have them taken away from ourselves. As states attempt to bolster border control we all pay a price. Those most precarious are worst affected. Yet these policies have implications for us all.

Appendix

Measuring the quality of life in detention detainee questionnaire

Part I

This survey is being carried out as part of a research project to measure the quality of life in THIS IRC. I will not be writing anything in your record or discussing any of your answers with anyone else. All of your answers and comments will remain confidential and anonymous.

Part I asks for some background information.

Part II asks about your quality of life in THIS Removal Centre.

If you would like to have anything explained, or have any difficulties with reading or writing, please ask for assistance.

Today's Date:_____

1. **What is your nationality?**...
2. **What is your ethnic group?** *(eg Kurdish, Asian, Arab etc)*..........................
3. **What is your religion?** ....
4. **How old are you?**...............................
5. **What is your marital status?**...............................
6. **How long have you been living in the UK?**...............................
7. **Do you have family members in the UK?**   Yes/No
8. **Do you have any children?**   Yes/No

9. If yes, where are they and with whom are they living?...................
....

10. How long have you been in this removal centre? ....
....

11. Were you previously in another removal centre in the UK?   Yes/No

12. If yes, which one(s) and for how long were you there?.........................
....

13. How does this centre compare to others you have experienced in the UK?
....

....

14. Have you ever been held a detention centre in any other country?
                                                                    Yes/No

15. If yes, where and when were you held? For how long were you there?
....

....

16. Before being in a removal centre, were you in prison in the UK?   Yes/No

17. If yes, how long was your sentence?

Less than one year	10 years but less than life
1 year but less than 2 years	Life (not including IPP)
2 years but less than 4 years	IPP
4 years but less than 10 years	Other (how long?)

The next set of questions concern your immigration/ asylum status:

1. Have you ever been granted the legal right to enter or remain in the UK?   Yes/No

2. Have you ever been granted indefinite leave to remain in the UK?   Yes/No

3. Did you over-stay a visa?   Yes/No

If yes, which visa did originally have (eg work, student) and when did it expire?
....

4. Do you have an immigration solicitor?   Yes/No

5. If yes, are you in regular contact?   Yes/No

6. Is your immigration solicitor paid for by Legal Aid?   Yes/No

7. Have you ever applied for *(please tick each box that is relevant):*

	Never	Once	Twice	3–5 times	5–10 times	More than 10 times
Asylum						
Bail						
Temporary Admission						
Judicial Review						
Review at the European Court						

8. **Are you currently appealing your immigration/asylum case?** Yes/No

9. **Have you appealed an immigration/asylum decision before?** Yes/No

10. **If yes, how many times have you appealed?**....................................

11. **Have your removal directions (flight) from the UK been set?** Yes/No

12. **If yes, when are you scheduled to leave/what day?**..........................

Thinking now about your detention:

1. **At this removal centre, what unit/wing are you on?**

....

2. **What incentives and privileges level are you on?** *(please circle relevant answer)*

    Basic   Standard   Enhanced   Don't know

3. **What do you do each day in this removal centre?**

....

....

4. **Have you ever been removed from Association at this centre?** Yes/No

5. **If Yes, how many times?**..

6. **Were you placed on Rule 40 or Rule 42?** Yes/No/Don't know

7. **Have you been on a hunger strike/food refusal at this removal centre?** Yes/No

8. **If Yes, how many times and for how long?**................................

9. Do you receive visits in this removal centre?   Yes/No
10. If yes, who visits you?...
....

11. Are you in regular contact with members of your family?   Yes/No
12. Are you in regular contact with outside organisations?   Yes/No
13. If yes, which ones?...
....

The next set of questions concern your health and how you are coping with detention

Below is a list of problems and complaints that people sometimes have. Read each one carefully, and select one of the descriptors that best describes **how much discomfort that problem has caused during the past Seven days (7 days) including today**. Place a tick in the appropriate box to the right of the problem. **Only one tick should be recorded for each question.**

How much were you distressed by:	Not at all	A Little bit	Quite a bit	Extremely
Feeling low in energy, slowed down				
Blaming yourself for things				
Crying easily				
Poor appetite				
Difficulty falling, staying asleep				
Feeling hopeless about the future				
Feeling sad				
Feeling lonely				
Thoughts of ending your life				

Feeling of being trapped or caught				
Worrying too much about things				
Feeling no interest in things				
Feeling everything is an effort				
Feelings of worthlessness				

14. Have you ever been on an ACDT (Assessment, Care in Detention and Teamwork) plan while in detention?

Don't know

No, never on ACDT   Yes, in another removal centre

Yes, in this removal centre   Yes, in this and another removal centre

15. Did you have a problem with drug or alcohol misuse before you arrived?

No problem with either   Yes, only with drugs

Yes, only with alcohol   Yes, with both drugs *and* alcohol

If you had a drug/alcohol misuse problem before coming into removal centre:

16. Did you need help to detox from drugs or alcohol on arrival in removal centre?

No, didn't need any detox   Yes, needed alcohol detox only

Yes, needed drug detox only   Yes, needed drug *and* alcohol detox

17. Do you have any other health problems or concerns?   Yes/No

18. If yes please list..

....

....

....

....

19. Are you on any medication?   Yes/No

20. If Yes, please list and give estimate of how long you have been taking the medication(s) (ie was it prescribed by a doctor in THIS removal centre, or before you arrived?)..

....

MEASURING THE QUALITY OF REMOVAL CENTRE LIFE

Part II

Part II of the questionnaire asks about how you feel about the quality of life you experience in *this* removal centre. It is important that you only answer in relation to the removal centre you are in now and not any other removal centres you may have been in before.

Please read each statement carefully and circle the answer that best describes how you feel. Only circle <u>one</u> answer for each statement and take care to answer each question. Please ask if there are any statements or words that you do not understand. Thank you for your co-operation.

QUESTION	FOR EACH QUESTION BELOW, PLEASE PUT A CIRCLE AROUND THE RESPONSE THAT BEST DESCRIBES HOW YOU FEEL					
	Strongly agree	Agree	Neither agree nor disagree	Disagree	Strongly disagree	Don't Know/Not applicable
1. **Most officers here are kind to me**	Strongly agree	Agree	Neither agree nor disagree	Disagree	Strongly disagree	Don't Know/Not applicable
2. **I am not being treated as a human being in here**	Strongly agree	Agree	Neither agree nor disagree	Disagree	Strongly disagree	Don't Know/Not applicable
3. **Most of the immigration staff here show concern and understanding towards me**	Strongly agree	Agree	Neither agree nor disagree	Disagree	Strongly disagree	Don't Know/Not applicable
4. **The quality of my living conditions is poor**	Strongly agree	Agree	Neither agree nor disagree	Disagree	Strongly disagree	Don't Know/Not applicable
5. **The food at this centre is good**	Strongly agree	Agree	Neither agree nor disagree	Disagree	Strongly disagree	Don't Know/Not applicable
6. **In this detention centre they do not care about me, they just want me to be deported.**	Strongly agree	Agree	Neither agree nor disagree	Disagree	Strongly disagree	Don't Know/Not applicable
7. **Most officers address and talk to me in a respectful manner**	Strongly agree	Agree	Neither agree nor disagree	Disagree	Strongly disagree	Don't Know/Not applicable

FOR EACH QUESTION BELOW, PLEASE PUT A CIRCLE AROUND THE RESPONSE THAT BEST DESCRIBES HOW YOU FEEL

QUESTION	Strongly agree	Agree	Neither agree nor disagree	Disagree	Strongly disagree	Don't Know/Not applicable
8. Most detainees do not address and talk to each other in a respectful manner	Strongly agree	Agree	Neither agree nor disagree	Disagree	Strongly disagree	Don't Know/Not applicable
9. Most immigration staff treat me with respect and listen to me properly	Strongly agree	Agree	Neither agree nor disagree	Disagree	Strongly disagree	Don't Know/Not applicable
10. I have been helped significantly by an officer in this centre with a particular problem	Strongly agree	Agree	Neither agree nor disagree	Disagree	Strongly disagree	Don't Know/Not applicable
11. I do not feel cared for by the staff in the healthcare unit	Strongly agree	Agree	Neither agree nor disagree	Disagree	Strongly disagree	Don't Know/Not applicable
12. This centre helps people who have been victims of rape or domestic violence get the care they need	Strongly agree	Agree	Neither agree nor disagree	Disagree	Strongly disagree	Don't Know/Not applicable
13. This centre helps people who have been victims of torture get the care they need	Strongly agree	Agree	Neither agree nor disagree	Disagree	Strongly disagree	Don't Know/Not applicable

	Strongly agree	Agree	Neither agree nor disagree	Disagree	Strongly disagree	Don't Know/Not applicable
14. Most staff members in this centre are honest and truthful	Strongly agree	Agree	Neither agree nor disagree	Disagree	Strongly disagree	Don't Know/Not applicable
15. The doctors here do not believe me when I tell them about my health problems	Strongly agree	Agree	Neither agree nor disagree	Disagree	Strongly disagree	Don't Know/Not applicable
16. I trust most of the immigration staff in this centre	Strongly agree	Agree	Neither agree nor disagree	Disagree	Strongly disagree	Don't Know/Not applicable
17. I do not trust most of the other detainees at this centre	Strongly agree	Agree	Neither agree nor disagree	Disagree	Strongly disagree	Don't Know/Not applicable
18. I have to be careful about everything I do in this removal centre, or it can be used against me in my immigration case	Strongly agree	Agree	Neither agree nor disagree	Disagree	Strongly disagree	Don't Know/Not applicable
19. I do not feel safe in this removal centre	Strongly agree	Agree	Neither agree nor disagree	Disagree	Strongly disagree	Don't Know/Not applicable
20. There is not enough to do at this centre	Strongly agree	Agree	Neither agree nor disagree	Disagree	Strongly disagree	Don't Know/Not applicable

QUESTION	FOR EACH QUESTION BELOW, PLEASE PUT A CIRCLE AROUND THE RESPONSE THAT BEST DESCRIBES HOW YOU FEEL				
21. I spend most of my day in my room	Strongly agree	Agree	Neither agree nor disagree	Disagree	Strongly disagree	Don't Know/Not applicable
22. To get things done in this removal centre you have to ask and ask and ask	Strongly agree	Agree	Neither agree nor disagree	Disagree	Strongly disagree	Don't Know/Not applicable
23. Staff do not bully or threaten me	Strongly agree	Agree	Neither agree nor disagree	Disagree	Strongly disagree	Don't Know/Not applicable
24. The other detainees threaten or bully me	Strongly agree	Agree	Neither agree nor disagree	Disagree	Strongly disagree	Don't Know/Not applicable
25. People who don't speak English have a hard time in here	Strongly agree	Agree	Neither agree nor disagree	Disagree	Strongly disagree	Don't Know/Not applicable
26. Since I arrived at this centre, I have thought about killing myself	Strongly agree	Agree	Neither agree nor disagree	Disagree	Strongly disagree	Don't Know/Not applicable
27. Anyone who harms themselves or attempts suicide gets the care and help from staff that they need	Strongly agree	Agree	Neither agree nor disagree	Disagree	Strongly disagree	Don't Know/Not applicable

	Strongly agree	Agree	Neither agree nor disagree	Disagree	Strongly disagree	Don't Know/Not applicable
28. I have never cut or hurt myself at this centre	Strongly agree	Agree	Neither agree nor disagree	Disagree	Strongly disagree	Don't Know/Not applicable
29. I can't receive enough visits in this centre	Strongly agree	Agree	Neither agree nor disagree	Disagree	Strongly disagree	Don't Know/Not applicable
30. This centre helps me stay in contact with my family	Strongly agree	Agree	Neither agree nor disagree	Disagree	Strongly disagree	Don't Know/Not applicable
31. I do not know where my children are	Strongly agree	Agree	Neither agree nor disagree	Disagree	Strongly disagree	Don't Know/Not applicable
32. I can speak often enough to my family/ friends on the telephone	Strongly agree	Agree	Neither agree nor disagree	Disagree	Strongly disagree	Don't Know/Not applicable
33. My children visit me here	Strongly agree	Agree	Neither agree nor disagree	Disagree	Strongly disagree	Don't Know/Not applicable
34. Most staff here do not treat detainees fairly when applying the centre rules	Strongly agree	Agree	Neither agree nor disagree	Disagree	Strongly disagree	Don't Know/Not applicable
35. Most of the immigration staff at this centre are good at explaining the decisions that concern my immigration/ asylum case	Strongly agree	Agree	Neither agree nor disagree	Disagree	Strongly disagree	Don't Know/Not applicable

QUESTION	FOR EACH QUESTION BELOW, PLEASE PUT A CIRCLE AROUND THE RESPONSE THAT BEST DESCRIBES HOW YOU FEEL					
36. Decisions made in my immigration/asylum case are made in good time	Strongly agree	Agree	Neither agree nor disagree	Disagree	Strongly disagree	Don't Know/Not applicable
37. If you do something wrong in this removal centre, officers do nothing	Strongly agree	Agree	Neither agree nor disagree	Disagree	Strongly disagree	Don't Know/Not applicable
38. I don't know how long I will be here	Strongly agree	Agree	Neither agree no disagree	Disagree	Strongly disagree	Don't Know/Not applicable
39. I don't know what is happening with my immigration/asylum case	Strongly agree	Agree	Neither agree nor disagree	Disagree	Strongly disagree	Don't Know/Not applicable
40. I don't think I will succeed in my immigration/asylum case	Strongly agree	Agree	Neither agree nor disagree	Disagree	Strongly disagree	Don't Know/Not applicable
41. Racist comments by staff are uncommon in this removal centre	Strongly agree	Agree	Neither agree nor disagree	Disagree	Strongly disagree	Don't Know/Not applicable

	Strongly agree	Agree	Neither agree nor disagree	Disagree	Strongly disagree	Don't Know/Not applicable
42. Detainees from different nationalities get along well in here	Strongly agree	Agree	Neither agree nor disagree	Disagree	Strongly disagree	Don't Know/Not applicable
43. Detainees from different religions do not get along well in here	Strongly agree	Agree	Neither agree nor disagree	Disagree	Strongly disagree	Don't Know/Not applicable
44. I mainly hang out with other detainees from the same country as me	Strongly agree	Agree	Neither agree nor disagree	Disagree	Strongly disagree	Don't Know/Not applicable
45. The shop does not provide for the needs of all ethnic and religious groups here	Strongly agree	Agree	Neither agree nor disagree	Disagree	Strongly disagree	Don't Know/Not applicable
46. Immigration staff treat all the detainees the same in this removal centre, no matter where they are from	Strongly agree	Agree	Neither agree nor disagree	Disagree	Strongly disagree	Don't Know/Not applicable
47. Healthcare provision here is as good as I would expect to receive outside	Strongly agree	Agree	Neither agree nor disagree	Disagree	Strongly disagree	Don't Know/Not applicable
48. I can usually see a doctor within a reasonable amount of time	Strongly agree	Agree	Neither agree nor disagree	Disagree	Strongly disagree	Don't Know/Not applicable

FOR EACH QUESTION BELOW, PLEASE PUT A CIRCLE AROUND THE RESPONSE THAT BEST DESCRIBES HOW YOU FEEL

QUESTION						
49. I cannot see a dentist within a reasonable amount of time	Strongly agree	Agree	Neither agree nor disagree	Disagree	Strongly disagree	Don't Know/Not applicable
50. The nurses in this removal centre look after me	Strongly agree	Agree	Neither agree nor disagree	Disagree	Strongly disagree	Don't Know/Not applicable
51. On the whole, relationships between officers and detainees in this centre are good	Strongly agree	Agree	Neither agree nor disagree	Disagree	Strongly disagree	Don't Know/Not applicable
52. I can always get help from an officer when I need it	Strongly agree	Agree	Neither agree nor disagree	Disagree	Strongly disagree	Don't Know/Not applicable
53. Personally, I do not like most of the officers here	Strongly agree	Agree	Neither agree nor disagree	Disagree	Strongly disagree	Don't Know/Not applicable
54. I have no real/good friends in this removal centre.	Strongly agree	Agree	Neither agree nor disagree	Disagree	Strongly disagree	Don't Know/Not applicable
55. It is not easy to get a translator when I need one	Strongly agree	Agree	Neither agree nor disagree	Disagree	Strongly disagree	Don't Know/Not applicable

	Strongly agree	Agree	Neither agree nor disagree	Disagree	Strongly disagree	Don't Know/Not applicable
56. I find it easy to make myself understood to immigration staff here	Strongly agree	Agree	Neither agree nor disagree	Disagree	Strongly disagree	Don't Know/Not applicable
57. I do not always understand what the officers are telling me	Strongly agree	Agree	Neither agree nor disagree	Disagree	Strongly disagree	Don't Know/Not applicable
58. The Induction process in this removal centre helped me to know what to expect each day	Strongly agree	Agree	Neither agree nor disagree	Disagree	Strongly disagree	Don't Know/Not applicable
59. When I am feeling really upset, there is someone here I can talk to	Strongly agree	Agree	Neither agree nor disagree	Disagree	Strongly disagree	Don't Know/Not applicable
60. I have no difficulty falling asleep at night	Strongly agree	Agree	Neither agree nor disagree	Disagree	Strongly disagree	Don't Know/Not applicable
61. I wake up a lot during the night	Strongly agree	Agree	Neither agree nor disagree	Disagree	Strongly disagree	Don't Know/Not applicable
62. I have regular bad dreams	Strongly agree	Agree	Neither agree nor disagree	Disagree	Strongly disagree	Don't Know/Not applicable
63. My religion helps me cope with detention	Strongly agree	Agree	Neither agree nor disagree	Disagree	Strongly disagree	Don't Know/Not applicable

QUESTION	Strongly agree	Agree	Neither agree nor disagree	Disagree	Strongly disagree	Don't Know/Not applicable
64. I am excited/happy about the future	Strongly agree	Agree	Neither agree nor disagree	Disagree	Strongly disagree	Don't Know/Not applicable
65. Officers help me to remain hopeful about my immigration/ asylum case here	Strongly agree	Agree	Neither agree nor disagree	Disagree	Strongly disagree	Don't Know/Not applicable
66. The other detainees help me to remain hopeful	Strongly agree	Agree	Neither agree nor disagree	Disagree	Strongly disagree	Don't Know/Not applicable
67. I feel it is impossible to make progress in my immigration/asylum case	Strongly agree	Agree	Neither agree nor disagree	Disagree	Strongly disagree	Don't Know/Not applicable
68. I am ready to go back	Strongly agree	Agree	Neither agree nor disagree	Disagree	Strongly disagree	Don't Know/Not applicable
69. I fear for my physical safety if I am removed from the UK	Strongly agree	Agree	Neither agree nor disagree	Disagree	Strongly disagree	Don't Know/Not applicable

	Strongly agree	Agree	Neither agree nor disagree	Disagree	Strongly disagree	Don't Know/Not applicable
70. **I am learning skills in here that will help with life after release**	Strongly agree	Agree	Neither agree nor disagree	Disagree	Strongly disagree	Don't Know/Not applicable
71. **The level of illegal drug use in this removal centre is quite high**	Strongly agree	Agree	Neither agree nor disagree	Disagree	Strongly disagree	Don't Know/Not applicable
72. **This removal centre is good at improving the well-being of detainees who have drug problems**	Strongly agree	Agree	Neither agree nor disagree	Disagree	Strongly disagree	Don't Know/Not applicable
73. **Illegal drugs cause a lot of problems between detainees in here**	Strongly agree	Agree	Neither agree nor disagree	Disagree	Strongly disagree	Don't Know/Not applicable

74. What are the three *worst* things for you about life in this removal centre?

   1...

   2...

   3...

75. What are the three most *positive* things for you about life in this removal centre?

   1...

   2...

   3...

Any other comments? *(feel free to go over the page as well if you like)*

Please take a moment or two to check that you have answered all the relevant
questions
Please put this questionnaire in the envelope provided.
Seal the envelope and hand it to a member of the research team
Thank you for taking part in the survey

References

Aas, K.F. (2013) 'The Ordered and the Bordered Society: Migration Control, Citizenship and the Northern Penal State', in K.F. Aas and M. Bosworth (eds) *The Borders of Punishment: Migration, Citizenship, and Social Exclusion*, Oxford: Oxford University Press, 21–39.

Aas, K.F. (2012) '"The Earth is one but the World is not": Criminological theory and its geopolitical divisions', *Theoretical Criminology*, 16(1): 5–20.

Aas, K.F. (2011) '"Crimmigrant" bodies and bona fide travellers: Surveillance, citizenship and global governance', *Theoretical Criminology*, 15(3): 331–46.

Aas, K.F. (2007a) *Globalization*, London: Sage.

Aas, K.F. (2007b) 'Analysing a world in motion: Global flows meet "criminology of the other"', *Theoretical Criminology*, 11(2): 283–303.

Aas, K.F. and M. Bosworth (eds) (2013) *The Borders of Punishment: Migration, Citizenship, and Social Exclusion*, Oxford: Oxford University Press.

Abu-Jamal, M. (1996) *Live from Death Row*, New York: Harper Perennial.

Agamben, G. (1998) *Homo Sacer: Sovereign Power and Bare Life*, Stanford, CA: Stanford University Press.

Agamben, G. (2004) *The State of Exception*, Chicago: University of Chicago Press.

Ahmed, S. (2004) *The Cultural Politics of Emotion*, London: Routledge.

Ahmed, S. (2000) *Strange Encounters: Embodied Others in Post-Coloniality*, London: Routledge.

Aliverti, A. (2013) *Crimes of Mobility: Criminal Law and the Regulation of Mobility*, Abingdon: Routledge.

Aliverti, A. (2012a) 'Exploring the Function of Criminal Law in the Policing of Foreigners: The Decision to Prosecute Immigration-related Offences', *Social & Legal Studies*, 21(4): 511–27.

Aliverti, A. (2012b) 'Making People Criminal: The Role of the Criminal Law in Immigration Enforcement', *Theoretical Criminology*, 16(4): 417–34.

Annison, H. (2014) 'Weeding the Garden: The Third Way, the Westminster Tradition and Imprisonment for Public Protection', *Theoretical Criminology*, 18(1): 38–55.

Arendt, H. (1963) *Eichmann in Jerusalem: A Report on the Banality of Evil*, Harmondsworth: Penguin.

Bacon, C. (2005) *Refugee Studies Centre Working Paper 27: The Evolution of Immigration Detention in the UK: The Involvement of Private Prison Companies*, Oxford: Refugee Studies Centre.

Baillot, H., S. Cowan, and V. Munro (2013) 'Second-hand Emotion? Exploring the Contagion and Impact of Trauma and Distress in the Asylum Law Context', *Journal of Law & Society*, 40(4): 509–40.

Baker, T. and J. Simon (eds) (2002) *Embracing Risk: The Changing Culture of Insurance and Responsibility*, Chicago, IL: University of Chicago Press.

Balibar, E. (2005) 'Difference, Otherness, Exclusion', *Parallax*, 11(1): 19–34.

Balibar, E. (2004) *We, the People of Europe? Reflections on Transnational Citizenship*, Oxford: Princeton University Press.

Barker, V. (2013a) 'Nordic Exceptionalism Revisited: Explaining the Paradox of a Janus-Faced Penal Regime', *Theoretical Criminology*, 17(1): 5–25.

Barker, V. (2013b) 'Democracy and Deportation: Why Membership Matters Most', in K. Aas and M. Bosworth (eds) *The Borders of Punishment: Citizenship, Migration, and Social Exclusion*, Oxford: Oxford University Press, 237–56.

Barker, V. (2012) 'Global Mobility and Penal Order: Criminalizing Migration, a View from Europe', *Sociology Compass*, 6(2): 113–21.

Bauman, Z. (2004) *Wasted Lives: Modernity and its Outcasts*, Cambridge: Polity Press.

Bauman, Z. (1998) *Globalization: The Human Consequences*, New York: Columbia University Press.

Bauman, Z. (1991) *Modernity and Ambivalence*, Cambridge: Polity Press.

Bauman, Z. (1989) *Modernity and the Holocaust*, Cambridge: Polity Press.

Beck, U. (1999) *World Risk Society*, Cambridge: Polity Press.

Beck, U. (1992) *The Risk Society: Toward a New Modernity*, London: Sage.

Beetham, D. (1991) *The Legitimation of Power*, London: Macmillan.

Benhabib, S. (2006) *Another Cosmopolitanism*, Oxford: Oxford University Press.

Benhabib, S. (2004) *The Rights of Others: Aliens, Residents and Citizens*, Cambridge: Cambridge University Press.

Bennett, J. (2012) 'The Working Lives of Prison Managers: An Exploration of Agency and Structure in the Late Modern Prison', Unpublished Ph.D. thesis, University of Edinburgh.

Bennett, J., B. Crewe, and A. Wahidin (eds) (2007) *Understanding Prison Staff*, Collumpton: Willan.

Bercher, H., S. Clements, and P. McMurray (2000) 'Asylum, Immigration Detention and Facilities: An Exploration of Perspectives on Campsfield House', Unpublished MSt dissertation, University of Oxford: Refugee Studies.

Bhui, H.S. (2013a) 'The Changing Approach to Child Detention and its Implications for Immigration Detention in the UK', *The Prison Service Journal*, 205: 23–8.

Bhui, H.S. (2013b) 'Introduction: Humanizing Migration Control and Detention', in K.F. Aas and M. Bosworth (eds) *The Borders of Punishment: Migration, Citizenship and Social Exclusion*, Oxford: Oxford University Press, 1–17.

Bigo, D. (2008) 'Globalized (In)Security: The Field and the Ban-Opticon', in D. Bigo and A. Tsoukala (eds) *Terror, Insecurity and Liberty: Illiberal Practices of Liberal Regimes after 9/11*, London: Routledge, 10–48.

Bigo, D. (2002) 'Security and Immigration: Towards a Critique of the Governmentality of Unease', *Alternatives*, 27: 63–92.

Bloch, A. and L. Schuster (2005) 'At the Extremes of Exclusion: Deportation, Detention and Dispersal', *Ethnic & Racial Studies*, 28(3): 491–512.

Bosniak, L. (2008) *The Citizen and the Alien: Dilemmas of Contemporary Membership*, Princeton, NJ: Princeton University Press.

Bosworth, M. (2013) 'Can Immigration Detention be Legitimate?', in K.F. Aas and M. Bosworth (eds) *The Borders of Punishment: Migration, Citizenship, and Social Exclusion*, Oxford: Oxford University Press, 149–65.

Bosworth, M. (2012) 'Subjectivity and Identity in Detention: Punishment and Society in a Global Age', *Theoretical Criminology*, 16(3): 123–40.

Bosworth, M. (2011a) 'Deporting Foreign National Prisoners in England and Wales', *Citizenship Studies*, 15(5): 583–95.

Bosworth, M. (2011b) 'Human Rights and Immigration Detention', in M. Dembour and T. Kelly (eds) *Are Human Rights for Migrants? Critical Reflections on the Status of Irregular Migrants in Europe and the United States*, Abingdon: Routledge, 165–83.

Bosworth, M. (2009) 'Governing the Responsible Prisoner: A Comparative Analysis', in Peter Triantafillou and Eva Sørensen (eds) *The Politics of Self-Governance*, Aldershot: Ashgate, 169–86.

Bosworth, M. (2008) 'Border Control and the Limits of the Sovereign State', *Social & Legal Studies*, 17(2): 199–215.

Bosworth, M. (2007a) 'Border Crossings: Immigration Detention and the Exclusive Society', in M. Lee (ed) *Human Trafficking*, Collumpton: Willan Publishing, 159–77.

Bosworth, M. (2007b) 'Creating the Responsible Prisoner: Federal Admission and Orientation Packs', *Punishment and Society*, 9(1): 67–85.

Bosworth, M. (1999) *Engendering Resistance: Agency and Power in Women's Prisons*, Aldershot: Ashgate.

Bosworth, M. and B. Bradford (forthcoming) 'Case Worker Decision Making and Legitimacy in Immigration Control'.

Bosworth, M. with D. Campbell, B. Demby, S.M. Ferranti, and M. Santos (2005) 'Doing Prison Research: Views from Inside', *Qualitative Inquiry*, 11(2): 1–16.

Bosworth, M. and E. Carrabine (2001) 'Reassessing Resistance: Gender, Race and Sexuality in Prison', *Punishment and Society*, 3(4): 501–15.

Bosworth, M., A. Fili, and S. Pickering (2014) 'Women's Immigration Detention in Greece: Gender, Control, and Capacity', in M.J Guia, V. Mitsilegas, and R. Khoulish (eds) *Immigration Detention, Risk and Human Rights*, New York: Springer.

Bosworth, M. and M. Guild (2008) 'Governing Through Migration Control: Security and Citizenship in Britain', *The British Journal of Criminology*, 48(6): 703–19.

Bosworth, M. and C. Hoyle (eds) (2011) *What is Criminology?*, Oxford: Oxford University Press.

Bosworth, M., C. Hoyle, and M. Dempsey (2011) 'Researching Trafficked Women: Some Thoughts on Methodology', *Qualitative Inquiry*, 17(9): 769–79.

Bosworth, M. and E. Kaufman (2011) 'Foreigners in a Carceral Age: Immigration and Imprisonment in the U.S.', *Stanford Law and Policy Review*, 22(1): 101–27.

Bosworth, M. and E. Kaufman (2013) 'Gender and Punishment', in J. Simon and R. Sparks (eds) *Handbook of Punishment and Society*, London: Sage, 186–204.

Bosworth, M. and B. Kellezi (2014) 'Citizenship and Belonging in a Women's Immigration Detention Centre', in C. Phillips and C. Webster (eds) *New Directions in Race, Ethnicity and Crime*, Abingdon: Routledge, 80–96.

Bosworth, M. and B. Kellezi (2013) 'Developing a Measure of the Quality of Life in Detention', *Prison Service Journal*, 205: 10–15.

Bosworth, M. and G. Slade (2014) 'In Search of Recognition: Gender and Staff-Detainee Relations in a British Immigration Detention Centre', *Punishment & Society*, 16(2): 169–86.

Bottoms, A.E. (1983) 'Neglected Features of Contemporary Penal Systems', in D. Garland and P. Young (eds) *The Power to Punish: Contemporary Penality and Social Analysis*, London: Heinemann, 166–202.

Bowling, B. (2010) *Policing the Caribbean: Transnational Security Cooperation in Practice*, Oxford: Oxford University Press.

Bowling, B. and J. Sheptycki (2011) *Global Policing*, London: Sage.

Broeders, D. (2010) 'Return to Sender? Administrative Detention of Irregular Migrants in Germany and the Netherlands', *Punishment & Society*, 12(2): 169–86.

Brotherton D. and L. Barrios (2013) 'The Social Bulimia of Forced Repatriation: A Case Study of Dominican Deportees', in K.F. Aas and M. Bosworth (eds) *The Borders of Punishment: Migration, Citizenship, and Social Exclusion*, Oxford: Oxford University Press, 201–17.

Brotherton D. and L. Barrios (2011) *Banished to the Homeland: Dominican Deportees and Their Stories of Exile*, New York: Columbia University Press.

Brotherton, D. and L. Barrios (2009) 'Displacement and Stigma: The Social-Psychological Crisis of the Deportee', *Crime, Media, Culture*, 5(1): 29–56.

Brown, W. (2010) *Walled States, Waning Sovereignty*, Boston, MA: MIT Press.

Bull, M., E. Schindeler, D. Berkman, and J. Ransley (2013) 'Sickness in the System of Long-term Immigration Detention', *Journal of Refugee Studies*, 26(1): 47–68.

Butler, J. (2009) *Frames of War: When is Life Grievable?*, New York: Verso.

Butler, J. (2005) *Giving an Account of Oneself*, New York: Fordham University Press.

Butler, J. (2004) *Precarious Life: The Powers of Mourning and Violence*, London: Verso.

Butler, J. (1997) *The Psychic Life of Power: Theories in Subjection*, Stanford, CA: Stanford University Press.

Butler, J. (1990) *Gender Trouble: Feminism and the Subversion of Identity*, New York: Routledge.

Butler, J. and G. Spivak (2009) *Who Sings the Nation State? Language, Politics, Belonging*, Chicago: University of Chicago Press.

Carlen, P. (2005) 'Alison Liebling, Prisons and their Moral Performance, book review', *Theoretical Criminology*, 9(2): 251–6.

Carlen, P. (1983) *Women's Imprisonment: A Study in Social Control*, London: Routledge & Kegan Paul.

Carlton, B. and M. Segrave (eds) (2013) *Women Exiting Prison: Critical Essays on Gender, Post-Release Support and Survival*, Oxford and New York: Routledge.

Carlton, B. and M. Segrave (2011) 'Women's Survival Post-Imprisonment: Connecting Imprisonment With Pains Past and Present', *Punishment & Society*, 13(5): 551–70.

Ceccorulli, M. and N. Labanca (eds) (2014) *The EU, Migration and the Politics of Administrative Detention*, Abingdon: Routledge.

Cesarani, D. and T. Kushner (eds) (1993) *The Internment of Aliens in Twentieth Century Britain*, London: Frank Cass.

Chacon, J. (2012) 'Overcriminalizing Immigration', *Journal of Criminal Law & Criminology*, 102(3): 613–52.

Christie, N. (1977) 'Conflicts as Property', *British Journal of Criminology*, 17(1): 1–15.

Cohen, R. (1994) *Frontiers of Identity: The British and Others*, London: Longman.

Cohen, S. (2001) *States of Denial: Knowing about Atrocities and Suffering*, Cambridge: Polity Press.

Cohen, S. (1988) *Against Criminology*, St Louis, WA: Transaction Publishers.

Cole, D. (2007) 'Against Citizenship as a Predicate for Basic Rights', *Fordham Law Review*, 75: 2541–8.

Cole, D. (2003) 'Their Liberties, Our Security: Democracy and Double Standards', *International Journal of Legal Information*, 31: 290–311.

Coleman, M. and A. Kocher (2011) 'Detention, Deportation, Devolution and Immigrant Incapacitation in the US, Post 9/11', *The Geographical Journal*, 177(3): 228–37.

Connell, R. (2005) *Masculinities, Second Edition*, Berkeley: University of California Press.

Cornelisse, G. (2010) *Immigration Detention and Human Rights: Rethinking Territorial Sovereignty*, Leiden and Boston: Martinus Nijhoff.

Crackanthorpe, M. (1892) 'Should Government Interfere?', in A. White (ed) *The Destitute Alien in Great Britain: A Series of Papers Dealing with the Subject of Foreign Pauper Immigration*, London: Swan Sonnenschein & Co, 39–70.

Crawley, E. (2006) *Doing Prison Work: The Public and Private Lives of Prison Officers*, Collumpton: Willan.

Crewe, B. (2011) 'Soft Power in Prison: Implications for Staff–Prisoner Relationships, Liberty and Legitimacy', *European Journal of Criminology*, 8(6): 455–68.

Crewe, B. (2009) *The Prisoner Community*, Oxford: Oxford University Press.

Crewe, B., A. Liebling, and S. Hulley (2011) 'Staff Culture, Use of Authority and Prisoner Quality of Life in Public and Private Sector Prisons', *Australian and New Zealand Journal of Criminology*, 44(1): 94–115.

Dauvergne, C. (2008) *Making People Illegal: What Globalization Means for Migration and Law*, Cambridge: Cambridge University Press.

Deakin, P. (1970) *Colour, Citizenship and British Society*, London: Panther Books.

Dembour, M.-B. (2006) *Who Believes in Human Rights? Reflections on the European Convention*, London: Cambridge University Press.

Dembour, M.-B. and T. Kelly (eds) (2011) *Are Human Rights for Migrants? Critical Reflections on the Status of Irregular Migrants in Europe and the United States*, Abingdon: Routledge.

Douglas, M. and A. Wildavsky (1982) *Risk and Culture: An Essay on the Selection of Technological and Environmental Dangers*, Berkeley, CA: University of California Press.

Dow, M. (2004) *American Gulag: Inside U.S. Immigration Prisons*, Berkeley, CA: University of California Press.

Drotbohm, H. (2011) 'On the Durability and the Decomposition of Citizenship: The Social Logics of Forced Return Migration in Cape Verde', *Citizenship Studies*, 15(3/4): 381–96.

Dudley M., Z. Steel, S. Mares, and L. Newman (2012) 'Children and Young People in Immigration Detention', *Current Opinion in Psychiatry*, 25(4): 285–92.

Earle, R. and C. Phillips (2012) 'Digesting Men? Ethnicity, Gender and Food: Perspectives from a "Prison Ethnography"', *Theoretical Criminology*, 16(2): 141–56.

Ehrenreich, B. and A. Hochschild (2003) 'Introduction', in B. Ehrenreich and A. Hochschild (eds) *Global Woman: Nannies, Maids, and Sex Workers in the New Economy*, New York: Metropolitan Books, 1–14.

Ericson, R. (2008) *Crime in an Insecure World*, Cambridge: Polity.

Ericson, R. (2007) 'Governing Through Risk and Uncertainty', *Economy & Society*, 3(4): 659–72.

Ericson, R.V. and K. Haggerty (1997) *Policing the Risk Society*, Oxford: Clarendon Studies in Criminology.

Evans, J.M. (1972) 'Immigration Act 1971', *The Modern Law Review*, 35(5): 508–24.

Fahrmeir, A. (2000) *Citizens and Aliens: Foreigners and the Law in Britain and the German States, 1789–1870*, New York: Berghahn Books.

Fassin, D. (2011) 'Policing Borders, Producing Boundaries. The Governmentality of Immigration in Dark Times', *Annual Review of Anthropology*, 40: 213–26.

Fazel, M., R. Reed, C. Panter-Brick, and A. Stein (2011) 'Mental Health of Displaced and Refugee Resettled in High-Income Countries: Risk and Protective Factors', *The Lancet*, 379(9812): 266–82.

Feeley, M. (1979) *The Process is the Punishment: Handling Cases in a Lower Criminal Court*, New York: The Russell Sage Foundation.

Feeley, M. and J. Simon (1994) 'Actuarial Justice: The Emerging New Criminal Law', in D. Nelken (ed) *The Futures of Criminology*, London: Sage, 173–201.

Feeley, M. and J. Simon (1992) 'The New Penology: Notes on the Emerging Strategy of Corrections and its Implications', *Criminology*, 30(4): 449–74.

Fili, A. (2013) 'The Maze of Immigration Detention in Greece: A Case Study of the Athens Airport Detention Facility', *Prison Service Journal*, 205: 34–8.

Fischer, N. (2013a) 'Bodies at the Border: The Medical Protection of Immigrants in a French Immigration Detention Centre', *Ethnic & Racial Studies*, 36(7): 1162–79.

Fischer, N. (2013b) 'The Detention of Foreigners in France: Between Discretionary Control and the Rule of Law', *European Journal of Criminology*, 10(6): 692–708.

Flavin, J. (2010) *Our Bodies, Our Crimes: The Policing of Women's Reproduction in America*, New York: New York University Press.

Flynn, M. (2012) 'Who Must Be Detained? Proportionality as a Tool for Critiquing Immigration Detention Policy', *Refugee Survey Quarterly*, 33(1): 1–29.

Foot, P. (1965) *Immigration and Race in British Politics*, Harmondsworth: Penguin.

Foucault, M. (2004) *Society Must Be Defended: Lectures at the College de France, 1975–1976*, London: Penguin.

Foucault, M. (1991) 'Governmentality', in G. Burchell, C. Gordon, and P. Miller (eds) *The Foucault Effect: Studies in Governmentality*, Chicago: University of Chicago Press, 87–104.

Foucault, M. (1979) *Discipline and Punish: The Birth of the Prison*, London: Penguin.

Foucault, M. (1978) *History of Sexuality, Volume 1: The Will to Knowledge*, London: Penguin.

Fraser, N. (2008) *Scales of Justice: Reimagining Political Space in a Globalizing World*, New York: Columbia University Press.

Fraser, N. (2007a) 'Feminist Politics in the Age of Recognition: A Two-Dimensional Approach to Gender Justice', *Studies in Social Justice*, 1(1): 23–35.

Fraser, N. (2007b) 'Transnationalizing the Public Sphere: On the Legitimacy and Efficacy of Public Opinion in a Post-Westphalian World', *Theory, Culture and Society*, 24(4): 71–2.

Fraser, N. (2003) 'Social Justice in the Age of Identity Politics: Redistribution, Recognition, and Participation', in N. Fraser and A. Honneth, *Redistribution or Recognition? A Political–Philosophical Exchange*, London: Verso and Frankfurt: Suhrkamp, 7–109.

Garland, D. (2001) *The Culture of Control*, Oxford: Oxford University Press.

Garland, D. (1996) 'The Limits of the Sovereign State: Strategies of Crime Control in Contemporary Society', *British Journal of Criminology*, 36(4): 445–71.

De Genova, N. (2010) 'The Deportation Regime: Sovereignty, Space and the Freedom of Movement', in N. De Genova and N. Peultz (eds) *The Deportation Regime: Sovereignty, Space, and the Freedom of Movement*, Durham, NC: Duke University Press, 33–68.

De Genova, N. (2002) 'Migrant "Illegality" and Deportability in Everyday Life', *Annual Review of Anthropology*, 31: 419–47.

De Genova, N. and N. Peultz (eds) (2010) *The Deportation Regime: Sovereignty, Space, and the Freedom of Movement*, Durham, NC: Duke University Press.

Gibney, M. (2013) 'Deportation, Crime, and the Changing Character of Membership in the United Kingdom', in K.F. Aas and M. Bosworth (eds) *The Borders of Punishment: Citizenship, Migration and Social Exclusion*, Oxford: Oxford University Press, 218–36.

Gibney, M. (2008) 'Asylum and the Expansion of Deportation in the United Kingdom', *Government and Opposition*, 43(2): 146–67.

Gibney, M. (2004) *The Ethics and Politics of Asylum: Liberal Democracy and the Response to Refugees*, Cambridge: Cambridge University Press.

Gill, N. (2009) 'Governmental Mobility: The Power Effects of the Movement of Detained Asylum Seekers around Britain's Detention Estate', *Political Geography*, 28(3): 186–96.

Gilroy, P. (2002) *There Ain't No Black in the Union Jack: The Cultural Politics of Race and Nation*, Abingdon: Routledge.

De Giorgi, A. (2010) 'Immigration Control, Post-Fordism, and Less Eligibility: A Materialist Critique of the Criminalization of Immigration Across Europe', *Punishment & Society*, 12(2): 147–67.

Girling, E., I. Loader, and R. Sparks (1999) *Crime and Social Change in Middle England: Questions of Order in an English Town*, London: Routledge.

Goffman, E. (1968) *Asylums*, Harmondsworth: Penguin.

Grewcock, M. (2011) 'Punishment, Deportation and Parole: The Detention and Removal of Former Prisoners Under Section 501 of the Migration Act 1958', *The Australian and New Zealand Journal of Criminology*, 44(1): 56–73.

Grewcock, M. (2010) *Border Crimes: Australia's War on Illicit Migrants*, Sydney: Federation Press.

Griffiths, M. (2014) '"Who Is Who Now?" Truth, Trust and Identification in the British Asylum and Immigration Detention System', Unpublished Doctoral dissertation, Anthropology, University of Oxford.

Griffiths, M. (2013) 'Living with Uncertainty: Indefinite Immigration Detention', *Journal of Legal Anthropology*, 1(3): 263–86.

Griffiths, M. (2012) 'Anonymous Aliens? Questions of Identification in the Detention and Deportation of Failed Asylum Seekers', *Population, Space and Place*, 18(6): 715–27.

Guild, E. (2009) *Security and Migration in the 21st Century*, Cambridge: Polity Press.

Hacking, I. (1990) *The Taming of Chance*, Cambridge: Cambridge University Press.

Hailbronner, K. (2007) 'Detention of Asylum Seekers', *European Journal of Migration and Law*, 9(2): 159–72.

Hall, A. (2012) *Border Watch: Cultures of Immigration, Detention and Control*, London: Pluto Press.

Hall, A. (2010) 'These People Could Be Anyone: Fear, Contempt (and Empathy) in a British Immigration Removal Centre', *Journal of Ethnic and Migration Studies*, 36(6): 881–98.

Hall, S. (2001) 'Conclusion: The Multicultural Question', in B. Hesse (ed) *UN/Settled Multiculturalisms: Diasporas, Entanglement, Transruptions*, London: Zed Books, 209–41.

Hannah-Moffat, K. (2011) 'Criminological Cliques: Narrowing Dialogues, Institutional Protectionism and the Next Generation', in M. Bosworth and C. Hoyle (eds) *What is Criminology?*, Oxford: Oxford University Press, 440–55.

Hannah-Moffat, K. (2005) 'Criminogenic Needs and the Transformative Risk Subject: Hybridizations of Risk/Need in Penality', *Punishment & Society*, 7(1): 29–51.

Hannah-Moffat, K. and P. O'Malley (eds) (2005) *Gendered Risks*, London: Routledge.

Hansen, R. (2000) *Citizenship and Immigration in Post-War Britain: The Institutional Origins of Multicultural Nation*, Oxford: Oxford University Press.

Hayter, T. (2004) *Open Borders: The Case Against Immigration Control*, London: Pluto Press.

Hemmings, C. (2012) 'Affective Solidarity: Feminist Reflexivity and Political Transformation', *Feminist Theory*, 13(2): 147–61.

Henne, K. (2013) 'Mapping the Margins of Intersectionality: Criminological Possibilities in a Transnational World', *Theoretical Criminology*, 17(4): 455–73.

Herd, D. (2011) '"Merely Circulating": The Movement of Persons and the Politics of Abandonment', *Parallax*, 17(2): 21–35.

Hernandez, D. (2008) 'Pursuant to Deportation: Latinos and Immigrant Detention', *Latino Studies*, 1(1/2): 35–53.

Hewett, H. (2009) 'Mothering Across Borders: Narratives of Immigrant Mothers in the United States', *Women's Studies Quarterly*, 37(3/4): 121–39.

Hill-Collins, P. (2000) *Black Feminist Thought: Knowledge, Consciousness and the Politics of Empowerment, Second Edition*, New York: Routledge.

Holmes, C. (1991) *A Tolerant Country: Immigrants, Refugees and Minorities in Britain*, London: Faber and Faber.

Holmes, C. (1988) *John Bull's Island: Immigration and British Society, 1871–1971*, Basingstoke: Macmillan.

Hondagneu-Sotelo, P. and E. Avila (1997) 'I'm Here But I'm There: The Meanings of Latina Transnational Motherhood', *Gender & Society*, 11(5): 548–71.

Honig, B. (2001) *Democracy and the Foreigner*, Princeton, NJ: Princeton University Press.

Hudson, V.M., D.L. Bowen, and P.L. Nielson (2011) 'What is the Relationship between Inequity in Family Law and Violence against Women: Approaching the Issue of Legal Enclaves', *Politics and Gender*, 7(4): 453–92.

Huysmans, J. (2006) *The Politics of Insecurity: Fear, Migration and Asylum in the EU*, London: Routledge.

Huysmans, J. and V. Squire (2009) 'Migration and Security', in M. Dunn Cavelty and V. Mauer (eds) *The Routledge Handbook of Security Studies*, London: Routledge, 169–79.

Irwin, J. (1970) *The Felon*, Englewood Cliffes, NJ: Prentice-Hall, Inc.

Isin, E.F. and G.M. Nielson (eds) (2008) *Acts of Citizenship*, London: Zed Books.

Jeyes, S.H. (1892) 'Foreign Pauper Immigration', in A. White (ed) *The Destitute Alien in Great Britain: A Series of Papers Dealing with the Subject of Foreign Pauper Immigration*, London: Swan Sonnenschein & Co, 167–91.

João Guia, M., M. van de Woude, and J. van Der Leun (eds) (2012) *Social Control and Justice: Crimmigration in the Age of Fear*, The Hague: Eleven International Publisher.

Johansen, N. (2013) 'Governing the Funnel of Expulsion: Agamben, the Dynamics of Force, and Minimalist Biopolitics', in K.F. Aas and M. Bosworth (eds) *The Borders of Punishment: Migration, Citizenship, and Social Exclusion*, Oxford: Oxford University Press, 257–72.

Joppke, C. (1999) *Immigration and the Nation State: The United States, Germany and Britain*, Oxford: Oxford University Press.

Kanstroom, D. (2012) *Aftermath: Deportation and the New American Diaspora*, New York: Oxford University Press.

Kaufman, E. (2014) *Punish and Expel: Border Control, Nationalism and the New Purpose of the Prison*, Oxford: Oxford University Press.

Kaufman, E. (2012) 'Finding Foreigners: Race and the Politics of Memory in British Prisons', *Population, Space and Place*, 18(6): 710–14.

Kaufman, E. and M. Bosworth (2013) 'Prison and National Identity: Citizenship, Punishment and the Sovereign State', in D. Scott (ed) *Why Prison?*, Cambridge: Cambridge University Press, 170–88.

Kimble, H. (1998) *Desperately Seeking Asylum: The View from Oxford*, Glasgow: Wild Goose Publications.

Klein, A. and L. Williams (2012) 'Immigration Detention in the Community: Research on the Experiences of Migrants Released from Detention Centres in the UK', *Population, Space and Place*, 18(6): 741–53.

Larsen, M. and J. Piché (2009) 'Exceptional State, Pragmatic Bureaucracy, and Indefinite Detention: The Case of the Kingston Immigration Holding Centre', *Canadian Journal of Law and Society*, 24(2): 203–29.

Lee, M. (2013) 'Human Trafficking and Border Control in the Global South', in K.F. Aas and M. Bosworth (eds) *The Borders of Punishment: Migration, Citizenship and Social Exclusion*, Oxford: Oxford University Press, 128–48.

Leerkes, A. and D. Broeders (2013) 'Deportable and Not So Deportable: Formal and Informal Functions of Administrative Immigration Detention', in B. Anderson, M. Gibney, and E. Paoletti (eds) *The Social, Political and Historical Contours of Deportation*, New York: Springer, 79–104.

Leerkes, A. and D. Broeders (2010) 'A Case of Mixed Motives? Formal and Informal Functions of Administrative Immigration Detention', *British Journal of Criminology*, 50(5): 830–50.

Lerman, A. and J. Page (2012) 'The State of the Job: An Embedded Work Role Perspective on Prison Officer Attitudes', *Punishment & Society*, 14(5): 503–29.

Liebling A. (2011) 'Distinctions and Distinctiveness in the Work of Prison Officers: Legitimacy and Authority Revisited', *European Journal of Criminology*, 8(6): 484–99.

Liebling, A. (2004) *Prisons and their Moral Performance*, Oxford: Clarendon Press.

Liebling, A. (2000) 'Prison Officers, Policing, and the Use of Discretion', *Theoretical Criminology*, 4(3): 333–57.

Liebling, A. and B. Crewe (2012) 'Prisons Beyond the New Penology: The Shifting Moral Foundations of Prison Management', in R. Sparks and J. Simon (eds) *Handbook of Punishment and Society*, London: Sage, 283–307.

Liebling, A., L. Durie, A. Stiles, and S. Tait (2005) 'Revisiting Prison Suicide: The Role of Fairness and Distress', in A. Liebling and S. Maruna (eds) *The Effects of Imprisonment*, Collumpton: Willan, 209–31.

Liebling, A., D. Price, and C. Elliott (1999) 'Appreciative Inquiry and Relationships in Prison', *Punishment & Society*, 1(1): 71–98.

Liebling, A., D. Price, and G. Shefer (2010) *The Prison Officer, Second Edition*, Abingdon: Willan.

Loader, I. (2006) 'Fall of the Platonic Guardians: Liberalism, Criminology and Political Responses to Crime in England and Wales', *British Journal of Criminology*, 46(4): 561–86.

Loader, I. and N. Walker (2007) *Civilizing Security*, Cambridge: Cambridge University Press.

Lorek A., K. Ehntholt, A. Nesbitt, E. Wey, C. Githinji, E. Rossor, and R. Wickramasinghe (2009) 'The Mental and Physical Health Difficulties of Children Held Within a British Immigration Detention Center: A Pilot Study', *Child Abuse and Neglect*, 33: 573–85.

Mainwearing, C. (2012) 'Constructing a Crisis: The Role of Immigration Detention in Malta', *Population, Space and Place*, 18(6): 687–700.

Makaremi, C. (2009a) 'Zone d'attente pour personnes en instance. Une ethnographie de la détention frontalière en France', Unpublished Ph.D. thesis, University of Montreal.

Makaremi, C. (2009b) 'Governing Borders in France: From Extra Territorial to Humanitarian Confinement', *Canadian Journal of Law and Society*, 24(3): 411–32.

Malloch, M. and E. Stanley (2005) 'The Detention of Asylum Seekers', *Punishment & Society*, 7(1): 53–71.

Melossi, D. (2013) 'People on the Move: From the Countryside to the Factory/Prison', in K. Aas and M. Bosworth (eds) *The Borders of Punishment: Migration, Citizenship and Social Exclusion*, Oxford: Oxford University Press, 273–90.

Melossi, D. (2003) '"In a Peaceful Life": Migration and the Crime of Modernity in Europe/Italy', *Punishment & Society*, 5(4): 371–97.

Michalon, B. (2013) 'Mobility and Power in Detention: The Management of Internal Movement and Governmental Mobility in Romania', in D. Moran, D. Conlon, and N. Gill (eds) *Carceral Spaces: Mobility and Agency in Imprisonment and Migration Detention*, Aldershot: Ashgate, 57–76.

Milgram, S. (1974) *Obedience to Authority: An Experimental View*, New York: Harper & Row.

Miller, T.A. (2002) 'The Impact of Mass Incarceration on Immigration Policy', in M. Mauer and M. Chesney-Lind (eds) *Invisible Punishment: The Collateral Consequences of Mass Imprisonment*, New York: The New Press.

Moran, D. (2014) *Carceral Geography: Spaces and Practices of Incarceration*, Aldershot: Ashgate.

Moran, D., D. Conlon, and N. Gill (eds) (2013) *Carceral Spaces: Mobility and Agency in Imprisonment and Migration Detention*, Aldershot: Ashgate.

Mountz, A. (2010) *Seeking Asylum: Human Smuggling and Bureaucracy at the Border*, Minneapolis: University of Minnesota Press.

Mountz, A. (2011a) 'Islands as Enforcement Archipelago: Haunting, Sovereignty, and Asylum', *Geography*, 30: 118–28.

Mountz, A. (2011b) 'Where Asylum-Seekers Wait: Feminist Counter-Topographies of Sites Between States', *Gender, Place and Culture*, 18(3): 381–99.

Mujuzi, J.D. (2011) 'Discrimination Against Homosexuals in Malawi: Lessons from the Recent Developments', *International Journal of Discrimination and the Law*, 11(3): 150–60.

Muzffar, S., O. Haque, and J. Sugden (1998) *An Evaluation of the Mental and Physical Health Standards at Campsfield House Detention Centre Kidlington*, Unpublished MSt thesis, Oxford: University of Oxford Refugee Studies.

O'Malley, P. (2004) *Risk, Uncertainty and Government*, London: Taylor & Francis.

Panayi, P. (1994) *Immigration, Ethnicity and Racism in Britain: 1815–1945*, Manchester: Manchester University Press.

Parreñas, R. (2010) 'Transnational Mothering: A Source of Gender conflicts in the Family', *North Carolina Law Review*, 88: 1825–56.

Pateman, C. (1992) 'Equality, Difference, Subordination: The Politics of Motherhood and Women's Citizenship', in G. Bock and S. James (eds) *Beyond Equality and Difference: Citizenship, Feminist Politics and Female Subjectivity*, New York: Routledge, 17–31.

Paul, K. (1997) *Whitewashing Britain: Race and Citizenship in the Postwar Era*, London: Cornell University Press.

Pedwell, C. and A. Whitehead (2012) 'Affecting Feminism: Questions of Feeling in Feminist Theory', *Feminist Theory*, 13(2): 115–29.

Phillips, C. (2012) *The Multicultural Prison: Ethnicity, Masculinity and Social Relations Among Prisoners*, Oxford: Oxford University Press.

Phillips, C. (2008) 'Negotiating Identities: Ethnicity and Social Relations in a Young Offenders' Institution', *Theoretical Criminology*, 12(3): 313–31.

Platt, C. (1991) *The Immigration Act 1988: A Discussion of its Effects and Implications*, Policy Paper in Ethnic Relations, No 16, University of Warwick Centre for Research in Ethnic Relations, <http://www2.warwick.ac.uk/fac/soc/crer/research/publications/policy/policyp_no.16.pdf>.

Pratt, A. (2005) *Securing Borders: Detention and Deportation in Canada*, Vancouver: University of British Columbia Press.

Pratt, A. (2001) 'Sovereign Power, Carceral Conditions and Penal Practices: Detention and Deportation in Canada', *Studies in Law, Politics and Society*, 23: 45–78.

Pratt, J. (2007) *Penal Populism*, London: Routledge.

Ramsay, P. (2012) *The Insecurity State*, Oxford: Oxford University Press.

Ramsay, P. (2010) 'Overcriminalization as Vulnerable Citizenship', *New Criminal Law Review*, 13(2): 262–85.

Roche, T.E. (1969) *The Key in the Lock: A History of Immigration Control in England from 1066 to the Present Day*, London: John Murray.

Rose, N. (2001) 'The Politics of Life Itself', *Theory, Culture & Society*, 18(6): 1–30.

Rose, N. (2000) 'Community, Citizenship and the Third Way', *The American Behavioral Scientist*, 43(9): 1395–1411.

Sabo, D. (2001) 'Doing Time, Doing Masculinity: Sports and Prison', in D. Sabo, T. Kupers, and W. London (eds) *Prison Masculinities*, Philadelphia: Temple University Press, 61–6.

Sanchez, G. and M. Romero (2010) 'Critical Race Theory in the US Sociology of Immigration', *Sociology Compass*, 4(9): 779–88.

Sassen, S. (2007) *The Sociology of Globalization*, New York: Norton.

Sassen, S. (1999) *Globalization and Its Discontents: Essays on the New Mobility of People and Money*, New York: The New Press.

Schinkel, W. (2011) 'Prepression: The Actuarial Archive and New Technologies of Security', *Theoretical Criminology*, 15(4): 365–80.

Schuster, L. (2005) 'A Sledgehammer to Crack a Nut: Deportation, Detention and Dispersal in Europe', *Social Policy and Administration*, 39(6): 606–21.

Schuster, L. and A. Bloch (2005) 'At the Extremes of Exclusion: Deportation, Detention and Dispersal', *Ethnic and Racial Studies*, 28(3): 491–512.

Schuster, L. and N. Majidi (2013) 'What Happens Post-Deportation? The Experience of Deported Afghans', *Migration Studies*, 1(2): 221–40.

Sherman, L. (2009) 'Evidence and Liberty: The Promise of Experimental Criminology', *Criminology & Criminal Justice*, 9(1): 5–28.

Silverman, S. and E. Massa (2012) 'Why Immigration Detention is Unique', *Population, Space and Place*, 18(6): 677–86.

Simon, J. (2000) 'The "Society of Captives" in the Era of Hyper-Incapacitation', *Theoretical Criminology*, 4(3): 285–308.

Simon, J. and R. Sparks (eds) (2012) *Handbook of Punishment and Society*, London: Sage.

Simpson, B. (1992) *In the Highest Degree Odious: Detention Without Trial in Wartime Britain*, Oxford: Oxford University Press.

Sitkin, L. (2013) 'The Right to Walk the Streets: Looking for Illegal Migration on the Streets and Stations of the UK and Germany', *The Prison Service Journal*, 205: 29–33.

Solomos, J. (1991) *Black Youth, Racism and the State: The Politics of Ideology and Policy*, Cambridge: Cambridge University Press.

Sparks, R., A.E. Bottoms, and W. Hay (1996) *Prisons and the Problem of Order*, Oxford: Clarendon Press.

Sparks, R. and A.E. Bottoms (1995) 'Legitimacy and Order in Prisons', *British Journal of Sociology*, 46(1): 45–62.

Spena, A. (2013) 'Injuria Migrandi: Criminalization of Immigrants and the Basic Principles of the Criminal Law', *Criminal Law and Philosophy*.

Spencer, I. (2002) *British Immigration Policy Since 1939: The Making of Multi-Racial Britain*, London: Routledge.

Spivak, G. (2000) 'Translation as Culture', *Parallax*, 6(1): 13–24.

Spivak, G. (1999) *A Critique of Postcolonial Reason: Towards a History of the Vanishing Present*, Calcutta/New Delhi: Seagull.

Spivak, G. (1998) 'Can the Subaltern Speak?', in C. Nelson and L. Grossberg (eds) *Marxism and the Interpretation of Culture*, London: Macmillan, 271–316.

Squire, V. (ed) (2010) *The Contested Politics of Mobility: Borderzones and Irregularity*, London: Routledge.

Steel, Z., D. Silove, S. Momartin, B. Alzuhairi, and I. Susljik (2006) 'Impact of Immigration Detention and Temporary Protection on the Mental Health of Refugees', *The British Journal of Psychiatry*, 188: 58–64.

Stevens, J. (2011) 'U.S. Government Unlawfully Detaining and Deporting U.S. Citizens as Aliens', *Virginia Journal of Social Policy and the Law*, 18(3): 606–719.

Stumpf, J. (2013) 'The Process is the Punishment in Crimmigration Law', in K.F. Aas and M. Bosworth (eds) *The Borders of Punishment: Migration, Citizenship and Social Exclusion*, Oxford: Oxford University Press, 58–75.

Stumpf, J. (2006) 'The Crimmigration Crisis: Immigrants, Crime, and Sovereign Power', *American University Law Review*, 56: 367.

Sykes, G. (1958) *Society of Captives: A Study of a Maximum Secure Prison*, Princeton, NJ: Princeton University Press.

Sykes, G. and D. Matza (1957) 'Techniques of Neutralization: A Theory of Delinquency', *American Sociological Review*, 22(6): 664–70.

Thomas, R. (2011) *Administrative Justice and Asylum Appeals: A Study of Tribunal Adjudication*, Oxford: Hart Publishing.

Thwaites, R. (2014) *The Liberty of Non-citizens: Indefinite Detention in Commonwealth Countries*, Oxford: Hart Publishing.

Twaddle, M. (1974) *Expulsion of a Minority: Essays on Ugandan Asians*, London: Athlone.

Ugelvik, T. (2012) 'Imprisoned On the Border: Subjects and Objects of the State in Two Norwegian Prisons', in S. Ugelvik and B. Hudson (eds) *Justice and Security in the 21st Century: Risks, Rights and the Rule of Law*, London: Routledge, 64–82.

Ugelvik, T. (2011) 'The Hidden Food: Mealtime Resistance and Identity Work in a Norwegian Prison', *Punishment and Society*, 13(1): 47–63.

Ugelvik, T. and S. Ugelvik (2013) 'Immigration Control in Ultima Thule: Detention and Exclusion Norwegian Style', *European Journal of Criminology*, 10(6): 709–24.

Vasquez, Y. (2011) 'Where Do We Go from Here? Advising Noncitizen Defendants on the Immigration Consequences of a Criminal Conviction after Padilla', *Fordham Urban Law Journal*, 39(1): 169–202.

Von Hirsch, A. (1976) *Doing Justice: The Choice of Punishments*, New York: Hill & Wang.

Wacquant, L. (2008) 'The Curious Eclipse of Prison Ethnography in the Age of Mass Incarceration', *Ethnography*, 3(4): 371–97.

Walters, W. (2011) 'Foucault and Frontiers: Notes on the Birth of the Humanitarian Border', in U. Bröckling, S. Krasmann, and T. Lemke (eds) *Governmentality: Current Issues and Future Challenges*, New York: Routledge, 138–64.

Walters, W. (2006) 'Border/Control', *European Journal of Social Theory*, 9(2): 187–204.

Walters, W. (2002) 'Deportation, Expulsion, and the International Police of Aliens', *Citizenship Studies*, 6(3): 265–92.

Webber, F. (2012) *Borderline Justice: The Fight for Refugee and Migrant Rights*, London: Pluto Press.

Weber, L. (2013) *Policing Non-Citizens*, Abingdon: Routledge.

Weber, L. and B. Bowling (2008) 'Valiant Beggars and Global Vagabonds: Select, Eject, Immobilize', *Theoretical Criminology*, 12(3): 355–75.

Weber, L. and S. Pickering (2011) *Globalization and Borders: Death at the Global Frontier*, London: Palgrave Macmillan.

Weil, P. (2005) *Access to Citizenship: A Comparison of Twenty-Five Nationality Laws*, Toronto: University of Toronto Press.

Welch, M. (2012) 'The Sonics of Crimmigration in Australia: Wall of Noise and Quiet Maneuvering', *British Journal of Criminology*, 52(2): 324–44.

Welch, M. (2002) *Detained: Immigration Laws and the Expanding I.N.S. Jail Complex*, Philadelphia: Temple University Press.

Welch, M. and L. Schuster (2005a) 'Detention of Asylum Seekers in the US, UK, France, Germany and Italy: A Critical View of the Globalizing Culture of Control', *Criminal Justice*, 5(4): 331–55.

Welch, M. and L. Schuster (2005b) 'Detention of Asylum Seekers in the UK and USA: Deciphering Noisy and Quiet Constructions', *Punishment & Society*, 7(4): 397–417.

White, A. (ed) (1892) *The Destitute Alien in Great Britain: A Series of Papers Dealing with the Subject of Foreign Pauper Immigration*, London: Swan Sonnenschein & Co.

Wilsher, D. (2012) *Immigration Detention: Law, History, Politics*, Cambridge: Cambridge University Press.

Wray, H. (2006) 'The Aliens Act 1905 and the Immigration Dilemma', *Journal of Law and Society*, 33(2): 302–33.

Young, J. (2003a) 'To These Wet and Windy Shores: Recent Immigration Policy in the UK', *Punishment & Society*, 5(4): 449–62.

Young, J. (2003b) 'Merton With Energy, Katz With Structure: The Sociology of Vindictiveness and the Criminology of Transgression', *Theoretical Criminology*, 7(3): 389–414.

Young, J. (1999) *The Exclusive Society: Social Exclusion, Crime and Difference in Late Modernity*, London: Sage.

Zedner, L. (2013) 'Is the Criminal Law only for Citizens? A Problem at the Borders of Punishment', in K. Aas and M. Bosworth (eds) *The Borders of Punishment: Citizenship, Migration, and Social Exclusion*, Oxford: Oxford University Press, 40–57.

Zedner, L. (2010) 'Security, the State and the Citizen', *New Criminal Law Review*, 13(2): 379–403.

Zedner, L. (2007a) 'Preventive Justice Or Pre-Punishment? The Case of Control Orders', *Current Legal Problems*, 60(1): 174–203.

Zedner, L. (2007b) 'Pre-Crime and post-Criminality', *Theoretical Criminology*, 11(2): 261–81.

Zedner, L. (2005) 'Securing Liberty in the Face of Terror', *Journal of Law and Society*, 32(4): 507–33.

Zedner, L. (2003) 'Too Much Security?', *International Journal of the Sociology of Law*, 31(3): 155–84.

REPORTS

Amnesty International (2013) *Frontier Europe: Human Right's Abuses on Greece's Border with Turkey*, London: Amnesty International.

Amnesty International (2010) *Greece: Irregular Migrants and Asylum-Seeker Routinely Detained in Substandard Conditions*, London: Amnesty International.

Ashford, M. (1994) *Detained Without Trial: A Survey of Immigration Act Detention*, London: Joint Council for the Welfare of Immigrants.

AVID (2014) *In Touch*, January 2014. London: AVID. Available at: <http://www. aviddetention.org.uk>.

BID (2013) *Fractured Childhoods: The Separation of Families by Immigration Detention*, London: BID.

BID (2010) *A Nice Judge on a Good Day: Immigration Bail and the Right to Liberty*. Available at: <http://www.biduk.org/420/bid-research-reports/a-nice-judge-on-a-good-day-immigration-bail-and-the-right-to-liberty.html>.

Bosworth, M. and B. Kellezi (2012) *Quality of Life in Detention: Results from the MQLD Questionnaire Data Collected in IRC Yarl's Wood, IRC Tinsley House and IRC Brook House, August 2010–June 2011*, Oxford: Centre for Criminology.

Bosworth, M., B. Kellezi, and G. Slade (2012) *Quality of Life in Detention: Results from Questionnaire Data Collected in IRC Morton Hall*, Oxford: Centre for Criminology.

Campbell S., M. Baqueriza, and J. Ingram (2011) *Last Resort or First Resort? Immigration Detention of Children in the UK*, London: BID.

D'Orey, S. (1984) *Immigration Prisoners: A Forgotten Minority*, London: Runnymede Trust.

Ellis, R. (1998) *Asylum-seekers and Immigration Act Prisoners—the Practice of Detention*, London: Prison Reform Trust.

Fordham, M., J. Stefanelli, and S. Eser (2013) *Immigration Detention and the Rule of Law: Safeguarding Principles*, London: British Institute of International and

Comparative Law (Bingham Centre). Available at: <http://www.biicl.org/files/6559_immigration_detention_and_the_rol_-_web_version.pdf>.

Gardner, E. (1980) *Who Do We Think We Are? An Inquiry Into British Nationality Law*, London: Conservative Political Centre.

Girma, M., S. Radice, N. Tsangarides, and N. Walter (2014) *Detained: Women Asylum Seekers Locked up in the UK*, London: Women for Refugee Women. Available at: <http://refugeewomen.com/wp-content/uploads/2014/01/WRWDetained.pdf>.

Gordon, I., K. Scanlon, T. Travers, and C. Whitehead (2009) *Economic Impact on London and the UK of an Earned Regularisation of Irregular Migrants in the UK*, London: Greater London Authority. Available at: <http://legacy.london.gov.uk/mayor/economic_unit/docs/irregular-migrants-report.pdf>.

Guild, E. (2006) *Briefing Paper: A Typology of Different Types of Centres for Third Country Nationals in Europe*, Brussels: European Parliament. Available at: <http://www.europarl.europa.eu/RegData/etudes/note/join/2006/378268/IPOL-LIBE_NT(2006)378268_EN.pdf>.

Hale, L. and L. Gelsthorpe (2012) *Criminalizing Migrant Women*, Cambridge: Institute of Criminology. Available at: <http://www.crim.cam.ac.uk/people/academic_research/loraine_gelsthorpe/criminalreport29july12.pdf>.

HMIP (2014a) *Detainees Under Escort: Inspection of Escort and Removals to Pakistan*, London: HMIP.

HMIP (2014b) *Detainees Under Escort: Inspection of Escort and Removals to Nigeria and Ghana by HM Chief Inspector of Prisons, 6–7 November 2013*, London: HMIP. Available at: <http://www.justice.gov.uk/downloads/publications/inspectorate-reports/hmipris/detainee-escort-inspections/nigeria-ghana-escorts-2013-rps.pdf>.

HMIP (2013) *Report on an Unannounced Inspection of Yarl's Wood Immigration Removal Centre, 17–28 June 2013, 30 September–1 October 2013*, London: HMIP. Available at: <http://www.justice.gov.uk/downloads/publications/inspectorate-reports/hmipris/immigration-removal-centre-inspections/yarls-wood/Yarls-Wood-2013.pdf>.

HMIP (2012a) *Report of Announced Visit to Cedar's Unit*, London: HMIP. Available at: <http://www.justice.gov.uk/downloads/publications/inspectorate-reports/hmipris/immigration-removal-centre-inspections/cedars/cedars-2012.pdf>.

HMIP (2012b) *Report on an Unannounced Short Follow-Up Visit to IRC Dover, 3–5 April 2012*, London: HMIP. Available at: <http://www.justice.gov.uk/downloads/publications/inspectorate-reports/hmipris/immigration-removal-centre-inspections/dover/dover-2012.pdf>.

HMIP (2012c) *Remand Prisoners: A Thematic Review*, London: HMIP. Available at: <http://www.justice.gov.uk/downloads/publications/inspectorate-reports/hmipris/thematic-reports-and-research-publications/remand-thematic.pdf>.

HMIP (2012d) *HM Chief Inspector of Prisons: Annual Report 2011–2012*, London: The Stationery Office, HC 613. Available at: <http://www.

justice.gov.uk/downloads/publications/corporate-reports/hmi-prisons/ hm-inspectorate-prisons-annual-report-2011-12.pdf>.

HMIP (2010a) *Report on an Unannounced Full Follow-Up Inspection of Colnbrook Immigration Removal Centre and Short-Term Holding Facility, 16–27 August 2010*, London: HMIP. Available at: <http://www.justice.gov.uk/downloads/ publications/inspectorate-reports/hmipris/immigration-removal-centre- inspections/conbrook/Colnbrook_2010_rps.pdf>.

HMIP (2010b) *Report on a Full Announced Inspection of Brook House Immigration Removal Centre, 15–19 March 2010*. Available at: <http:// www.justice.gov.uk/downloads/publications/inspectorate-reports/ hmipris/immigration-removal-centre-inspections/brook-house/Brook_ House_2010_rps_.pdf>.

HMIP (2008) *Expectations*, London: HMIP. Available at: <http://inspectorates. homeoffice.gov.uk/hmiprisons/docs/expectations-2008?view=Binary>.

HMIP (2007a) *Immigration Detention Expectations: Criteria for Assessing the Conditions for and Treatment of Foreign Detainees*, London: HMIP. Available at: <http://inspectorates.homeoffice.gov.uk/hmiprisons/docs/immigration- expectations-2007?view=Binary>.

HMIP (2007b) *Foreign Nationals in Prison: A Follow-Up Report*, London: HMIP. Available at: <http://inspectorates.homeoffice.gov.uk/hmiprisons/ thematic-reports1/Foreign_Nationals_follow-up1.pdf?view=Binary>.

HMIP (2002) *An Inspection of Campsfield House Immigration Removal Centre*, London: HMIP. Available at: <http://www.justice.gov.uk/downloads/publications/ inspectorate-reports/hmipris/immigration-removal-centre-inspections/ campsfield-house/campsfieldhouse02-rps.pdf>.

HMIP (1997) *Report on Tinsley House Immigration Detention Centre Gatwick Airport, 4–7 August 1997*, London: Her Majesty's Chief Inspector of Prisons for England and Wales.

HMIP (1994) *Report of an Unannounced Short Inspection of Campsfield House Immigration Detention Centre, September 1994*, London: Her Majesty's Chief Inspector of Prisons for England and Wales.

HMIP and CGPL (2013) *Report on Unannounced Joint Inspection of Coquelles and Calais Non-Residential Short-Term Holding Facilities*, London: HMIP. Available at <http://www.justice.gov.uk/downloads/publications/inspectorate-reports/ hmipris/short-term-holding-facility-reports/calais-coquelles-2012.pdf>.

HMIP and ICIBI (2012) *The Effectiveness and Impact of Immigration Detention Casework: A Joint Thematic Review*, London: HM Inspectorate of Prisons and the Independent Chief Inspector of Borders and Immigration. Available at <http://www.justice.gov.uk/downloads/publications/inspectorate-reports/ hmipris/thematic-reports-and-research-publications/immigration-detention- casework-2012.pdf>.

Home Office (2013a) *User Guide to Home Office Immigration Statistics*, London: Home Office. Available at <https://www.gov.uk/government/uploads/sys- tem/uploads/attachment_data/file/260910/user-guide-immig-statistics.pdf>.

Home Office (2013b) *Immigration Directorates' Instructions: Chapter 31 Section 1—Detention and Detention Policy in Port Cases.* Available at <http://www.ukba.homeoffice.gov.uk/sitecontent/documents/policyandlaw/IDIs/idichapter31detention/section1/sec1-detention-policy-port.pdf?view=Binary>.

Home Office (2013c) *Immigration Statistics: January to March 2013.* Available at <https://www.gov.uk/government/publications/immigration-statistics-january-to-march-2013/immigration-statistics-january-to-march-2013>.

Home Office (2012) *Detention Service Order DSO 06/2012*, London: Home Office. Available at: <http://www.ukba.homeoffice.gov.uk/sitecontent/documents/policyandlaw/detention-services-orders/>.

Home Office (2008) *Detention Service Order DSO 6/2008*, London: Home Office. Available at: <http://www.ukba.homeoffice.gov.uk/sitecontent/documents/policyandlaw/detention-services-orders/>.

Home Office (1984) *Managing the Long-Term Prison System. The Report of the Control Review Committee*, Cmd 3175, London: HMSO.

Home Office (1967) *Report of the Committee on Immigration Appeals (Wilson Committee)*, Cmnd 3387, London: HMSO.

Home Office (1965) *Immigration from the Commonwealth*, Cmnd 2739, London: HMSO.

Human Rights Watch (2013) *Unwelcome Guests: Greek Police Abuses of Migrant in Athens*, New York: Human Rights Watch.

IMB (2013) *Campsfield House Immigration Removal Centre Annual Report for 2012.* Available at <http://www.justice.gov.uk/downloads/publications/corporate-reports/imb/annual-reports-2013/campsfield-house-2012.pdf>.

IMB (2012) *Annual Report, 2012. Independent Monitoring Board Colnbrook Immigration Removal Centre.* Available at <http://www.justice.gov.uk/downloads/publications/corporate-reports/imb/annual-reports-2012/colnbrook-irc-2012.pdf>.

Jenkins, K. (1984) *The Closed Door: A Christian Critique of Britain's Immigration Policies*, London: British Council of Churches.

Liebling, A., H. Arnold, and C. Straub (2011) *An Exploration of Staff-Prisoner Relationships at HMP Whitemoor: 12 Years On*, Revised Final Report. Cambridge: Institute of Criminology. Available at <https://www.gov.uk/government/uploads/system/uploads/attachment_data/file/217381/staff-prisoner-relations-whitemoor.pdf>.

Lowe, K. (1993) *Britain's Forgotten Prisoners: Meeting the Needs of Immigration Act Detainees*, London: Detention Advice Service.

Medical Justice (2013) *Expecting Change: The Case for Ending Detention of Pregnant Women.* Available at <http://www.medicaljustice.org.uk/images/stories/reports/expectingchange.pdf>.

Medical Justice (2012) *'The Second Torture': The Immigration Detention of Torture Survivors*, London: Medical Justice. Available at <http://oppenheimer.mcgill.ca/IMG/pdf/Medical_Justice_-_Second_Torture_Report.pdf>.

Ministry of Justice (2012) *Criminal Casework: Multi-Agency Public Protection Arrangements (MAPPA)*, London: HMSO. Available at <http://www.ukba.homeoffice.gov.uk/sitecontent/documents/policyandlaw/modernised/criminality-and-detention/multi-agency-public?view=Binary>.

Ministry of Justice (2006) *Reducing Reoffending Through Skills and Employment*, London: HMSO.

Monaghan, K. (2013) *Inquest into the Death of Jimmy Kelenda Mubenga*. Report by the Assistant Deputy Coroner, Karon Monaghan, QC, Under the Coroner's Rules 1984, Rule 43. Available at <http://inquest.gn.apc.org/pdf/reports/Mubenga_R43.pdf>.

National Audit Office (NAO) (2009) *The Home Office: Management of Asylum Applications*, London: National Audit Office.

Palmer, M. (2005) *Inquiry into the Circumstances of the Immigration Detention of Cornelia Rau: Report*, Canberra, ACT: Commonwealth of Australia. Available at <http://rspas.anu.edu.au/asiarightsjournal/palmer-report.pdf>.

Parekh, B. (2000) *The Future of Multi-Ethnic Britain. The Parekh Report*, London: Runnymede Trust.

Phelps, J. (2009) *Detained Lives: The Real Cost of Indefinite Immigration Detention*, London: London Detainee Support Group. Available at <http://www.ldsg.org.uk/files/uploads/detainedlives-web.pdf>.

PICUM (2013) *The Silent Humanitarian Crisis in Greece: Devising Strategies to Improve the Situation of Migrants in Greece*, Brussels: PICUM.

Prison Reform Trust (2013) *Bromley Briefings Prison Factfile. Autumn 2013*, London: Prison Reform Trust. Available at <http://www.prisonreformtrust.org.uk/Portals/0/Documents/Factfile%20autumn%202013.pdf>.

Prison Reform Trust (2005) *Keeping in Touch: The Case for Family Support work in Prison*, London: PRT. Available at <http://www.prisonreformtrust.org.uk/Portals/0/Documents/KEEPING_IN_TOUCH.pdf>.

Race Relations Board (1967) *Report of the Race Relations Board*, London: HM Stationery Office.

Refugee Council (2007) *The New Asylum Model: Refugee Council Briefing*. Available at <http://www.refugeecouncil.org.uk/Resources/Refugee%20Council/downloads/briefings/Newasylummodel.pdf>.

Rose et al (1969) *Colour & Citizenship: A Report on British Race Relations*, London: IRR.

Royal Commission on Population (1949) *Royal Commission on Population*, Cmd 7695, London: HMSO.

Scarman, L. Lord (1981) *Brixton Disorders 10–12 April 1981: Report of an Inquiry by the Rt Hon the Lord Scarman, OBE* (Scarman Report), London: HMSO.

Shackman, J. (2002) *Criminal Treatment: The Imprisonment of Asylum Seekers*, London: Prison Reform Trust.

The Binational Migration Institute (2013) *A Continued Humanitarian Crisis at the Border: Undocumented Border Crosser Deaths Recorded by the Pima County Office of the Medical Examiner, 1990–2012.* Available at <http://bmi.arizona.edu/sites/default/files/border_deaths_final_web.pdf>.

UKBA (2011) *Operation Enforcement Manual,* London: Home Office. Available at: <http://www.ukba.homeoffice.gov.uk/policyandlaw/guidance/enforcement/>.

UKBA (2008) *Operating Standards for Immigration Removal Centres,* London: Home Office. Available at: <https://www.gov.uk/government/uploads/system/uploads/attachment_data/file/257352/operatingstandards_manual.pdf>.

UN Women (2011) *Progress of the World's Women: In Pursuit of Justice.* Available at <http://progress.unwomen.org/pdfs/EN-Report-Progress.pdf>.

Vine, J. (2011a) *Asylum: A Thematic Inspection of the Detained Fast Track.* London: Independent Chief Investigator of the UK Border Agency. Available at <http://icinspector.independent.gov.uk/wp-content/uploads/2012/02/Asylum_A-thematic-inspection-of-Detained-Fast-Track1.pdf>.

Vine, J. (2011b) *A Thematic Inspection of How the UK Border Agency Manages Foreign National Prisoners,* London: Independent Chief Inspector of the UK Border Agency.

Women in Prison (2013) *The State of the Estate: Women in Prison's Report on the Women's Custodial Estate, 2011–2012,* London: WIP. Available at <http://womeninprison.org.uk/userfiles/file/StateoftheEstateReport.pdf>.

NEWSPAPER ARTICLES

Allison, E. (2013) 'Asylum seeker death investigated by Home Office amid health-care concerns', *theguardian.com,* 14 April 2013. Available at <http://www.theguardian.com/uk/2013/apr/14/asylum-seeker-death-investigated>.

Australian Associated Press (2014) 'Reza Berati was "knocked downstairs and then beaten to death"', *theguardian.com,* 21 March 2014. Available at: <http://www.theguardian.com/world/2014/mar/21/reza-barati-was-knocked-down-stairs-and-then-beaten-to-death>.

Brogen, P. (1970) 'An Asian odyssey that ended in a cul de sac', *The Times,* 18 August: 10.

Daily Mail Reporter (2011) '"Undesirable and dangerous" immigrant criminals cannot be deported from Britain, say Euro judges', *Daily Mail Online,* 28 June 2011.

Davies, L. (2013a) 'Lampedusa boat tragedy is "slaughter of innocents" says Italian president', *The Guardian,* 4 October 2013: 1. Available at <http://www.theguardian.com/world/2013/oct/03/lampedusa-boat-tragedy-italy-migrants>.

Davies, L. (2013b) 'Italy boat wreck: scores of migrants die as boat sinks off Lampedusa', *theguardian.com,* 3 October 2013. Available at <http://www.theguardian.com/world/2013/oct/03/lampedusa-migrants-killed-boat-sinks-italy>.

Evans, P. (1970) '90 Gaoled on UK Arrival', *The Times,* 5 February: 3.

Hayter, T. (1998) 'Trial of the Campsfield Nine', *Red Pepper,* 52.

Hillingdon Mirror (1980) 'Harmondsworth Detention Centre', September 1980, *Hillingdon Mirror*.

Hirsch, A. (2013) 'Niger migrants died from thirst, after stranding in Sahara desert', *The Guardian*, 1 November 2013: 34. Available at <http://www.theguardian. com/world/2013/oct/31/niger-migrants-found-dead-sahara-desert>.

Hornsby-Smith, P. (1968) *The Telegraph*, 27 April 1968.

L'Humanité (2013) 'Khatchik Khachatryan: "Ma place est en France"' in *L'Humanité*. Available at <http://www.humanite.fr/societe/551656>.

Mapondera, G. and D. Smith (2012) 'Malawi Suspends anti-Gay laws as MPs debate repeals', *theguardian.com*, 5 November 2012. Available at <http://www. guardian.co.uk/world/2012/nov/05/malawi-gay-laws-debate-repeal>.

McVeigh, K. (2011) 'Yarl's Wood detainees "paid 50p an hour"', *The Guardian*, 3 January 2011: 5. Available at <http://www.guardian.co.uk/uk/2011/jan/02/ yarls-wood-detainees-paid-50p-hour>.

Mulholland, H. and A. Stratten (2010) 'Nick Clegg: "shameful" detention of children in asylum centres to end by May', *theguardian.com*, 16 December 2010. Available at <http://www.theguardian.com/politics/2010/dec/16/nick-clegg- shameful-detention-children-end>.

Rawlinson, K. (2014) 'Immigration minister pledges full investigation over Yarl's Wood death', *theguardian.com*. Available at: <http://www.theguardian.com/ uk-news/2014/apr/01/immigration-sercogroup>.

O'Hagan, E.M. (2012) 'Britain Shames itself by detaining immigrants indefinitely', *theguardian.com*, Comment is Free. Available at <http://www.guardian.co.uk/ commentisfree/2012/dec/18/britain-detaining-immigrants-indefinitely>.

Our Home Affairs Correspondent (1970) 'Immigrant care plan "disgraceful"', *The Times*, 24 July: 2.

Strafford, P. (1978) 'Immigrants in the Harmondsworth limbo', *The Times*, 11 October 1978: 3. The Times Digital Archive. Accessed 19 September 2012.

Taylor, D. (2014) 'Yarl's Wood immigration centre detainee dies', 31 March 2014: 12. Available at: <http://www.theguardian.com/uk-news/2014/mar/30/yarls- wood-immigration-centre-detainee-dies>.

Taylor, M. (2014) 'Jimmy Mubenga: Three G4S guards to be charged with manslaughter', *The Guardian*, 21 March 2014: 2. Available at <http:// www.theguardian.com/uk-news/2014/mar/20/jimmy-mubenga-death- three-g4s-guards-charged-manslaughter>.

The Times (1970) 'Review of Asians' case after 3-week shuttle', *The Times*, 31 October: 3.

Townsend, M. (2013) 'Detainees at Yarl's Wood immigration centre "facing sexual abuse"', *The Observer*, 15 September 2013: 1. Available at <http://www. theguardian.com/uk-news/2013/sep/14/detainees-yarls-wood-sexual-abuse>.

Wansell, G. (1973) 'Immigrants attack conditions in Jail', *The Times*, 5 March 1973: 1–2.

Wilson, A. (1975) 'Heathrow's Cul-de-sac', *The Guardian*, 1 December 1975: 12.

PARLIAMENTARY DEBATES

House of Commons

HC Deb 22 January 1969, vol 776 col 509.
HC Deb 22 January 1969, vol 776 cols 489–567.
HC Deb 2 August 1972, vol 842 cols 862–3.
HC Deb 17 February 1982, vol 18 cols 126–9.
HC Deb 14 February 1986, vol 91 cols 567–8.
HC Deb 1 May 1987, vol 115 cols 259–60.
HC Deb 8 July 1988, vol 136 cols 1375–84.
HC Deb 13 March 1989, vol 149 cols 9–10.
HC Deb 24 January 1991, vol 184 col 300.
HC Deb 14 October 1991, vol 196 cols 17–24.
HC Deb 17 March 1994, vol 239 col 780.
HC Deb 5 May 1994, vol 242 col 623.
HC Deb 4 June 1996, vol 278 cols 330–1.
HC Deb 3 April 2014, col 757.
HC Deb 9 April 2014, col 248.
HC Written Answers 17 January 2014, cols 720–1, Available at: <http://www.publications.parliament.uk/pa/cm201314/cmhansrd/cm140117/text/140117w0002.htm>.

House of Lords

HL Deb 27 March 1969, vol 300 cols 1418–55.
HL Deb 27 March 1969, vol 300 cols 1426–32.
HL Deb 27 March 1969, vol 300 col 1434.
HL Deb 9 June 1978, vol 392 col 1677.
HL Deb 9 June 1978, vol 392 col 1678.
HL Deb 16 May 1980, vol 409 cols 538–9.
HL Deb 20 October 1980, vol 413 cols 1749–50.
HL Deb 6 April 1989, vol 505 cols 1193–5.

LEGISLATION

Immigration Act 2014
Borders, Citizenship and Immigration Act 2009
Criminal Justice and Immigration Act 2008
UK Borders Act 2007

Immigration, Asylum and Nationality Act 2006
Prevention of Terrorism Act 2005
Asylum and Immigration (Treatment of Claimants, etc) Act 2004
Nationality, Immigration and Asylum Act 2002
Anti-Terrorism, Crime and Security Act 2001
The Detention Centre Rules 2001
Immigration and Asylum Act 1999
The Prison Rules 1999
Human Rights Act 1998
Asylum and Immigration Act 1996
Immigration and Asylum Appeals Act 1993
British Nationality Act 1981
Race Relations Act 1972
Nationality Act 1971
Immigration Appeals Act 1969
Race Relations Act 1968
Commonwealth Immigrants Act 1968
Race Relations Act 1965
Commonwealth Immigrants Act 1962
Prison Act 1952
British Nationality Act 1948
Aliens Restriction (Amendment) Act 1919
Aliens Restriction Act 1914
Aliens Act 1905

INTERNATIONAL CONVENTIONS, TREATIES, AND LEGAL INSTRUMENTS

European Union Returns Directive 2008/115/EC
Council of Europe Convention on Action Against Trafficking in Human Beings, 16 March 2005 (entered into force 1 February 2008)
Convention against Transnational Organized Crime, 15 November 2000 (entered into force 29 September 2003)
Protocol against the Smuggling of Migrants by Land, Sea and Air (entered into force 28 January 2004)
Protocol to Prevent, Suppress and Punish Trafficking in Persons, especially Women and Children (entered into force 25 December 2003)
European Union Dublin Convention, 15 June 1990 (entered into force 1 September 1997)
Council Regulation (EC) No 604/2013, 26 June 2013 (Dublin III)
Council Regulation (EC) No 343/2003, 18 February 2003 (Dublin II)
International Convention on Civil and Political Rights (ICCPR), 16 December 1966 (entered into force 23 March 1976)

International Covenant on Economic, Social and Cultural Rights, 16 December 1966 (entered into force 3 January 1976)

Convention Relating to the Status of Refugees, 28 July 1951 (Refugee Convention) (entered into force 22 April 1954)

Protocol Relating to the Status of Refugees (entered into force 4 October 1967)

European Convention for the Protection of Human Rights and Fundamental Freedoms (ECHR) 4 November 1950 (entered into force 3 September 1953)

CASE LAW

R (on the application of Giwa) v Secretary of State for the Home Department [2013] EWHC 3189 (Admin).

A and others v Secretary of State for the Home Department [2004] UKHL 56.

R v Governor of Durham Prison ex parte Hardial Singh [1984] 1 WLR 704.

POLITICAL SPEECH

Clegg, N. (2010) *Nick Clegg confirms end to child detention* (full speech) <http://www.libdems.org.uk/speeches_detail.aspx?title=Nick_Clegg_confirms_end_to_child_detention_(full_speech)&pPK=d73b587e-f837-4b16-b7d5-a14b1bfa8a9b>.

May, T. (2013) *Speech to Conservative Party Conference.* Available at: <http://www.ein.org.uk/news/home-secretary-announce-massive-shake-immigration-law>.

ARCHIVES

Bowden, Herbert (1965) Commonwealth Immigration, Memorandum to Cabinet by the Lord President of the Privy Council, 23 July 1965. National Archives. CAB 129/122/9.

CM 18/18 (1981) 'Gatwick Permanent Detention accommodation', National Archives, London.

CM 8 121/1 (1988) National Archives, London.

CM 8 121/2 (1990) National Archives, London.

Doherty, H.A. (1988) Relocation Detention Centre Harmondsworth. Letter from H.A. Doherty HM Inspector from Appeals Section Harmondsworth, dated 31 May 1988, signed Iris Russell (pp) to Mr Harris. IS/88 41/25/1, in File CM 8 121/1. National Archives, London.

Hillingdon Borough Council, London. Harmondsworth Detention Centre Plans and planning application (1969) L.B.H. T/P 8190B/6662. Uxbridge: Planning Department.

Home Office: Aliens Department, HO 396 (1939–1947).

Hooper, G. (1969) Letter from Mr George Hooper to Ministry of Public Buildings and Works, 27 May 1969, in Microfiche L.B.H. T/P8190B/6662, Hillingdon Council Archives, Uxbridge Planning, London.

IS/8841/25/1 in File CM 8 121/1. National Archives, London.

KV2, The Security Service: Personal (PF series) Files, National Archives, London.

KV4, The Security Service: Policy (Pol F series) Files, National Archives, London.

KV 4/339, Policy and Procedure re detention of aliens at the Royal Patriotic Schools, National Archives, London.

KV 4/342, Policy and Procedure re detention of aliens at the Royal Patriotic Schools, National Archives, London.

Records of the Metropolitan Police 1918–1957, MEPO 35, National Archives, London.

Report of the Committee on Immigration Appeals (Wilson Committee): notes and papers. LAB 8/3398, National Archives, London.

Shingleton, B.L. (1982) Letter from B.L. Shingleton Home Office, Whittington House, London WC1E 7EJ to D. Vine, dated 22 February 1982. In File CM 18/18, National Archives, London.

The National Committee for Commonwealth Immigrants, 1965–1968, HO 231.

Wheeler, B.A. (1990) Letter from B.A. Wheeler Chief Immigration Officer, HM Immigration Office, Terminal 1 London (Heathrow) Airport to Mr D. Matthewson, PSA, St Christopher House, dated 24 April 1990. In File CM 8 121/2, National Archives, London.

Index

Introductory Note

References such as '178–9' indicate (not necessarily continuous) discussion of a topic across a range of pages. Because the entire work is about 'immigration detention', the use of this term (and certain others which occur constantly throughout the book) as an entry point has been minimized. Information will be found under the corresponding detailed topics.

Printed and bound by CPI Group (UK) Ltd, Croydon, CR0 4YY